The Protest Psychosis

"Jonathan Metzl offers a richly textured story of the confluence of race, psychiatric diagnoses, and social upheaval. The result is an absorbing account of how schizophrenia became a highly racialized label."

—EARL LEWIS, author of *Love on Trial* and
To Make Our World Anew, and provost, Emory University

"*The Protest Psychosis* is the most important book on schizophrenia in years. Jonathan Metzl shows how schizophrenia was transformed from a largely white, middle-class, nonmenacing disorder to one that is widely perceived as dangerous and threatening, precisely at the time of the U.S. civil rights movement. Metzl demonstrates convincingly that fears associated with urban violence and the rise of black power in the 1960s became an essential part of the very definition of schizophrenia.

—BYRON GOOD, author of *Medicine, Rationality, and Experience*
and professor of medical anthropology, Harvard Medical School

"*The Protest Psychosis* offers a compelling and expertly crafted study of the ways in which racial tensions are structured into medical interactions and shape its disease categories. This innovative historical portrait of the interaction of race and medicine should provoke deep reflection on how racial meanings become attached to docility, rage, and aggression, and become reified in psychiatric nomenclature and practice."

—KEITH WAILOO, author of *Dying in the City of the Blues:
Sickle Cell Anemia and the Politics of Race and Health*

"In this riveting book, Jonathan Metzl anatomizes the ways in which social forces, cultural anxieties, and political protests shaped schizophrenia as a black disease. The story that emerges is fascinating and heartbreaking from the first word to the last."

—EMILY MARTIN, author of *Bipolar Expeditions:
Mania and Depression in American Culture*

"*The Protest Psychosis* is an incisive and unexpectedly riveting book, equal parts medical history, social criticism, and investigative journalism. A very impressive work of scholarship."

—CARL ELLIOTT, author of *Better than Well:
American Medicine Meets the American Dream*

THE PROTEST PSYCHOSIS

The Protest Psychosis

HOW SCHIZOPHRENIA BECAME A BLACK DISEASE

Jonathan M. Metzl

BEACON PRESS · BOSTON

Beacon Press
25 Beacon Street
Boston, Massachusetts 02108-2892
www.beacon.org

Beacon Press books
are published under the auspices of
the Unitarian Universalist Association of Congregations.

13 12 11 10   8 7 6 5 4 3 2 1

This book is printed on acid-free paper that meets the uncoated paper
ANSI/NISO specifications for permanence as revised in 1992.

Composition by Wilsted & Taylor Publishing Services

Library of Congress Cataloging-in-Publication Data

Metzl, Jonathan,
   The protest psychosis : how schizophrenia became a black disease / Jonathan M. Metzl.
      p. cm.
   Includes bibliographical references and index.
   ISBN 978-0-8070-8592-9 (alk. paper)
   1. African Americans—Mental health—Case studies. 2. Schizophrenia—
Case studies. I. Title.
   RC451.5.N4.M48 2009
   362.196'8980089960973—dc22   2009016610

To Rumpa

The Protest Psychosis

THIS BOOK TELLS THE STORY of how race gets written into the definition of mental illness. It uncovers the surprising ways anxieties about racial differences shape clinical encounters, even when the explicit races of doctors and patients are not at issue. The book also shows how historical concerns about racial protest reverberate through treatment institutions and subvert even well-intentioned efforts to diagnose people or to help them. Ultimately, the book explores the processes through which American society equates *race* with *insanity;* and through which our definitions of both terms change as a result.

It is well known, of course, that race and insanity share a long and troubled past. In the 1850s, American psychiatrists believed that African American slaves who ran away from their white masters did so because of a mental illness called *drapetomania.* Medical journals of the era also described a condition called *dysaesthesia aethiopis,* a form of madness manifest by "rascality" and "disrespect for the master's property" that was believed to be "cured" by extensive whipping. Even at the turn of the twentieth century, leading academic psychiatrists shamefully claimed that "Negroes" were "psychologically unfit" for freedom.[1]

We have undoubtedly progressed since that time. Terms such as *drapetomania* fill the dustbin of history, and rightly so. Yet, in unintended and often invisible ways, psychiatric definitions of insanity continue to police racial hierarchies, tensions, and unspoken codes in addition to separating normal from abnormal behavior. Sometimes, the boundaries of sanity align closely with the perceived borders of the racial status quo. Mainstream culture then defines threats to this racial order as a form of madness that is, still, overwhelmingly located in the minds and bodies of black men. At other times, members of minority communities use the language of insanity to describe the psychical effects of living in racist societies. In these instances and others, questions of who is mentally ill and why orbit around American race relations and their discontents. And seemingly hermetic clinical encounters between psychiatrists and patients unconsciously mirror larger conversations about the politics of race.

As a beginning illustration of the book's main point, consider a prominent story that appeared on the front page of the *Washington Post* on June
28, 2005. "Racial Disparities Found in Pinpointing Mental Illness" read the
headline. The article detailed a discovery that was at once shocking and sadly
familiar. Researchers had examined the largest American registry of psychiatric patient records looking for "ethnic trends" in schizophrenia diagnoses. As the *Post* described it, schizophrenia, "a disorder that often portends
years of powerful brain-altering drugs, social ostracism and forced hospital-
izations . . . has been shown to affect all ethnic groups at the same rate." And
yet, the large government study uncovered striking categorical differences in
its analysis of 134,523 case files: doctors diagnosed schizophrenia in African
American patients, and particularly African American men, *four times* as
often as in white patients. The *Post* cited the study's lead author, John Zeber,
who explained that doctors overdiagnosed schizophrenia in African American men even though the research team uncovered no evidence that "black
patients were any sicker than whites," or that patients in either group were
more likely to suffer from drug addiction, poverty, depression, or a host of
other variables. According to Zeber, "the only factor that was truly important was race."[2]

Paradoxically, we live in an era when the opposite is supposed to be the
case: race should be entirely unimportant to psychiatric diagnosis. Present-
day psychiatry believes that mental illness results from disordered brain
biology at levels that are presumably the same in people of all races and ethnic backgrounds. And psychiatrists consider schizophrenia to be the most
biologically based of the mental illnesses. Leading journals routinely attribute symptoms of the illness—officially defined as *delusions, hallucinations,
disorganized speech, disorganized or catatonic behavior,* or so-called *negative symptoms* such as *affective flattening*—to defects in specific brain structures, peptides, or neurotransmitters. Articles that describe research into the
causes of the illness thus carry titles such as "Conserved Regional Patterns
of GABA-Related Transcript Expression in the Neocortex of Subjects with
Schizophrenia" or, incredibly, "Smaller Nasal Volumes as Stigmata of Aberrant Neurodevelopment in Schizophrenia." Meanwhile, textbooks routinely
claim that, as a biological disorder, schizophrenia is an illness that should occur in *1 percent* of any given population, or one out of every hundred persons
regardless of where they live, how they dress, who they know, or what type of
music they happen to prefer.[3]

Yet, in the real world, 1 percent is a delusion. Not only do stories such as
the *Post* article appear with regularity—they persist over time. In the 1960s,

National Institute of Mental Health studies found that "blacks have a 65% higher rate of schizophrenia than whites." In 1973, a series of studies in the *Archives of General Psychiatry* discovered that African American patients were "significantly more likely" than white patients to receive schizophrenia diagnoses, and "significantly less likely" than white patients to receive diagnoses for other mental illnesses such as depression or bipolar disorder. Throughout the 1980s and 1990s, a host of articles from leading psychiatric and medical journals showed that doctors diagnosed the paranoid subtype of schizophrenia in African American men five to seven times more often than in white men, and also more frequently than in other ethnic minority groups.[4]

Everyday racism seems a reasonable explanation for these findings. Though we might wish otherwise, medical training does not wholly free clinicians from preexisting racial beliefs, assumptions, or blind spots. While medicine has undoubtedly made significant progress toward addressing multicultural issues in clinical practice, some doctors undoubtedly harbor negative opinions about particular patients based on stereotyped cultural assumptions. As Francis Lu, a psychiatrist at the University of California at San Francisco, explains it "physician bias is a very real issue . . . we don't talk about it—it's upsetting. We see ourselves as unbiased and rational and scientific."[5]

This book makes a broader claim: from a historical perspective, race impacts medical communication because racial tensions are structured into clinical interactions long before doctors or patients enter examination rooms. To a remarkable extent, anxieties about racial difference shape diagnostic criteria, health-care policies, medical and popular attitudes about mentally ill persons, the structures of treatment facilities, and, ultimately, the conversations that take place there within.

Stokely Carmichael, the civil rights activist, once described such a process as institutional racism, by which he meant forms of bias embedded not in actions or beliefs of individuals, but in the functions of social structures and institutions. "I don't deal with the individual," he said. "I think it's a cop-out when people talk about the individual." Instead, Carmichael protested the silent racism of "established and respected forces in the society" that functioned above the level of individual perceptions or intentions, and that worked to maintain the status quo through such structures as zoning laws, economics, schools, and courts. Institutionalized racism, he argued, "is less overt, far more subtle, less identifiable in terms of specific individuals committing the acts, but is no less destructive of human life."[6]

In a perfect world, interactions between doctors and patients should be immune from any process deemed destructive to health. The Hippocratic Oath decrees that the primary aim of medical encounters is to restore, not to harm. Most physicians, myself included, enter the practice of medicine out of a desire to help people. And most patients seek the aid of physicians in times when they require palliation and care.

However, as the pages that follow reveal, institutional forces supersede even the best individual intentions when race and insanity are the topics of diagnostic interaction. The book looks closely at changing twentieth-century American assumptions about race and schizophrenia through sources including American medical journals, newspapers, popular magazines, pharmaceutical advertisements, historically black newspapers, studies of popular opinion, music lyrics, films, and civil rights memoirs. Most important are a series of previously unstudied "White" and "Negro" case files from the archives of the Ionia State Hospital for the Criminally Insane in Ionia, Michigan, where racial tensions dominated interactions between doctors and patients. Taken together, these sources suggest that, far from being a timeless phenomenon, institutional racism waxes and wanes, becoming more powerful in the context of specific moments when racial tensions rise to the fore of American consciousness.

The Protest Psychosis traverses the period from the 1920s to the present day, but focuses mainly on a series of transformations that occurred during the American civil rights era of the 1960s and 1970s. During this vital period, new clinical ways of defining mental illness unintentionally combined with growing cultural anxieties about social change. Meanwhile, reports about new "psychochemical" technologies of control merged with concerns about the "uncontrolled" nature of urban unrest. As these historical contingencies evolved, the American public, and at times members of the scientific community, increasingly described schizophrenia as a violent social disease, even as psychiatry took its first steps toward defining schizophrenia as a disorder of biological brain function.

It was not always so. Prior to the civil rights movement, mainstream American medical and popular opinion often assumed that patients with schizophrenia were largely white, and generally harmless to society. From the 1920s to the 1950s, psychiatric textbooks depicted schizophrenia as an exceedingly broad, general condition, manifest by "emotional disharmony," that negatively impacted white people's abilities to "think and feel." Authors of research articles in leading psychiatric journals, many of whom were psychoanalysts, described patients with schizophrenia, and, all too often, their "schizophrenogenic mothers," as "native-born Americans" or immigrants of "white European ancestry." Psychiatric authors frequently assumed that such patients were nonthreatening, and were therefore to be psychotherapeutically nurtured by their doctors, as if unruly children, but certainly not feared.[7]

Leading mainstream American newspapers in the 1920s to the 1950s similarly described schizophrenia as an illness that occurred "in the seclusive, sensitive person with few friends who has been the model of behavior in childhood," or that afflicted white women or intellectuals. In 1935, for instance, the *New York Times* described how many white poets and novelists demonstrated a symptom called "grandiloquence," a propensity toward flowery prose believed to be "one of the telltale phrases of schizophrenia, the mild form of insanity known as split personality." Meanwhile, popular magazines such as *Ladies' Home Journal* and *Better Homes and Gardens* wrote of unhappily married, middle-class white women whose schizophrenic mood swings were suggestive of "Doctor Jekyll and Mrs. Hyde," a theme that also appeared in Olivia de Havilland's infamous depiction of a "schizophrenic housewife" named Virginia Stuart Cunningham in the 1948 Anatole Litvak film, *The Snake Pit.*[8]

Of course, it was far from the case that all persons who suffered from a disease called schizophrenia during the first half of the twentieth century were members of a category called white. Rather, American culture marked schizophrenia as a disease of the mainstream in ways that encouraged identification with certain groups of people while rendering other groups invisible. For example, popular magazines in the 1920s to the 1950s incorrectly assumed that schizophrenia was a psychoanalytic condition connected to neurosis, and as a result affixed the term to middle-class housewives. Meanwhile, researchers conducted most published clinical studies in white-only wards. Such strategies occluded recognition of the countless men and women diagnosed with schizophrenia who resided in so-called Negro hospitals and suffered well outside most realms of public awareness.[9]

American assumptions about the race, gender, and temperament of schizophrenia changed beginning in the 1960s. Many leading medical and popular sources suddenly described schizophrenia as an illness manifested not by docility, but by rage. Growing numbers of research articles from leading psychiatric journals asserted that schizophrenia was a condition that also afflicted "Negro men," and that black forms of the illness were marked by volatility and aggression. In the worst cases, psychiatric authors conflated the schizophrenic symptoms of African American patients with the perceived schizophrenia of civil rights protests, particularly those organized by Black Power, Black Panthers, Nation of Islam, or other activist groups.

As but one example, the title of this book comes from a 1968 article that appeared in the prestigious *Archives of General Psychiatry*, in which psychiatrists Walter Bromberg and Frank Simon described schizophrenia as a "protest psychosis" whereby black men developed "hostile and aggressive feelings" and "delusional anti-whiteness" after listening to the words of Malcolm X, joining the Black Muslims, or aligning with groups that preached militant resistance to white society. According to the authors, the men required psychiatric treatment because their symptoms threatened not only their own sanity, but the social order of white America. Bromberg and Simon argued that black men who "espoused African or Islamic" ideologies, adopted "Islamic names" that were changed in such a way so as to deny "the previous Anglicization of their names" in fact demonstrated a "delusional anti-whiteness" that manifest as "paranoid projections of the Negroes to the Caucasian group."[10]

Advertisements for new pharmaceutical treatments for schizophrenia in the 1960s and 1970s depicted similar themes. As I discuss in a later chap-

FIG. 1 *Advertisements for the antipsychotic drug Haldol from the 1970s depicted black men with clenched fists, under the headline "Assaultive and belligerent?"* (Archives of General Psychiatry 31, no. 5 (1974): 732-33.)

ter, advertisements for the antipsychotic medication Haldol in leading psychiatric journals showed angry black men with clenched, Black Power fists in urban scenes whose symptoms of social belligerence required chemical management.

Meanwhile, mainstream white newspapers in the 1960s and 1970s described schizophrenia as a condition of angry black masculinity, or warned of crazed black schizophrenic killers on the loose. "FBI Adds Negro Mental Patient to '10 Most Wanted' List'" warned a *Chicago Tribune* headline in July 1966, above an article that advised readers to remain clear of "Leroy Ambrosia Frazier, an extremely dangerous and mentally unbalanced schizophrenic escapee from a mental institution, who has a lengthy criminal record and history of violent assaults." Hollywood films such as Samuel Fuller's 1963 B-movie classic, *Shock Corridor,* similarly cast the illness as arising in black men, and particularly men who participated in civil rights protests.[11]

Schizophrenia's rhetorical transformation from an illness of white feminine docility to one of black male hostility resulted from a confluence of social and medical forces. Some of these forces were obvious, such as the biased actions of individual doctors, researchers, or drug advertisers, while others functioned at structural levels beyond individual perceptions. One of the key pieces of evidence I use to uncover this later process is an analysis of shifting language associated with the official psychiatric definition of schizophrenia. Prior to the 1960s, psychiatric classification systems often posited that schizophrenia was a psychological "reaction" to a splitting of the basic functions of personality. Official descriptors emphasized the generally calm nature of such persons in ways that encouraged associations with middle-class housewives. But the frame changed in the 1960s. In 1968, in the midst of a political climate marked by profound protest and social unrest, psychiatry published the second edition of the *Diagnostic and Statistical Manual* (DSM). That text recast the paranoid subtype of schizophrenia as a disorder of masculinized belligerence. "The patient's attitude is frequently hostile and aggressive," the DSM-II claimed, "and his behavior tends to be consistent with his delusions." Growing numbers of research articles from the 1960s and 1970s used this language to assert that schizophrenia was a condition that also afflicted "Negro men," and that black forms of the illness were more hostile and aggressive than were white ones.[12]

As we will see, the shifting frame surrounding schizophrenia had dire consequences for African American men held at the Ionia State Hospital during the civil rights era. Prior to this era, Ionia doctors considered schizophrenia to be an illness that afflicted nonviolent, white, petty criminals, including the hospital's considerable population of women from rural Michigan. Charts emphasized the negative impact of "schizophrenogenic styles" on these women's abilities to perform their duties as mothers and wives. By the early 1970s, however, schizophrenia was a diagnosis disproportionately applied to the hospital's growing population of African American men from urban Detroit. Ionia doctors used the DSM-II and other diagnostic tools to link these men's symptoms to a host of era-specific racial anxieties, even if the men had no direct involvement in the civil rights movement. As a result, individual attempts to help these men took a backseat to structural attempts to control them. And patients who by all reasonable criteria should have been treated based on their character and intellect were instead interned because of the color of their suddenly schizophrenic skins.

Changing notions of schizophrenia in the 1960s and 1970s had wider implications as well. New psychiatric definitions of schizophrenic illness impacted persons of many different racial and ethnic backgrounds. Some patients *became* schizophrenic because of changes in diagnostic criteria rather than in their clinical symptoms. Others saw their diagnoses changed to depression, anxiety, or other conditions because they did not manifest hostility or aggression. Emerging understandings of the illness shaped American cultural fears about mental illness more broadly, particularly regarding cultural stereotypes of persons with schizophrenia as being unduly hostile or violent. In an important counternarrative that I discuss extensively in later chapters, new notions of schizophrenia also provided powerful language for civil rights leaders, who argued that insanity and rage arose not because of defects in black bodies, but because of violent racist ideals that emanated from the white society in which these bodes lived and worked.[13]

In no way is my telling of this history meant to suggest that schizophrenia is a socially fabricated disease or, worse, that people's suffering is somehow inauthentic. As a psychiatrist, I have seen the tragic ways in which hallucinations, delusions, social withdrawal, cognitive decline, and profound isolation rupture lives, careers, families, and dreams in profoundly material ways. I know that such symptoms afflict persons of many different social, economic, and racial backgrounds, most of whom are deeply aware of the sense of loss that their disease represents, even if society is less attuned. I agree with the clinician and activist E. Fuller Torrey, who writes that "the lives of those affected [by schizophrenia] are often chronicles of constricted experiences, muted emotions, missed opportunities, unfulfilled expectations . . . the fate of these patients has been worsened by our propensity to misunderstand."[14]

I also strongly believe that persons diagnosed with schizophrenia and other mental illnesses benefit from various forms of treatment or social support, and that our society should invest more in the care and well-being of the severely mentally ill. This reality was largely overlooked by leaders of the largely white "anti-psychiatry" movement of the 1970s, who argued that schizophrenia was a wholly political diagnosis whose constraints needed to be lifted in the name of emancipation. Thomas Szasz, David Cooper, and R. D. Laing were but a few of the activist psychiatrists who contended that mental illness was a "myth," or that psychiatry merely policed societal norms by pathologizing and controlling deviance. Claims about the mythic nature of mental illness emerged during a social moment when mistrust of many forms of authority, including doctors, shaped political thought. Yet in formatting arguments that were later seamlessly taken up by conservative ideologues, anti-psychiatrists overlooked the reality that, once free of the constraints of psychiatric terms or institutions, the newly liberated psychiatric patients often had nowhere to go and no one to turn to for help.

At the same time, this book centrally explores how the material reality of schizophrenia is shaped by social, political, and, ultimately, institutional factors in addition to chemical or biological ones. Too often, we assume that medical and cultural explanations of illness are distinct entities, or engage in frustratingly pointless debates about whether certain mental illnesses are either socially constructed or real. These debates often position political forces as existing outside of psychiatry's purview. *Psychiatry focuses on dopamine,* the logic goes, *and leaves the social stuff to others.* The current edition of the DSM goes so far as to separate genuine psychiatric illness, termed an Axis I diagnosis, from "Psychosocial and Environmental Factors," which are relegated to Axis IV.

Arguments for a clean divide between dopamine and culture misrepresent the profound interrelatedness of these two seemingly distinct explanations in clinical settings. Make no mistake, we psychiatrists want to know what causes mental disease, and biological science offers promising clues about nosology. But we are not there yet. We do not diagnose schizophrenia, depression, traumatic stress, or a host of other illnesses solely through X-rays, brain scans, or specific laboratory tests. Instead, we query, listen, observe, categorize, and expertly surmise. Thus, even in an era dominated by neuroscience, diagnosis remains a projective act, one that combines scientific understanding with a complex set of ideological and, as I will show, political assumptions. Cloaking our observations under the seemingly objective rubric of biological science renders these ideological functions all the more difficult to discern or critique.[15]

Another misnomer that this book takes aim at is the belief that stigma against psychiatric illness cannot be changed because stigmatizing attitudes against the mentally ill are timeless, eternal, and, ultimately, immutable. *Beliefs about the volatility of madmen are as old as time itself,* we might say, and indeed we would be right. As the eminent historian Roy Porter aptly describes it, narratives of insane violence "may be as old as mankind," and course through disparate religious texts and object lessons. Yet arguments about the timeless nature of stigma against schizophrenia often fail to address the impact of relatively recent events on present-day attitudes and beliefs. As we will soon see, *schizophrenia* was a European term, invented in the early twentieth century and imported to the United States around 1915. For decades, schizophrenia connoted white, American neurosis. Only during the civil rights era did emerging scientific understandings of schizophrenia become enmeshed in a set of historical currents that marked particular bodies, and particular psyches, as crazy in particular ways. The tensions of that era then changed the associations that many Americans made about persons with schizophrenia in ways that altered not just stigma against the illness, but the definition of the illness itself. Ultimately, recent American racial history altered more than the meaning of mental illness: it changed the meaning of mental health as well.[16]

As the *Washington Post* article demonstrates, this history continues to impact the lives of African American men. Research suggests that even African American doctors overdiagnose schizophrenia in African American men. African American men also receive higher dosages of antipsychotic medications than do white male psychiatric patients, and are more likely to be described by health care professionals as being hostile or violent. Such disparities have been remarkably resistant to interventions such as "cultural competency training" or "standardized" diagnostic encounters. For instance, the U.S. Department of Health and Human Services recently developed "Cultural Competence Standards" to help clinicians better understand, and communicate with, patients of diverse ethnic backgrounds. And the San Francisco General Hospital psychiatry department opened a "Black Focus Unit," complete with clinicians of color, African art, and, as reported in the *Post,* "pictures of Vanessa Williams, Maya Angelou and Oprah Winfrey" on the walls.[17]

Yet, the problem of race-based misdiagnosis persists. Perhaps part of the reason why such interventions fail is that they focus exclusively on the race of the patient and of the doctor, and define the problem as arising in the intersection of these two races. By so doing, they align with the work of scholars of social interactions, from Erving Goffman to Glenn Loury, who assume that stigmatizing encounters occur between individuals when visual markers of difference—such as skin color—stand in for larger assumptions about good and bad. While valid, such an approach leaves free from scrutiny the third race that functions in the examination room: *that of the diagnosis,* and its structurally developed links to protest, resistance, racism, and other associations that work against therapeutic communication between doctors and patients.

History also lives on in instances where associations between schizophrenia and race suggest a "loosening of associations," to use historian Keith Wailoo's insightful description of the ways assumptions about the virulence of particular racial groups expand to impact all sufferers of a particular disease. For instance, negative perceptions of persons with schizophrenia as being unduly hostile or violent thrive in American society, even though these persons are exponentially more likely to be the victims than the perpetrators of violent acts. Meanwhile, as is well-known, people diagnosed with schizophrenia in the present day reside more often in penal than in psychiatric care facilities. While many complex economic and social factors contribute to such issues, their current composition also depends on a racialized logic that comes directly from the 1960s and 1970s, whereby schizophrenia represents both a mental illness and a threat to civilized society.[18]

In sum, then, this book tells the story of how civil rights-era anxieties about racial protest catalyzed associations between schizophrenia, criminality, and violence. It deeply respects psychiatric attempts to uncover the ontology of mental illness. But it also recognizes that the search for ontology is an ongoing process, and that the frames aggregating certain symptoms into particular psychiatric diagnoses exist in an ongoing state of flux. Such flux can be a positive force, to be sure: it allows psychiatry to redefine illnesses in ways that are more scientifically precise. But flux can also have abjectifying or stigmatizing consequences if its politics are not closely watched. Thus was the case in the 1960s and 1970s, when the newly narrowed frame surrounding paranoid schizophrenia circumscribed and helped create the category of angry, black, male schizophrenic subjects, while casting women, neurotics, manic depressives, and other thereby nonthreatening persons into expanding categories of depression, bipolar disorder, or anxiety disorders. Racial concerns, and at times overt racism, were thereby written into diagnostic language in ways that are invisible to us now. The book concludes by discussing how understanding this past enables new ways of addressing the implications of racial schizophrenia in the present. I specifically discuss antistigma efforts, approaches to the role of race in clinical interactions, ways of understanding mistrust of psychiatry by members of minority communities, and efforts to combat linkages between criminality and mental illness.

My argument is indebted to many important scholars whose work deals with similar themes in far more comprehensive ways than I do here. Vital texts such as Harriet Washington's *Medical Apartheid,* Wailoo's *Dying in the City of the Blues,* and W. Michael Byrd and Linda A. Clayton's *An American Health Dilemma* detail the long history of injustice perpetuated by the American medical system to African American patients and communities. Masterworks such as Michel Foucault's *Madness and Civilization,* Gerald Grob's *The Mad Among Us,* David Rothman's *The Discovery of the Asylum,* and Nancy Tomes's *The Art of Asylum-Keeping* document the complex genealogies of psychiatric institutions in ways that provide context for my reading of the Ionia charts. Taylor Branch's trilogy, *America in the King Years,* remains a gold standard of civil rights–era histories. And writings by critical race studies scholars such as Angela Davis (*Women, Race and Class; Are Prisons Obsolete?*), Ruth Frankenberg (*White Women, Race Matters*), and Kimberlé Crenshaw ("The Intersection of Race and Gender") uncover the vital ways in which social categories such as race are never inherently pure, but instead *intersect* with other categories such as gender and social class. Davis, for instance, details how economic, social, and, ultimately, gender anxieties lie beneath American cultural beliefs about the volatility of black men, while Frankenberg deploys a feminist analysis of whiteness to argue, in language reflective of Carmichael, that "racism appears not only as an ideology or political orientation chosen or rejected at will; it is also a system and set of ideas embedded in social relations."[19]

To be sure, we inhabit a current cultural moment in which American racial systems, ideas, and social relations promise improvement. The election of an African American president and a new national attention to matters of race suggests transformation not just in governance, but in long-held attitudes, beliefs, and everyday practices. Change is here, the moment tells us, and change will come.

Yet, the hospital charts, medical writings, and popular documents I examine in this book provide cautionary tales about the complex ways in which moments of change, and particularly moments that portend changed race or gender relations, produce anxieties about the stability of the status quo. The battles that follow—when the idea of change begins to produce actual change—appear for all the world to play out on the public stage: in an election, for instance, or in the White House, or in other, highly visible sites where newfound leaders, freedoms, or rights become markers of progress for some people and symbols of inquietude for others.

History teaches us, however, that the brunt of the pushback against change is borne most by persons who, for various reasons, are least able to defend themselves or, as this book shows, to protest. These persons then become doubly or triply stigmatized based on unfounded generalizations about deviance, perceived volatility, abnormality, or other characteristics that remain acceptable modes of discrimination. Public concern about the actions or proclivities of these persons then grows, even as they themselves are rendered less than full citizens or are progressively removed from public life. As we know all too well from plagues past, the rhetorics of health and illness become effective ways of policing the boundaries of civil society, and of keeping these people always outside.

Thus was the case with schizophrenia in the 1960s and 1970s. Far beneath the national glare of bus boycotts, sit-ins, and marches, another hidden civil rights–era history unfolded in response to national events. Here, the currency was neither liberation nor equality, but containment. And the result was not increased voting rights, legal protections, educational access, or other hard-fought liberties. Instead, the civil rights era catalyzed a shift in the structure of buildings, institutions, diagnostic codes, and even in the structure of minds, attitudes, and identities. Schizophrenia literally, and then figuratively, became a black disease. And prisons emerged where hospitals once stood.

PART I

Ionia

FIG. 2 *An aerial view of the Ionia State Hospital for the Criminally Insane,
circa 1932. (Source: Archives of Michigan, RG77-3, B2 F8)*

CHAPTER 1

Homicidal

CECIL PETERSON HAD NO HISTORY with the police. Even on the day the white stranger insulted his mother, Peterson simply wanted to eat lunch. He sat in his usual seat at the counter of the diner on Woodward Street and ordered his usual BLT and coffee. Somehow he caught the stranger's eye in the squinted way that begets immediate conflict between men. The stranger glared. Peterson was not one to walk away from confrontation, but he knew the implications of glaring back. One should not glare back at a white man. So he looked down. But the two men crossed paths again after Peterson paid his tab and walked outside. And then came the remark. And then came the fight.

Two white Detroit police officers happened to be passing by the diner that September day in 1966. They ran to the altercation and tried to separate the combatants. At that point, according to their formal report, Peterson turned on the officers and struck them "without provocation." According to the report, Peterson knocked one officer down and "kicked him in the side." A second police team arrived and assisted in apprehending the "agitated" Mr. Peterson. Medics took the first officers on the scene to the Wayne County Hospital emergency room. The ER physician's report noted that both officers had "bruises," though neither required treatment. The white stranger was not charged.

Peterson was twenty-nine, African American, and an unmarried father of four who worked the line at Cadillac Motor Company. He had not previously come to the attention of the state. He had not been diagnosed or treated for any physical or mental illness. Nor had he been held for crimes or misdemeanors. He had limited interactions with white people and preferred to stay close to home. But on that September day in 1966 his life changed along with his identity. He became a prisoner. And then he became a patient.

The Wayne County court convicted Mr. Peterson of two counts of "assault on a police officer causing injury requiring medical attention" and sent him to the Wayne County jail on a two- to ten-year sentence. After several weeks of incarceration, prison notes described Mr. Peterson as "extremely paranoid and potentially explosive," screaming that "the white stranger" had "insulted my mother" and that his "civil rights" were being violated. The prison psychiatrist provided a diagnosis of "sociopathic personality distur-bance with antisocial reaction," and recommended seclusion, restraint, and continuous doses of Thorazine at 200 milligrams. Within six months, Mr. Peterson's unprovoked outbursts became so severe that he earned the dis-tinction of being a "problem inmate" who was "dangerous on the basis of his presenting a threat to the guards." Soon thereafter, he began to ramble incoherently. One guard's note explained that Mr. Peterson "occasionally gri-maces, remains silent for long minutes, then looks up toward the ceiling with his eyes rolling in all directions." A year into his incarceration, Mr. Peterson loudly accused the prison staff of "depriving him of women." They observed him to be "hostile, suspicious, and increasingly annoyed" without any appar-ent provocation. He soon escalated, and the prison psychiatrist was called again. This time the psychiatrist recommended transferring Mr. Peterson to the notorious Ionia State Hospital for the Criminally Insane. The transfer sheet described Mr. Peterson as "HOMICIDAL."

The drive to Ionia took four hours, much of which Mr. Peterson slept off in the back of the police car. But he stiffened when the vehicle pulled into the winding drive that led up to Ionia Hospital; and his attention reached the level of panic when the car doors opened onto the expansive, forty-one-building campus of bricks and chimneys and yards and fences and crazy people as far as the eye could see.

Dragged inside one of the largest of these buildings, Mr. Peterson shouted and struggled to get away. He said he was an "African warrior" and spoke gib-berish, which he claimed to be his native African language. Then, in English, he loudly accused the guards of detaining him against his will. He claimed to be under attack by all white men.

Sylvan Cabrioto was not fazed. He had been the on-call physician at the Ionia receiving hospital since 1958, fully ten years before Cecil Peterson ap-peared in his examination room. A first-generation psychiatrist and second-generation American, Cabrioto was an authoritative, robust man of fifty-three who had a different bow tie for each day of the week. Treating the steady flow of burglars, peeping toms, pedophiles, and murderers who came through the Ionia doors gave Cabrioto a detached air of competence that undoubtedly re-sulted from having seen it all before. So he was not intimidated, at least not overtly, when Peterson appeared in the receiving hospital, or when the two prison guards drove off, or even when, after his handcuffs were taken off, Mr. Peterson "doubled up his fists" and gestured in a manner that was "irritable, disturbed, and sarcastic."

It was, after all, a stance Cabrioto had seen in nearly every one of the growing number of "Negro" patients brought to the Ionia State Hospital for the Criminally Insane in the 1960s. One man heard the voice of Jesus telling him to come home. Another was certain that loved ones were trying to poison him. Another performed "mystic voodoo movements" while claiming an "eternal struggle against the white man."

Like Peterson, most of the men came from "deteriorated neighborhoods" of Detroit. Most nonetheless held gainful employment. Like Peterson, each was convicted of a crime against person or property, ranging from larceny to murder to various forms of civil unrest. Few of the men had seen psychiatrists prior to their convictions, though this was not surprising since few psychiatrists resided in the urban sections of Detroit in the 1960s and 1970s. The men passed through various courts, prisons, and other state institutions. By the time they arrived at Ionia, they were nothing if not psychotic. Like Peterson, they hallucinated and ideated, or acted withdrawn, suspicious, paranoid, or combative. They argued, and fought, and resisted, and projected. And, according to Cabrioto and his colleagues, these actions were easily explained with a single diagnosis.

CHAPTER 2

Ionia

IONIA, MICHIGAN, IS A TOWN of 10,569 residents whose claim to fame these days is the Chili-Dawg Challenge, an annual competition of hot-dog eating prowess that draws contestants from throughout Ionia and Clinton counties. If, as Michiganders often claim, the state of Michigan is shaped like an open hand, then Ionia resides somewhere near the fourth metacarpal. The city Web site boasts that Ionia "has a diverse economy, including auto parts manufacturing, metal fabrication, and playing host each July/August to the Ionia County Free Fair." The Web site also advertises that Ionia hosts "plenty of small businesses." Yet even the most cursory tour through the three-block downtown suggests that Ionia's fate is linked not to an investment boom but to Michigan's declining economy. Many shops on the red-brick Main Street remain boarded up or empty. At noon in the Blue Water Café sit men who might, in better times, have held gainful employment. The 88¢ Superstore inexplicably holds a "half price sale." Perhaps not surprisingly, the only businesses that appear to be thriving reside in the strip malls outside of town: Walmart and Instant Cash Advance/Bondsmen.[1]

You might drive through Ionia on a sunny day and never have a clue about Ionia's other past, the past covered over by the tranquility of decline, the past seemingly far removed from a not unrecent time when being sent to Ionia was synonymous with a life sentence of electrotherapy, straightjackets, and padded cells.

Between 1885 and 1976, Ionia was home to one of the nation's most notorious mental asylums. The hospital opened as the Michigan Asylum for Insane Criminals, making it the second hospital for criminal offenders in the United States. The asylum resided for five years in the vacated compound of the Michigan Reformatory, a small set of buildings adjacent to the State House of Corrections. In 1890, Superintendent O. R. Long successfully argued that it was not "conducive to recovery" to house mental patients near a penal institution or "in cramped quarters without access to fresh air." The hospital then purchased an eighty-acre farm on a bluff overlooking the Grand River Valley along County Road 468 and was renamed the Ionia State Hospital for the Criminally Insane.[2]

During its heyday in the 1920s, '30s, '40s, and '50s, the Ionia Hospital grounds grew to an expansive 529 acres. An imposing skyline of forty-one buildings, many gothic and made of stone, occupied the high ground overlooking the Grand River Valley. Nine of these buildings housed men patients, including separate buildings for the senile, psychopathic, convalescent, volatile, and "semi-disturbed." Building 5, a four-storey structure constructed in 1908, hosted the hospital's smaller population of women. Building 8 contained several large dining rooms and a chapel. Building 2 was used for recreation, and held an auditorium and a gym. Building 7 was a full-service hospital, complete with receiving wards, a tubercular unit, an "intensive treatment" facility, a pharmacy, an electroshock center, and a dentist's office. In addition, the hospital boasted its own patient library, greenhouse, dairy farm and milk-pasteurization plant, swineherd, industrial workshop, horse barn, and chicken house. The superintendent lived in a lavish Savannah-style home, complete with columns and a porch swing. Many of the other physicians, nurses, orderlies, and guards lived in separate homes, or else in the brick, three-storey employee dormitory. Hospital-owned farmland, as far as the eye could see, provided space where the prisoners-cum-patients were sent to work off their particular forms of insanity.

Ionia Hospital's annual census hovered above 1,500 patients throughout the middle part of the twentieth century. These men and women were a combination of society's damned, condemned, labeled, and feared, accompanied by a good number of the just unlucky. They came from four main referral sources. State penal institutions, including the Detroit House of Correction, the Michigan Reformatory, and the State Prison of Southern Michigan transferred prisoners who developed "mental disease." Criminal courts sent people under arrest or charged with crimes but found to be exhibiting symptoms of insanity. Civil state hospitals, including Kalamazoo State, Eloise, Traverse City, and Ypsilanti State hospitals, unloaded violent or difficult-to-control patients. And the probate court sent ex-convicts or former patients found to show a mental illness of one form or another.[3]

Throughout the first half of the twentieth century, life at Ionia resembled something closer to a summer camp for the hyperactive than the current stereotype of an asylum. To be sure, misery was the main currency of daily life. Patients received regular courses of insulin shock, Metrazol-induced shock, and electrotherapy. Even those who did not suffer from insanity caused by syphilitic involvement of the central nervous system were at times subjected to hyperpyrexia, a "therapeutic fever" induced through malaria inoculation or via an electric dynatherm machine. Yet, Ionia also enacted a philosophy of rechanneling pent-up energy through innumerable chores, activities, and events. "Too much stress cannot be given to a very elaborate recreation program in an institution caring for the criminally insane," Superintendent P. C. Robertson wrote in his 1937–38 annual report. Because these patients were in constant need of "a sane outlet in a physical way," Robertson championed "the advantages obtained from active and vigorous occupational and recreational programs . . . to reduce to a minimum friction among patients on the wards." Male patients worked in the hospital kitchen, horse barn, dairy, or with the swineherds; they made signs, repaired shoes, made clay models and pottery, and manufactured mop heads. Women, meanwhile, made shirts, aprons, handkerchiefs, suspenders, dresses, laundry bags, caps, sponges, toys, and, perhaps most surprising, surgeons' masks and robes. The hospital regularly hosted tea parties for these women, seamstresses who, like all unpaid laborers at Ionia, brought income to the hospital through their efforts.[4]

In their spare time, patients participated in an extensive program of calisthenics and intra- and extramural activities. In 1937, male patients played in 82 basketball games, 97 softball games, and 13 baseball games, including a good number against local men's teams, while women enjoyed weekly picnics or bus rides. Patients also took music lessons, played in the hospital orchestra, performed amateur theatrical productions, and participated in song festivals, "with an average of 276 patients attending" each week. Many patients attended biweekly moving-picture shows and seasonal parties that included terpsichorean-inducing performances by outside entertainers. Others wrote, edited, and published a monthly newspaper, the *Aurora*, which contained stories of daily life in the hospital from "the patient's perspective." Still others worked on the hospital's elaborate annual patient float for the Michigan State Fair parade.[5]

Ionia housed its share of celebrity convicts. The Razor Madmen slept there, as did Holshay, the notorious bandit and desperado of the Central West. Eugene and Pearl Burgess, a Michigan couple convicted of killing an elderly neighbor because they believed she was a witch, spent time at Ionia. So did Dr. Kenneth Small, the dentist who famously slew his wife's lover at a posh New York resort. An eighteen-year resident and serial rapist named Louis Smith gained national notoriety for volunteering to undergo experimental ablative psychosurgery to cure his perversions, and for then recanting before the procedure. Perhaps the most famous resident of Ionia was not a person, but a cow. Ionia Aggie Sadie Vale, a registered Holstein in the state hospital herd, was hailed by the Holstein Friesian Association of America in July 1940 as the "new all-time champion lifetime producer" after giving 230,723 pounds of milk.[6]

But the hospital's primary tenants were run-of-the-mill perverts, burglars, larcenists, shoplifters, alcoholics, and parole violators. All were sent to Ionia after failing the so-called three-prong sanity test that assessed whether they understood the nature of their crimes, comprehended their roles in the crimes, and demonstrated the ability to assist in their defenses "in a rational or reasonable manner." All participated in Ionia's daily blend of treatment, work, and leisure activities. And since, on average, only fifteen patients per year were deemed sane, many spent the rest of their lives working, fighting, playing, and striving within Ionia State Hospital's frenetic, pastoral city of miscreants and maladjustables.

Today, however, these patients, and indeed the hospital itself, live silently inside cardboard boxes entombed deep within concrete storage rooms at the State Archive of Michigan in Lansing. That is because, in the 1970s, the hospital underwent a shattering transformation. In January 1965, the patient population of Ionia Hospital was a robust 1,568, including 1,454 men and 114 women. Superintendent A. A. Birzgalis complained about "dangerous overcrowding" that persisted in spite of the new men's building. But only seven years later, workers razed the first of the hospital's grand stone buildings, and "security updated" most of the others. The 1972 census dropped below 700, leading Superintendent Birzgalis to plead to the Michigan legislature for the continued viability of the hospital as the state's "best maximum security facility." His calls went unanswered, and the Ionia State Hospital Medical Audit Committee recommended that the hospital "should be phased out" and recast.[7]

According to in-house memos, the threat of closure hung ominously over patients and staff. Extra layers of security grew around the perimeter like ripples in a lake. The census count dropped below 400 in 1974, and then dropped again. Ionia State Hospital morphed briefly into a regional hospital in 1976. The state released many long-term patients, who then wandered the streets of Ionia looking for food, shelter, and community. Meanwhile, workers placed the hospital's institutional memory—nearly a century of patient charts, reports, photographs, ledgers, and other artifacts—into storage. Bureaucrats slated the documents for disposal, and the collection would certainly have been discarded were it not for the efforts of two archivists in Lansing, Dave Johnson and Mark Harvey, who fought successfully for transfer to the state holdings.[8]

I first came to Lansing to study the Ionia files in the summer of 2004, after an extensive twelve-month clearance process from various state review boards. I knew that Ionia Hospital was part of an extensive state system that included such notorious institutions as the Kalamazoo State Hospital, the State Psychopathic Hospital of Ann Arbor, the Ypsilanti State Hospital, and the Northern Michigan Asylum for the Insane at Traverse City. Of course, as a hospital for insane criminals, Ionia generally housed patients that the state deemed to be law breakers, in addition to being mentally ill. Ionia was also one of the few asylums for which records remained. Most archives suffered the same fate as the institutions themselves, bulldozed, discarded, or fatally neglected in the surge of hospital closures that began in the 1970s.

I knew that the Ionia Hospital had much in common with the grand asylums made famous by classic social texts of the past half-century. For instance, Ionia functioned as a total institution, a term coined by Erving Goffman, based on his observations at Saint Elizabeth's Hospital in Washington, D.C. Like Saint Elizabeth's, Ionia was a hierarchical social system that forced its inhabitants into positions of subordination in relation to authority figures such as guards, physicians, and, ultimately, the superintendent. Ionia also functioned as an institution that reified power by defining a host of socially or economically aberrant behaviors as mental illnesses in ways suggestive of sociologist Michel Foucault's description, in *Madness and Civilization,* of the Hôpital Général in Paris. Ionia similarly brought to mind asylums described by the historians David Rothman, Gerald Grob, and Nancy Tomes, each of whom has shown how life within asylum walls reflects and, in perverse ways, benefits local economies. Such institutions, Rothman aptly wrote in *The Discovery of the Asylum,* "cannot function free of the societies in which they flourished."[9]

Yet I quickly learned that Ionia was unique because of its geographic locale, in rural environs but a mere 130 miles from Detroit, a city historically shaped by racial tensions. The archive made clear that the racial and gender demographics of the hospital shifted along with the shifting fate of Detroit. For instance, according to the official census, the hospital averaged 150 admissions per year between 1920 and 1950. In name, Ionia was a desegregated Northern hospital. Yet, on average, Ionia classified 122 of these admissions per year as "U.S.-White" and only 17 admissions/year as "U.S.-Negro." Most patients hailed from the rural Midwest, and in some years up to 35 admits were women who were hospitalized after convictions for such offenses as public disturbances, suicide attempts, or shoplifting. Doctors diagnosed schizophrenia or its earlier iteration, dementia praecox, in roughly

35 percent of all cases. These charts read as if ripped from the pages of the *New York Times* or *Ladies' Home Journal*. "This patient wasn't able to take care of her family as she should," or "This patient is not well adjusted and can't do her housework," or "She got confused and talked too loudly and embarrassed her husband."[10]

However, the hospital became increasingly African American, male, and "schizophrenic" between the mid-1950s and the early 1970s. In 1955, the hospital classified 135 of its 243 admissions as "Male-U.S. Negro," and by the late 1960s upwards of 60 percent of the entire census was composed of "dangerous, paranoid" black, schizophrenic men. Most hailed from urban Detroit. Meanwhile, the hospital's population of "U.S.-White" patients, and particularly white women, dropped precipitously.[11]

I will not soon forget my first day at the archive. I entered the reading room and filled out a request for my first set of charts, thinking that I would simply look through the admissions notes in order to catalogue information about patients and diagnoses. As a psychiatrist, I naively assumed that I had enough experience with medical charts to readily locate and transcribe each patient's identifying information, admitting symptoms, diagnosis, treatment plan, and other relevant details, as recorded by Ionia physicians.[12]

I soon realized that my assumptions about medical charts reflected my experiences as a practitioner trained in the era of litigation, brief admissions, and electronic records. For instance, in my hospital-based clinic, I dictate recollections of each patient encounter by telephone using a template of the patient's "subjective complaints," my "objective" observations, my "assessment/ diagnosis," followed by the treatment plan. My notes are then processed at outsourcing centers and, after edits, posted on the clinic's secure Web site. Each patient's chart—really a Web site—appears largely uniform in structure, form, and even content. Encounter notes appear in chronological order, and the language I use in dictating often follows a standard set of DSM-based observations. The voice constructing the record is largely my own, though I often mediate quotes from the patient, from other doctors and nurses, and, occasionally, from the transcribers (who ask for clarification, for instance).

I recognized just how much the Ionia charts were of another era the moment that the archivist wheeled out the first box of charts. Many folders made the New York City phone book seem small by comparison. Each contained documentation well in excess of what is seen today. Detailed observations made by doctors, nurses, and attendants combined with prolonged assessments of each patient's developmental milestones, family and marital relationships, jobs, legal histories, hobbies, and other information. Some charts contained hundreds of pages of these notes, carefully typed and mimeographed by what must have been a massive typing pool. Each chart also included family and developmental histories filled out by hand by the nearest relation, as well as complete sets of handwritten correspondence between relatives and physicians. Letters often complained of poor treatment or unjustified hospitalization, questioned diagnoses, or praised the care that their relatives received. Many also included personal documentation that ranged from commissary receipts to eyeglass prescriptions to field trip reports to birthday cards to telegrams.

Reading, I felt a mixture of responsibility and deep sadness. For better and largely for worse, the Ionia charts documented the lives of the marginalized and the forgotten in novel-like detail, and in ways that made the medical records of today seem impersonal and flat. This was because the charts recorded people in two conflicting ways: in their roles as patients and convicts, as defined by interactions with the state hospital complex and the courts, and in their roles as sons, daughters, fathers, husbands, wives, or loners, as defined by letters, cards, and other texts. The charts also documented in minute detail the tragedy of what it meant to be warehoused in a state asylum at mid-century—and in particular, in an asylum where short sentences devolved into lifelong incarceration. A number of charts contained yearly notes from patients to their doctors voicing such sentiments as "Doc, I really think I am cured," or "Dear Doctor, I believe I am ready to go home," or "You have no right to keep me here after my sentence is over." These letters stacked thirty-deep in some charts, signifying years of pleading and longing and anger, together with thirty years' of responses from clinicians urging, "You are almost there" or "Perhaps next year." Invariably, the last note in each stack was a death certificate from the Ionia coroner.

I visited the archive regularly over the next four years. With the help of my research assistant, I analyzed and catalogued hospital administrative records and the charts of nearly six hundred randomly selected patients admitted to the hospital between the late 1920s and the early 1970s, under the agreement that I significantly alter all personal identifying information about patients, as I have done in the case descriptions that appear in this book. Names, dates, and places have been changed, and vignettes represent condensed and extrapolated aggregates drawn from the rich case materials. All doctor-patient dialogue and text in quotation marks is reproduced verbatim. I also visited Ionia on numerous occasions and conducted a series of oral histories with surviving members of the hospital staff, though, perhaps tellingly, I located no surviving patients despite numerous attempts.[13]

What stories boxes tell. Ionia was its own planet, walled off, orbiting, a place where real people worked and lived and died. Then came a series of public scandals, the advent of psychopharmaceuticals, and changes in legal systems and penal codes. Decreased public funding followed, along with encroachment by regional forensic centers. Finally, the transformation. The boxes were but light-years of this implosion, vapor trails, found poems, measurable heat. Disembodied voices that told silent stories of what it meant to be incarcerated, or neglected, or entrenched, or immured.

Deinstitutionalization, that failed social experiment of the 1960s and 1970s, seemed a viable explanation for Ionia's stunning demise. Deinstitutionalization combined economic considerations with reactions to appalling conditions in mental asylums to push for the liberation of persons warehoused in state psychiatric hospitals. In the United States, the movement's crowning achievement was the Community Mental Health Act of 1963, which undercut large mental institutions by transferring funding to nonresidential community mental-health centers. According to the psychiatric epidemiologist Richard Lamb, the result was "mass exodus of mentally ill persons from living in hospitals to living in the community . . . in 1955, when numbers of patients in state hospitals reached their highest point, 559,000 persons were institutionalized in state mental hospitals out of a total population of 165 million; in 1998, there were 57,151 for a population of more than 275 million."[14]

Ionia suffered a similar fate. Administrators worried that the Community Mental Health Act provided cover for the state legislature to cut funding for hospital operations. Concern turned to near panic in the aftermath of local amendments such as Michigan House bills 3344, 3342, and 3343, which effectively reclassified many criminally insane patients as simply insane. Key referral sources disappeared overnight, and long-incarcerated patients walked free. By the mid-1970s, as longtime Ionia ward attendant Louise Cook recalls, patients could be seen "shuffling down city streets, talking to themselves." "Some patients couldn't make it on their own," added another former employee, Naomi Lutz. "So they would on occasion walk back to the hospital and ask to be readmitted. But we couldn't keep them, of course." Another former attendant, who asked that his name not be used, remembers thinking that deinstitutionalization was a conspiracy: "What better way for the Russians to get even with us than to let all of the mental patients loose!"[15]

However, the more I read, the more it became clear to me that Ionia did not let *all* of the patients loose, and that deinstitutionalization did not tell the whole, fateful tale of the hospital and its inhabitants. If deinstitutionalization told the whole narrative, then why did so many charts from the 1960s and

1970s describe unruly male patients admitted and contained well after the process of hospital closure had begun? Like Cecil Peterson, these men were blue-collar workers from Detroit. Many were sent to Ionia after convictions for crimes that ranged from homicide to armed robbery to property destruction during periods of civil unrest, such as the Detroit riots of 1968. Some of the men entered the system half-crazed already. "Family reports long history of hearing voices," or "suspicious that neighbors poisoned his food." Others, such as Mr. Peterson, developed their symptoms only after incarceration, and likely abuse, in state prisons. "Nine months in solitary . . . Now markedly combative . . . appears delusional." In both instances, ward notes emphasized how hallucinations and delusions rendered these men as threats not only to other patients, but to the authority represented by clinicians, ward attendants, and society itself. "Paranoid against his doctors and the police." Or, "would be a danger to society were he not in an institution."

Ionia held these men using little-known loopholes in deinstitutionalization amendments that stipulated that the hospital would continue to receive or contain patients deemed too violent for state correctional institutions, or who posed "dangerousness to the community" even after most other patients were set free. The word NEGRO appeared on the upper right corner of the face page in eight out of every ten of these charts. And *schizophrenia, paranoid type* was overwhelmingly the most common diagnosis applied to these men, these institutionalized black bodies that deinstitutionalization left behind.[16]

How did a group of African American men from Detroit become deinstitutionalization's invisible, inevitable undertow? The most obvious answers turned out to be incomplete. Race-based misdiagnosis, the racist intentions of doctors, and even the actions or symptoms of the men themselves did not fully explain why Ionia incarcerated these men for periods well beyond their original sentences. Rather, the men's confinement resulted from a longer process of racialization in which schizophrenia morphed from an illness of pastoral, feminine neurosis into one of urban, male psychosis, not just within American society, but within the asylum's increasingly sturdy walls.

Scholars have long argued that medical and governmental institutions code threats to authority as mental illnesses during moments of political turmoil. Much of the best-known literature on the subject comes from outside the United States. International human rights activists such as Walter Reich have long chronicled the ways in which Soviet psychiatrists in so-called Psikhushka hospitals diagnosed political dissidents with schizophrenia. Meanwhile, Michel Foucault often cited French hospitals as examples to support his belief that the discourses of the human sciences produce and discipline deviant subjects in the larger project of maintaining particular power hierarchies. Foucault also importantly developed a theory of "state racism," whereby governments use emancipatory discourses of what he called "race struggle" as excuses for the further oppression of minority groups. Meanwhile, the Martinique-born psychiatrist Frantz Fanon called on his experiences in Algeria to describe a North African syndrome in which political and medical subjugation literally created psychiatric symptoms in colonized subjects. Fanon's important schema, discussed at length below, focused on the ways in which racist social structures reproduce themselves not only in political or economic institutions, but also in the "damaged" psyches of people it needs to control.[17]

The more I learned about the men at Ionia, the more I came to believe that, far from the national glare, a similar process may have taken place in the United States. Ionia's schizophrenic patients in the 1930s, 1940s, and 1950s often appeared as if downtrodden Olivia de Havillands, lower-middle-class women and men down on their luck. To be sure, the hospital did admit very small numbers of African American women—on average, only three admissions per year. But, the hospital classified the majority of women as "U.S.-White," which was not surprising given the demographics of rural Michigan and the anything-but-desegregated admissions policies of this nominally desegregated hospital. The next section describes one such case, a woman I have called Alice Wilson who was admitted to Ionia in the 1940s after creating a public disturbance while shopping at a general store.

Yet, as later chapters detail, 1960s-era changes in hospital demographics, mental-health policies, popular attitudes, national events, and a host of other variables altered the meaning of schizophrenia in profoundly political ways. *Parens patriae* gave way to police *patriae*. Increasingly biological and chemical definitions of mental illness made it ever more difficult for doctors and patients to recognize how clinical issues mirrored structural ones. The state classified fewer and fewer women as criminally insane—and then shut the women's ward completely. Civil unrest filled the airwaves and the streets. Detroit burned. Ionia transformed. Only at the end of this diagnostic, cultural, and, ultimately, *institutional* shift were unruly black men from Detroit viewed as suffering from a disease called schizophrenia. And only then did the Michigan mental-health system treat these men, and retain them, as such.

When read through the lens of the racial politics of the 1960s, the archived charts suggested that, at Ionia at least, deinstitutionalization was far from a monolithic process. Its oratory demanded freedom for mental patients. But the revolution's on-the-ground practice took intimate account of race as well. In this sense, deinstitutionalization did not simply dictate which patients the state set free; it also decided which patients the state held onto.

Ultimately, the charts served as object lessons in the story I now turn to tell: how the rhetorics of liberation, from deinstitutionalization to civil rights, also produce anything-but-emancipatory anxieties about social change. And, how, as a result of these anxieties, a hospital for insane criminals became something else instead.

PART II

Alice Wilson

FIG. 3 *Patient activities at Ionia State Hospital for the Criminally Insane*
included knitting, sewing, and building floats for the Michigan State Fair.
Above is a patient-built float from the 1933 Ionia County centennial parade.
(Source: Archives of Michigan, RG77-3, B2 F8)

CHAPTER 3

She Tells Very Little about Her Behavior Yet Shows a Lot[1]

ALICE WILSON WORE HER SHAME like a thin coat on a cold day, and no one could take it away—not her husband, not her neighbors, and certainly not her doctors. She knew she had embarrassed her family. She scolded and neglected them. She had not cooked or cleaned. She had not mended or sewn. At times she had not cared, though most often she struggled to keep it in by swallowing her sadness and her pain. But then came the trip, and the outburst, and the arrest. And then came the treatment.

Alice Wilson, née Alice Perkins, was born in March 1910 into a family of farmers in Nashville, Michigan, a town named after George Nash, chief engineer of the Michigan Central Railroad. She would have settled in Nashville were her life not altered by tragedy. When Alice was three, her mother, Nora Perkins, contracted smallpox during her second pregnancy and died while giving birth to a stillborn son. Alice was too young to remember the details, but in her early years she heard neighbors recount how her mother suffered and fought against fever, pain, and exhaustion in an attempt to save her own life and that of her child. Nora's screams carried out to the country road. But after three days she screamed no more.

Alice's father, Gus Perkins, arranged a quick burial in the night. He lay all of Nora's clothes, blankets, letters, and combs neatly on the ground outside the house in an attempt to let sunlight kill the smallpox. Perhaps the sun worked against the germs, but it did little to inoculate Gus against despair. He could scarcely take care of himself, let alone his left alone daughter. Alice moved in with nearby cousins, though she would one day regret that she did not stay by her father's side. Two years later, Gus died of pneumonia, and Alice moved in with her grandparents in Lansing.

Was it any wonder that Alice waited to start her own family? A robust girl of some pulchritude, she rejected all suitors and concentrated instead on schoolwork and music. She became a straight-A student and an accomplished pianist. Alice's teachers described her as a "quiet, timid, eventempered" child who was perpetually "cheerful" and "friendly." Her hospital chart later asserted that Alice showed "no knowledge about sex" and remained in every way virginal throughout her teen years.

Alice took a teaching job after high school, believing that she would live life as a spinster. But her plans changed when, at twenty-three, she met George Wilson, a square-jawed reporter for the local newspaper. A marriage, two sons, and a daughter followed, and Alice spent the next seven years happily keeping home while George worked as a reporter and then as an editor.

Wives often receive gifts of bronze to mark their eighth year of marriage. But Alice got schizophrenia instead. As George saw it, the symptoms came on suddenly, though in retrospect she had been off for a while. Normally a meticulous cleaner, she let dishes pile up in the sink and dust build up in the corner. Normally a proud dresser, she remained in her bedclothes until noon. Normally self-assured, she cried, fretted, or chastised herself aloud for "not doing a good job rearing my children." Families have ways of accommodating such warning signs, perhaps because the need for cohesion forces blindness toward individual deviations from the norm. Alice and George's family was no different. But in retrospect, perhaps they should have known.

There was no ignoring what happened on the vacation of 1941. Ever the reporter, George provided most of the details when he testified in front of the judge. The family planned a trip to visit George's father in Biloxi, Mississippi. George, Alice, and the children left Nashville and drove 711 miles, halfway through Arkansas, before stopping to rest at a motel. Tired and sore, the family checked in and went out to buy groceries, Coke, and playing cards. At the general store, Alice suddenly began to fill her shopping cart with underpants. "The children need clean undergarments," she explained in an eerie, disconnected voice. "I forgot to pack them." She grew angry when George contradicted her, but she allowed him to empty her cart. Crisis averted, he thought.

George and the children paid and started to walk to the car with the bagged groceries and supplies when Alice began to cry. "Why do we need these things? We do not need them. I am such a bad mother," she moaned. "I provide for no one. I am worthless." She pulled items from the shopping bags. Then she fell to the ground. George tried to comfort her, but she could not be assuaged. The store manager demanded that she "pipe down." Officers soon arrived on a call for disturbing the peace. "I am worthless," she cried. "I am inferior."

She repeated these words to the judge, who wished simply to mete out a misdemeanor and send the family on its way. But between tears, Alice—pointing to her family—mentioned that she had no idea who these people were and wondered why she should drive off with a strange man. Was her sudden amnesia inadvertent? Was it intentional? Was it calculated? Was it unconscious? No one knew for sure, but all agreed on the course of action: professional help. Biloxi could wait. And thus began the long journey back to Michigan, to Kalamazoo, and ultimately to Ionia.

Alice Wilson was admitted to the Ionia women's ward on September 1, 1941. The admission face sheet summarized her identifying information as follows.

> Age: 31. Nativity: Native Born of Native Born Parents. Color: White. Occupation: Housewife. Religious Denomination: Protestant. Clothing: From Home. Reason for Admission: Disturbing the Peace. Got Confused and Embarrassed Husband.

An extensive workup ensued. Alice's examining psychiatrist was R. Barry Leroy, a staid, impeccable man of forty-four who hailed from Lansing. Barry Leroy's approach to examination coated sharp skepticism behind a veneer of empathic concern. He was no psychoanalyst. Leroy resented the ivory tower analysts he met at professional meetings because of their disdain for the so-called directive-organic psychiatrists like himself. At the same time he believed firmly in Freudian notions of disease, and readily adopted a psychoanalytic stance of evenly hovering attention—or more aptly, evenly hovering mistrust—that interpreted presenting symptoms as but incomplete markers of unconscious conflicts.

Dr. Leroy began his inquiry with a physical examination. "Patient," as Alice was now called, "is a clean white female who came readily for the examination and was cooperation [*sic*] throughout," he wrote in the chart. "Hair is blonde, eyes are blue. There is a mole on the left shoulder. There is no significant asymmetry of the body." Dr. Leroy found all aspects of the physical exam to be normal, and wrote in capital letters that "PATIENT HAS BLADDER AND BOWEL CONTROL AND EXCERCISES THIS."

The mental portion of the exam was next. Dr. Leroy noted first that Alice "came readily for examination and was neat in appearance," and that "patient readily gives her attention to the interviewer, does not appear distractible." Trust established, Dr. Leroy lit two cigarettes, one for himself and one for the patient, and then began with the usual questions meant to assess constitution.

DR. LEROY: Can you tell me, please, your full name?
ALICE: Alice Wilson, formerly Alice Perkins. From Nashville.

DR. LEROY: And Alice, what are you?

ALICE: I am a housewife.

DR. LEROY: Very good. Can you tell me the date, month, and year?

ALICE: I have lost track of the date—I only just arrived here. I believe it is the first week of September. We are in 1936, I am sure of that.

DR. LEROY (LIGHTING SECOND CIGARETTE): Correct—today is September first. Please also tell me—who am I?

ALICE: I am sick, I am in the hospital, I miss my family. I need to get home to my family. . . . You just examined me. You must be the doctor. Am I right?

DR. LEROY: Exactly. As I told you before, my name is Doctor Leroy. I am examining you in order to determine your diagnosis. Then I will be taking care of you so that you may better take care of your family, as you say—but more about that later. For now, I wish to ask some questions meant to evaluate your intellect.

Dr. Leroy then posed the seventeen standard intelligence questions, noting Alice's responses in the chart. These included the following:

Say the alphabet ("said well")
Count from 1 to 50 ("counted well")
Name the months ("named well")
Repeat the Lord's Prayer ("repeated well")
Sing some school song or recitation ("not able to")
What is the largest river in America? ("Mississippi")
What is the largest city in the world? ("doesn't know")
Name some states touching Michigan ("Indiana, Illinois, Wisconsin")
What was the War of the Revolution? ("Evasive. Claims not to remember.")
What was the Civil War? ("Evasive. Claims not to remember.")
Who is the Governor of Michigan? ("Evasive. Claims not to know.")
Who is the ruler of England? ("Claims not to know.")
What is seven times nine? ("63")
What is eighty-four minus twenty-five? ("69")
What is twelve times thirteen? ("doesn't know")

Dr. Leroy's diagnostic sensors stirred only slightly when Alice failed to identify, among other trivia, that George VI was king of the United Kingdom and the British Dominions, and that Winston Churchill served as prime minister, first lord of the Treasury, and minister of defense. "Perhaps a low fund of knowledge," he thought, "though intellect is intact." But he sat forward in his chair when, in reply to the seemingly straightforward query "What is the reason you are here?" Alice replied: "I thought about drowning myself a few months back, but taking one's life is a sin. So I sat at home. I was mentally disturbed at that time and I wasn't able to take care of my family as I should. I felt I couldn't do my housework, and I was not well adjusted."

DR. LEROY: But why are you here now?

ALICE: We were on the way to Biloxi. My husband said I talked too loudly and got out of my head. I know I let my family down. (Leroy notes: "Patient grins, stifles laughter.")

DR. LEROY: Were you out of your mind?

ALICE: Well, I don't think I'm the person to say. I don't know. I mean, don't men become disturbed? (Leroy notes: "Patient ambivalent, evasive.")

DR. LEROY: Were people against you?

ALICE (TAKING HER TIME): No, that's when we drove home. The trip— it was all hazy to me—the trip coming home. (Leroy notes: "Possibly evasive, circumstantial.") I don't feel safe here, if that's what you mean.

DR. LEROY: Do you hear voices when there is no one around?

ALICE: No.

DR. LEROY: Did you?

ALICE: No. (Leroy notes: "Confusion, delusion about the incident. Staff earlier reported patient responding to internal stimuli. Patient denies.")

DR. LEROY: Thank you, Alice. That will be all.

ALICE: When can I go home?

After the examination, Dr. Leroy strode down the corridor to his office. He lit a third cigarette, followed soon by a fourth, called in his secretary, and began to dictate.

Alice Wilson is a white woman of thirty-one years who appears to have passed through a very confused period. . . . This patient has taken reasonable care of her husband until late. . . . Symptoms include a delusional sadness and irascible feelings of guilt. . . . The patient is evasive and tells very little about her behavior and yet shows a lot. . . . Hospital staff has observed patient responding to internal stimuli, though she has only once admitted to being hallucinated. . . . Overwhelmed by guilt feelings about proper care of her family. Likely date back to her formative years, and feelings of failure regarding care of her widowed father. . . . Guarded and mistrustful. . . .

For Dr. Leroy, the diagnosis was clear.

CHAPTER 4

Loosening Associations

THERE WERE OTHERS. DAVID MORRIS, a twenty-seven-year-old Navy veteran from Flint, Michigan, had sex with his sister. Carol Sue Adams, twenty-two years old from Adrian, Michigan, stole a purse. On her way to jail, guards noticed that Adams was "very dejected and out of contact with reality." Minnie Briggs, the youngest of eleven siblings from Yale, Michigan, and once a state violin champ, forged her mother's name on a check, got caught, cried for three days, and then tried to hang herself. Milmouth Hunt, always drunk, was convicted of entering without breaking. He would have been a free man if he could have just kept to himself his unassailable belief that the State Prison of Southern Michigan was located in mainland China. And Frank St. Clair, a forty-six-year-old repetitive handwasher from Gary, Indiana, may or may not have taken indecent liberties with his neighbor's teenage daughter.

Why did Dr. Leroy and the other Ionia psychiatrists believe that these patients from the 1930s and 1940s suffered from schizophrenia of the paranoid type? Your first response might be to say that they did not. You might point out that these women and men did not demonstrate month-long periods of delusions or hallucinations, nor did they experience moments of unexplained theophany. Their speech was not disorganized, their behavior far from catatonic. Perhaps depression, obsessive-compulsive disorder, or substance abuse disorders were correct diagnoses instead?

You would in many ways be right. For instance, if Alice Wilson appeared at a psychiatrist's office in the present day, she would very likely receive a diagnosis other than paranoid schizophrenia. Major depressive disorder with psychotic features would be one option, the so-called Axis II personality disorders such as borderline or histrionic personality disorder would be another. Obsessive-compulsive disorder might garner consideration as well. Alice would likely receive antidepressant medications in this present-day visit, and she would be an unlikely candidate for admission to a psychiatric hospital.

But you would also be wrong for one important reason: Alice Wilson was not diagnosed today, or yesterday, or even the day before. Instead, her interaction with Dr. Leroy took place in a historical moment very different from our own, when era-specific social conditions, assumptions about illness and health, and interactions between doctors and patients shaped understandings of schizophrenia that were dissimilar from ours in form as well as in content.

In this sense, diagnosing Alice Wilson as suffering from depression, obsessive-compulsive disorder, or other present-day definitions of mental illness can be described as an error of what is called historical presentism. In his classic text, *Historians' Fallacies: Toward a Logic of Historical Thought*, the historian David Fischer describes presentism as a logical fallacy in which present-day values or perspectives are anachronistically introduced into depictions or interpretations of the past. As Fisher writes, "The fallacy of presentism is a complex anachronism, in which the antecedent in a narrative series is falsified by being denied or interpreted in terms of the consequent."[1]

Well-intentioned researchers commit errors of analytic presentism when they use modern-day illness categories to diagnose historical figures. For instance, based on a quantitative analysis of the poetry and letters of Emily Dickinson, Dr. John McDermott writes that the poet's "sudden, spontaneous anxiety attack at age 24 . . . clearly meet[s] DSM-IV criteria for a panic attack," and that "data" from Dickinson's poems suggest a seasonal "bipolar pattern." Dr. Dietrich Blumer similarly diagnoses Vincent van Gogh based on his observation that "van Gogh suffered two distinct episodes of reactive depression, and there are clearly bipolar aspects to his history. Both episodes of depression were followed by sustained periods of increasingly high energy and enthusiasm." And, in their article "Witchcraft, Religious Fanaticism and Schizophrenia—Salem Revisited," Thurman Sawyer and George Bundren argue that "it is our belief that schizophrenia was present in Salem in 1692, and that the type most prevalent was the chronic undifferentiated type."[2]

These and other observations rely on state-of-the-art understandings of illness. But they fail to account for the ways that state-of-the-art diagnoses, though considered accurate in our own era, encapsulate assumptions that render their transport across space and time difficult if not impossible.

Of course, it is more than reasonable to make comparative judgments about other historical moments. Condemning a woman as a witch in Salem was undoubtedly more morally repugnant than diagnosing someone with schizophrenia today. But suggesting that women in Salem actually *had* schizophrenia, an illness not yet "discovered" in 1692, is a more difficult claim because present-day definitions of schizophrenia make sense to us only in the context of contemporary doctor-patient interactions, diagnostic imaging technologies, insurance battles, pharmaceutical treatments, health-care aesthetics, social networks, and a host of other variables that were simply not relevant three centuries ago. In this sense, diagnosing these women with schizophrenia reveals more about present-day categories and beliefs than it does about actual conditions in 1692.

From a historical perspective, a better question than whether Alice Wilson had schizophrenia might be why Dr. Leroy *thought* Alice Wilson had schizophrenia, as he understood the illness in 1941. The answer might surprise you, because in the context of the 1930s and 1940s, far from being a victim of mistaken diagnosis, Alice Wilson was in many ways a textbook case.

IT SEEMS IRONIC that the story of why a woman from Nashville looked schizophrenic to a doctor from Ionia originated in a nature-versus-nurture debate between two Europeans. But that is precisely what happened.

Emil Kraepelin lost the debate, though, as a consolation, he would later become known as the father of modern psychiatry. Kraepelin was a German psychiatrist and director of an eighty-bed clinic at the Universität Dorpatat in then–Soviet Estonia during the latter part of the nineteenth century. At the time, conventional wisdom avowed that specific actions and life events caused specific types of insanity. Pauper lunacy resulted from habitual intemperance, poverty, and destitution, treated by a diet of wholesome digestible bread, milk porridge, or milk thickened with various farinaceous substances, and good broth, along with occasional topical bleedings and counterirritations. Masturbatory insanity came from onanistic self-corruption and led to a form of idiocy manifest by sallow skin, lusterless eyes, flabby muscles, loose stools, and, of course, cold and clammy hands. And old maid's insanity was, as the name implied, the insanity of old maids.[3]

Kraepelin was foremost among a group of European clinicians who defined insanity not according to causes or symptoms, but according to course and prognosis. This movement began with the work of John Haslam, superintendent of Bethlem Hospital in London. In 1809, Haslam described an insanity that afflicted adolescents of prompt capacity and lively disposition who suffered a "diminution of the ordinary curiosity" and a marked reduction in "affection toward their parents and relations." In its most severe cases, according to Haslam, the illness transformed "promising and vigorous young intellects into slavering and bloated idiots." That same year, the famed French reformer Phillipe Pinel published parallel observations about patients under his care at the Bicêtre and Salpêtrière asylums. Pinel called the illness *démence,* and argued that these patients should not be kept in chains like criminals, as was common practice, but should rather be shown empathic kindness. In 1852, a French physician and follower of Pinel named Benedict Morel similarly noted an illness that afflicted adolescents whose "brilliant intellectual facilities underwent in time a very distressing arrest." According to Morel, patients who once displayed brilliance and intellectual energy suddenly lived lives of "torpor akin to hebetude," or dullness and lethargy. He described these patients as suffering from *démence précoce,* literally premature dementia.[4]

Kraepelin studied the longitudinal case histories of institutionalized patients. His major insight, published in the sixth edition of his *Lehrbuch der Psychiatrie* in 1899, was a classification system that divided insanity into two genera: one that ultimately resulted in dementia and one that did not. In the latter category were patients with manic-depressive psychosis, circumscribed psychotic episodes along with emotional disturbances from which they ultimately recovered. By contrast, patients who exhibited "hallucinations, delusions, incongruous emotivity, impairment of attention, negativism, and progressive mental dilapidation" to the point of "simplicity" suffered from an illness that Kraepelin named with the Latinized version of Morel's diagnostic term: *dementia praecox,* the "development of a peculiar simple condition of mental weakness occurring at a youthful age."[5]

Kraepelin believed that dementia praecox was a biological illness caused by underlying organic lesions or faulty metabolism. A prolific researcher, Kraepelin earlier discovered an organic basis of what is now known as Alzheimer's disease, and he was confident that he would someday identify the pathologic basis of dementia praecox as well. Kraepelin argued that, because praecox resulted from irreversible biological changes, the prognosis was dismal, with over 75 percent of cases progressing to incurable dementia.[6]

Paul Eugen Bleuler disagreed. In 1911, the Swiss psychiatrist and onetime student of Kraepelin published a lasting critique titled *Dementia Praecox or the Group of Schizophrenias.* While working at a psychiatric hospital in Rheinau, Germany, and later at the Burghölzli Hospital in Zurich, Bleuler observed that praecox was neither a dementia, nor did it always occur in young people. "The older term [dementia praecox]," he wrote only a decade after the publication of Kraepelin's classic text, "is a product of a time when not only the very concept of dementia, but, also that of precocity, was applicable to all cases at hand. But it hardly fits our contemporary ideas of the scope of this disease-entity."[7]

According to Bleuler, the underlying mechanism in praecox was "loosening of associations," a process in which patients existed in the real world and at the same time turned away from reality ("autism") into the world of fantasy, wishes, fears, and symbols. As an early proponent of Freud, Bleuler placed psychosis on a spectrum with neurosis as a developmental disorder with childhood origins. Bleuler argued that the condition described by Kraepelin was not a biological disorder, but was instead a psychical splitting of the basic functions of the personality. He thus maintained that the term *dementia praecox* should be replaced by a name that combined the Greek words for "split" (*schizo*) and "mind" (*phrene*). "I call dementia praecox '*schizophrenia*,'" he wrote, "because the 'splitting' of the different psychic functions is one of its most important characteristics."[8]

Bleuler believed that emotional splitting was accompanied not by violence, but by symptoms such as indifference, creativity, passion, and even fanaticism. He wrote,

> Even in the less severe forms of illness, indifference seems to be the external sign of their state; an indifference to everything—to friends and relations, to vacation or enjoyment, to duties or rights, to good fortune or bad. "I don't care one way or another," is what a patient of Binswanger said. Generally the defect shows itself most strikingly in relation to the most vital of the patient's interests and it does not make any difference whether or not their comprehension requires complicated thinking. A mother might show right at the beginning of her illness that she is indifferent to the weal and woes of her children. . . . There are many schizophrenics who display lively affect at least in certain directions. Among them are the active writers, the world improvers, the health fanatics, the founders of new religions.[9]

Obvious overlap existed between the two men and their theories. Perhaps that was why their correspondence grew nasty over time, as academic debates often do. Kraepelin defended his observations and attacked Bleuler as unscientific. Bleuler, meanwhile, criticized Kraepelin as resistant to change. Ultimately, however, Bleuler's diagnostic term prevailed. *Schizophrenia* became standard psychiatric nomenclature, while *dementia praecox* fell from vocabularies, textbooks, and tongues.[10]

Historians of psychiatry often assert that schizophrenia replaced praecox for clinical reasons, and rightly so. Bleuler's definition more adeptly encapsulated the prognostic trajectory, and the free market of medicine invested in the accurate term while devaluing the inaccurate one. But a second reason explains why schizophrenia rhetorically defeated praecox when the terms crossed the Atlantic and came to the United States: American physicians and the general public associated dementia praecox with the marginalized, and schizophrenia with the mainstream. Moreover, the categories of marginal and mainstream reflected early twentieth-century American beliefs not just about mental illness, but about race, class, and nativity as well.[11]

Ironically, Kraepelin believed that, because praecox functioned at a biological substrate beneath culture or context, the illness occurred in all peoples equally. To prove this point he once traveled to Singapore and Java to study "Malaysians, Javanese, and Chinese" patients. After the trip, he concluded that praecox was not caused by race, climate, food, or life circumstance, but by underlying biology common to "mankind."[12]

Yet, when the German psychiatrist's terminology came to the United States in the 1910s and 1920s, the Kraepelinian emphasis on brain biology fit easily into existing beliefs that "Negroes" were biologically unfit for freedom. This troubling argument emerged from the work of the American surgeon Samuel Cartwright, who wrote in 1851 in the *New Orleans Medical and Surgical Journal* that the tendency of slaves to run away from their captors was a treatable medical disorder. Cartwright described two types of insanity among slaves. Drapetomania resulted when "the white man attempts to oppose the Deity's will, by trying to make the Negro anything else than 'the submissive knee-bender' (which the Almighty declared he should be) by trying to raise him to a level with himself, or by putting himself on an equality with the Negro." According to Cartwright, such unnatural kindness led to a form of mania whose sole symptom was the propensity of slaves to run away. Similarly, *dysaesthesia aethiopis* was Cartwright's term for the "rascality" and "disrespect for the master's property" that resulted when African Americans did not have whites overseeing their every action. Cartwright theorized that both conditions resulted from biological lesions, and he advised treating both with whipping, hard labor, and, in extreme cases, amputation of the toes.[13]

The historian Sander Gilman has shown that Cartwright's ideas influenced early twentieth-century medical researchers, who argued that the incidence of insanity rose dramatically in African Americans after emancipation. Such ideas suffused American psychiatry as well. Psychiatric authors combined Cartwright's drapetomania with Kraepelin's praecox in order to contend that African Americans were psychologically unfit for freedom. For instance, in 1913, Arrah Evarts, a psychiatrist from the Government Hospital for the Insane in Washington, D.C., wrote an article in the *Psychoanalytic Review* titled "Dementia Praecox in the Colored Race," in which she described dramatic increases in the illness in "colored" patients. Evarts's patients included a woman of "primitive character" who, upon leaving her job as an assistant cook at a Virginia plantation, "became greatly excited and beat her head against the wall" and then "sang hymns and repeated verses from the bible"; an "undisciplined" schoolteacher who went mute for three years; and a woman who believed, on the word of a faith healer, that her abdomen was occupied by snakes.[14]

Like Cartwright, Evarts linked the appearance of praecox in these and other patients to the pressures of freedom—pressures for which "Negroes," she argued, were biologically unfit. Speaking of slavery, Evarts wrote,

> This bondage in reality was a wonderful aid to the colored man. The necessity of mental initiative was never his, and his racial characteristic of imitation carried him far on the road. But after he became a free man, the conditions under which he must continue his progress became infinitely harder. He must now think for himself, and exercise forethought if he and his family are to live at all; two things which has [*sic*] so far not been demanded and for which there was no racial preparation. It has been said by many observers whose words can scarce be doubted that a crazy Negro was a rare sight before emancipation. However that may be, we know he is by no means rare today.

The good doctor's racist words reflected the beliefs of European colonizers in places such as Africa and Algeria, who had for centuries argued that colonial servitude aided blacks by civilizing them. Dr. Evarts and other physicians of the 1910s and 1920s modified this lineage through the deployment of state-of-the-art Kraepelinian terminology. Following Kraepelin's emphasis on brain biology, Evarts wrote that dementia praecox was "essentially a deteriorating psychosis," caused by "lipoid degeneration, reticular degeneration of the ganglion cells, proliferation of neurogliar tissue, and Kornchen cells."[15]

American popular culture similarly associated Kraepelin's schema with marginalized others. Praecox perhaps sounded like smallpox, and practically every mention of the illness in major American newspapers between 1910 and 1930 referenced the term in relation to anxieties about "Negroes," immigrants, criminals, or "subnormals." For example, in 1912, the American media was rife with stories of an invasion of the United States by legions of "alien insane." Dr. Spencer Dawes, New York's special commissioner for matters of alien sanity, issued a statement in December of that year describing how immigrants with dementia praecox had overrun American ports,

courts, and hospitals. According to Dawes, "more than 64 percent" of patients in U.S. mental asylums in 1910 were "foreign-born" or "of foreign-born
parents," numbers that "increased by 48.3 percent" each decade. Aliens included Italians, Jews, Irish, Germans, Canadians, and "Negro immigrants
from the West Indies." These findings led to calls for laws assuring that each
steamship that landed in the United States would be met by a trained alienist
who would test immigrants for dementia praecox using an expanded version
of the mental status questions that Barry Leroy asked Alice Wilson. Those
aliens who answered twenty-five to thirty questions "intelligently" would be
assumed sane and permitted access to America, while those found to have
dementia praecox would be slated for immediate deportation.[16]

Praecox was also frequently associated with crime. Throughout the 1910s
and 1920s, newspapers reported steady increases in crimes committed by
"demented criminals"—a term likely condensed from dementia praecox
—including several high-profile murder cases. Herbert Jerome Dennison, a
convicted killer of two six-year-old boys, was a diagnosed praecox patient let
loose on the street, as was Porter Charlton, an Italian immigrant who shot
his wife, Mary. Forensic research in 1915 "discovered" that up to 60 percent
of arrests and 15 percent of violent crimes involved praecoxial perpetrators.
A series of articles by the author French Strothers in the early 1920s claimed
that dementia praecox, or emotional insanity, "is practically the cause of all
crime." Strothers paraphrased Kraepelin to argue that the disease, and thus
the crime, was "hereditary and incurable."[17]

In a landmark speech to the Russell Sage Foundation in New York in
1915, Chief Justice Harry Olson of the municipal court of Chicago described
the establishment of a forensic laboratory whose purpose was to determine
which criminals suffered from dementia praecox and which did not. Olson
argued that insane crime was extracting an enormous cost on U.S. society.
He urged the national adoption of a mental test to identify insanity in adolescents before they had "progressed so far as to commit murder or other
serious crimes." In the projective test, youthful offenders of minor crimes
were made to "gaze for ten seconds at a drawing of a scroll and a box" and
then draw these figures from memory. According to Olson, drawings by diseased people always showed "the same kind of faults and mannerisms, and
according to the style of their work the subjects are quickly classified as sufferers from dementia praecox, drug users, alcoholics, etc." Once so identified,
Olson maintained, these individuals could then be selectively sterilized. As
the *New York Times* reported on November 20, 1915, under the headline "DE-
CLARES INSANITY CAN BE EXTIRPATED":

An extension of the system all over the country, [Olson] said, would in time enable society to recognize practically all who were suffering from mental disease and finally to extirpate it. He said that Charles Benedict Davenport of the Eugenics Record Office of Cold Spring Harbor, L.I., had said to him recently, "If we had the power we need to deal with the subject, we could abolish insanity in this country in thirty years." The insane men who suddenly commit murders could all have been identified as dangerously insane many years before their outbreaks, he said, and the mental tests if universally applied to all offenders when they first get into difficulties, usually of a minor nature, would enable society to protect itself by preventing the individual from committing insane acts and by preventing the reproduction of insane stock.[18]

Such rhetoric grew louder during the 1920s and 1930s thanks to the shameful American eugenics movement. Eugenicists such as Olson combined Kraepelin's biology with American bias and fear to define persons with dementia praecox as "subnormal" scourges on the good seed of humanity. For instance, on September 2, 1923, a *Times* headline read "CHECK ON SOCIETY'S DEFECTIVES SEEN AS URGENT NEED OF NATION: LABORATORY EXPERIMENTS IN CHICAGO SHOW THAT AID FOR THE UNFIT ENCOURAGES THEIR SPREAD—MUNICIPAL CHIEF JUSTICE WOULD CURB THE SUBNORMAL AND DEVELOP BETTER STOCK." In the article, Olson claimed that "with the organization of the Eugenical Society of the United States of America, the application of biological results is only beginning, and beginning with a tardiness that is a reproach to our foresight." Olson warned that the "defective insane" were "multiplying as never before in the history of the race," and that efforts to aid the mentally ill through alms or asylums enabled "this degenerate stream to become wider." Examples of the defectives he discovered included people who sounded strikingly similar to the patients described by Arrah Evarts, such as

Case K.W. . . . Since his fourteenth birthday he has been in the *Boy's Court* seven times for various offenses ranging from petit larceny to automobile thievery. The psychopathic laboratory finds him a middle grade moron, plus dementia praecox katatenia [*sic*], somewhat effeminate.

Exploring the family history, Olson found that

K.W. is one of a family of two boys and five girls. The other boy, now 31 years old, is but 14 years mentally. Three of the five girls are alive. The first is a high-grade moron and a dementia praecox. The second is a high-grade moron plus dementia praecox katatonia. The third is a high-grade borderland moron plus dementia praecox katatonia. The fourth died an infant and the fifth at 13 of diphtheria.

Crafting arguments that would later appear with a vengeance in Nazi Germany, Olson proposed that society deal with such patients via "race betterment" through "positive, negative, and prophylactic methods" such as "segregating and sterilizing defective stocks so that they may not reproduce their kind" and active "encouragement of larger families on the part of competent and healthy members of society."[19]

HOW DIFFERENT WAS the American reception for schizophrenia, how different were its associations.

Late in his career, Bleuler made the unfortunate mistake of espousing beliefs similar to those of Dr. Evarts, that "lower races" had "germinal predispositions" to schizophrenia. He argued that "Negroes, who as slaves had no percentage of insanity worth mentioning, become insane in greater numbers the more they approach the manner of living of the whites." Yet, when his nomenclature crossed the Atlantic between the 1920s and the 1950s, doctors and the public frequently linked the Swiss psychiatrist's definition of illness not with the marginalized, but with the mainstream. A condition associated with marginalized populations, dementia praecox afflicted people who functioned beneath the radar of popular perception, or who threatened the functioning of the American nation. Schizophrenia, however, hit close to home. If praecox was a diagnosis of *them*, then schizophrenia in many ways became a diagnosis of *us*.[20]

Psychiatrists frequently highlighted Bleuler's insistence that schizophrenia was an illness of personality instead of biology. Descriptions of patients remained largely, though by no means entirely, free of connections to violence, invasions, crime, impurity, and other eugenic staples. Psychiatrists instead described patients with schizophrenia as academics, poets, women, eccentrics, and others who perhaps deviated from, but remained largely within, the norm. In sharp contrast to dementia praecox, schizophrenia often implied an illness not of the black body, but of the white mind.[21]

Psychiatric textbooks frequently demonstrated such usage. Textbook authors cited Bleuler's emphasis on the intellect and personality to depict schizophrenia as a disease of white male genius—a lineage that combined the Aristotelian alignment between great minds and madness with the work of William Awl and other psychiatrists who held that the Anglo-Saxon race was "especially vulnerable to insanity because of high intellectual achievements." For instance, when the psychiatrist Arthur P. Noyes wrote in support of a switch from dementia praecox to schizophrenia in the 1927 edition of his *Textbook of Psychiatry,* he did so by emphasizing terms taken directly from Bleuler. Noyes described a rupture in "the fundamental basis of personality" that resulted in a disorder of "feeling and thinking." Noyes called on the work of German psychiatrist and ardent anti-eugenicist Ernst Kretschmer, author of *The Psychology of Men of Genius,* to argue that persons prone to schizophrenia included "sensitive" persons who maintained "child-like facial expressions far past the usual age—an expression of vagueness and dreaminess."[22] Such patients were,

> Quiet, serious, shy, easily embarrassed and without sense of humor. In school or college he never takes part in rough games. He is teased but never learns how to defend himself by a return in kind. . . . He chooses studies of an abstract nature, particularly of a philosophical type. He has vague schemes for bettering humanity. If he has intellectual opportunities he may attempt to write poetry, particularly of a dreamy, idealistic type. He has a genuine love of nature and is often found alone in the woods and fields; he may be extravagantly enraptured by a beautiful sunset.[23]

Like other psychiatrists of his era, Noyes believed that schizophrenia resulted from early-life psychological trauma. The first (1927) and second (1936) editions of his textbook used psychoanalytic language to explain how the ultimate cause of the illness was "intrapsychic conflict" that "weakened the forces of sublimation or of repression," leading to disorders of the "emotions":

> The patient fails to show interest in the things which formerly appealed to him. There is a progressive dulling of his inner feelings; the amenities of human relations are discarded. The patient becomes moody . . . matters of the utmost intimate importance become of no concern. Home and family no longer command affection or stimulate ambition. . . . There may be a lack of harmony between the content of an idea and the accompanying expression of emotion. . . . This lack of unity and coordination in emotions constitutes part of the schizophrenia or emotional splitting.[24]

Similarly, when schizophrenia first appeared in the 1918 edition of the National Committee for Mental Hygiene's *Statistical Manual for the Use of Institutions for the Insane,* which was in many ways the precursor of the DSM, the text claimed, "The term 'schizophrenia' is now used by man writers instead of dementia praecox. The illness afflicts . . . the seclusive type of personality or one showing other evidences of abnormality in the development of instincts or feelings."[25]

Given this flowery framework, it is not surprising that many psychiatrists believed that persons with schizophrenia—and particularly white persons with schizophrenia—were neither to be feared as if criminals nor selectively eliminated as if subnormals. Noyes, for instance, urged clinicians to nurture patients as if they were underdeveloped children by finding the "sensitive and tender nature" hidden behind a patient's "cold and unresponsive exterior," thereby helping patients progress beyond "infantile" regressions. In addition to talk therapies, Noyes advocated teaching patients how to function as adults through activities that substituted "objective reality for phantasy" such as occupational therapy, physical exercise, and the encouragement of participation in "dances, concerts, and other opportunities for social contact."[26]

Similar arguments appeared in many, though by no means all, scientific articles about schizophrenia throughout the 1920s to the early 1950s. Writing in the *American Journal of Psychiatry,* psychiatrist M. G. Martin described a hospital program that surrounded "the most miserable male schizophrenic patients" with "flowering plants," taught them to "play baseball," and engaged them in "simple gardening chores." The psychoanalyst Otto Fenichel, among others, described schizophrenia as a "special kind of neurosis" amenable to psychoanalytic talk therapies. Psychiatrist Barbara Betz also encouraged physicians to conduct psychotherapy with people with schizophrenia in order to counter the forces of psychological regression. Betz advised physicians to act as if "kind, strong, fair" parents to their patients, and suggested that "with kindness, even 'tough-guy patients'" would become "touched and responsive."[27]

Schizophrenia reflected its Bleulerian origins when the term entered American popular vernacular. Schizophrenia often appeared in popular magazines and newspapers as a personality disorder brought by the pressures of white civilization, and was as such assumed to be one of the "Psychic Ills that Trouble Us," as the *New York Times* explained in August 1936. "Us" in this context meant those who lived in society rather than those who invaded it: "since all life moves in polar tensions, the oscillating interactions between the poles must be considered as normal." In 1937, *Harper's Magazine* declared that Americans lived in an "Age of Schizophrenia," a "dazzling world of bright light and swift movement and flashing communications in which the man of flesh and blood makes it impossible to make a home."[28]

Schizophrenia's wide usage resulted from a very different set of rhetorical connections than dementia praecox. Schizophrenia probably sounded like schism, and Bleuler's terminology seamlessly aligned with American notions of the conscious/unconscious binary popularized by that other European import, psychoanalysis. Psychoanalysis famously gave American culture neurosis, a set of symptoms that rendered white middle-class women unable to fulfill their roles as house mothers and as housewives. Bleuler's insistence on a split in personality, and the psychoanalytic underpinnings of his work, allowed for easy conflation. The *New York Times* described schizophrenia as a disorder of "dual personality" found in men of luminosity. Articles explained how brilliant white poets and novelists were touched by what they called "grandiloquence," a propensity toward flowery prose believed to be one of the "telltale phrases of schizophrenia, the mild form of insanity known as split personality."[29]

Meanwhile, feature stories in *Collier's Weekly* told of white families who "adopted" docile, white people with schizophrenia, and asked readers to similarly consider "sharing" their dinner tables with the mentally ill. A series of high-profile articles in the health magazine *Hygeia* detailed how the emerging science of occupational therapy helped women mental patients produce surprisingly beautiful pottery, sculptures, jewelry, and home goods. In one such article Dr. William Alanson White defined occupational therapy as "one of the avenues of approach in our attempts to solve the problem of psychotic behavior, and to accelerate, if process, the process of social and economic readjustment." To that end, *Hygeia* showed posed photographs of white women in art studios, silversmithing classes, and, most important, in the "dietetics laboratory" where "young homemakers learn the art of cooking." [30]

Many popular articles described middle-class women driven to insanity by the dual pressures of housework and motherhood. "Are we all going quietly mad?" asked an article in *Better Homes and Gardens* titled "Don't Tell Them We're All Going Crazy," which, once again, located madness within the mainstream. "Are you neurotic now? And if you are, does it mean that tomorrow you'll be psychotic or schizophrenic?" The sine qua non of such insanity, according to the *Ladies' Home Journal* article "Are You Likely to Be a Happily Married Woman?" were schizophrenic mood swings suggestive of "Doctor Jekyll and Mrs. Hyde."[31]

In 1932, another Chicagoan, Dr. W. A. Evans, the health commissioner of Chicago and a professor of psychiatry at Northwestern University Medical School, famously diagnosed Mary Todd Lincoln, the oft-maligned wife of the occasionally maligned president. In his own act of diagnostic presentism, Dr. Evans wrote a book titled *Mrs. Abraham Lincoln: A Study of Her Personality and Her Influence on Lincoln* that observed how Mrs. Lincoln diligently did her housework and gave birth to four children before suffering a "weakening of her personality." After her husband's election, according to Dr. Evans, Mary traveled to New York and began "a long series of extravagant purchases which by the end of Lincoln's first term had saddled her with debts amounting to $70,000." Evidence of her "eccentricities" grew, as the first lady vacillated between sharp-tongued and venomous and emotionally isolated and withdrawn. Such bipolarity pointed to a psychiatric diagnosis, though that diagnosis was not bipolar disorder. "She had," wrote Dr. Evans, "a mild emotional insanity which caused her to act as does a case of schizophrenia."[32]

Surely the most notorious woman with schizophrenia was Virginia Stuart Cunningham, the heroine of Mary Jane Ward's autobiographical 1946 novel, *The Snake Pit*. Virginia was a "beautiful, happily married writer" who "blacked out one day, broken by the strains of modern living." Her schizophrenic hallucinations open the book. "Virginia sits alone in the yard at Juniper Hill asylum. 'Do you hear voices?' he asked. You think I am deaf? 'Of course,' she said, 'I hear yours.'" Trying to rationalize her sanity, Virginia explained that "I am just me, Virginia Stuart Cunningham. There is just one of me and it is having a hard enough time thinking for one, let alone splitting into two."[33]

Critics hailed *The Snake Pit* for revolutionizing American assumptions about schizophrenia. *New York Times* writer Isa Kapp praised the "Novelist's Dramatic View of Schizophrenia" that "transformed" understandings of the illness, and *Los Angeles Times* cinema critic Edwin Schallert later described the infamous 1948 film version as "one of the most challenging pictures of all time." Yet, part of *The Snake Pit*'s popularity clearly resulted from the ways in which, in addition to shocking viewers and readers, the story reaffirmed comfortable stereotypes and beliefs about schizophrenia as an illness of whiteness. Virginia Stuart Cunningham personified the popular narrative in which early-life trauma rendered white, middle-class women unable to function as wives and mothers without psychoanalytic intervention. "Stirring and intensely moving," the book's back cover explains, "this is the story of a beautiful woman's mental breakdown and her thrilling recovery with the aid of a devoted and understanding husband and a wise psychiatrist." The maternal narrative was reaffirmed even in articles about the making of the film: in a December 1948 exposé, the gossip columnist Hedda Hopper detailed how Olivia de Havilland prepared for her two most important roles, playing Virginia in the film and "having a baby" in real life. Meanwhile, Orville Prescott's important review of the book in the *New York Times* sounded very much like *Harper's Magazine*'s description of the Age of Schizophrenia, in which insanity resulted from the pressures of white mainstream culture. "As the pressure of modern civilization bears more and more heavily upon *us all,*" Prescott wrote, "the incidence of mental disease mounts."[34]

Of special note, similar representational strategies appeared in advertisements for early antipsychotic medications in leading medical and psychiatric journals. For instance, advertisements for Serpasil (reserpine) in the *American Journal of Psychiatry* in the 1950s touted the ways in which the

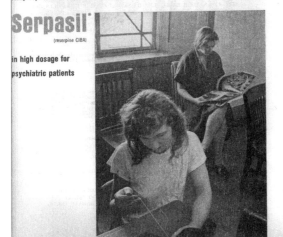

"CLEAN, COOPERATIVE, AND COMMUNICATIVE"

Under the influence of Serpasil, patients who had been destructive, resistant, hostile, withdrawn, untidy, or troubled with hallucinations became, in a short period of time, "clean, cooperative, and communicative persons."[1]

Serpasil has been shown to be effective even in violently disturbed psychotics *if sufficiently high dosage is used.* After 6 to 8 weeks of Serpasil therapy in 127 chronic schizophrenics "the result was frequently astounding, even to psychiatrists of long clinical experience."[1]

In similar studies, the worst behavior problems in the hospital showed improvement, chiefly ". . . a reduction of motor activity, of tension, of hostility, and aggressiveness."[2] Many reports have indicated that Serpasil may be substituted for electro- or insulin shock and that it sharply reduces destruction and assaults in the violent back wards.

Adequate trial is essential – a minimum of 3 months, beginning with "parenteral doses of at least 5 mg. of reserpine and continued daily doses of 2 to 8 mg. orally."[1] "The occurrence of the turbulent phase (with exaggeration of symptoms) is *not* an indication for discontinuing treatment."[2]

1. Hollister, L. E., Krieger, G. E., Kringel, A., and Roberts, R. H.: Ann. New York Acad. Sc. *61*:92 (April 15) 1955.
2. Hoffman, J. L., and Konchegul, L.: Ann. New York Acad. Sc. *61*:144 (April 15) 1955. 3. Kline, N. S., and Stanley, A. M.: Ann. New York Acad. Sc. *61*:85 (April 15) 1955.

Parenteral Solution, 2-ml. ampuls, 2.5 mg. Serpasil per ml. *Tablets,* 4.0 mg. (scored), 2.0 mg. (scored), 1.0 mg. (scored), 0.25 mg. (scored) and 0.1 mg. *Elixir,* 1.0 mg. and 0.2 mg. Serpasil per 4-ml. teaspoon.

Serpasil
(reserpine CIBA)

in high dosage for
psychiatric patients

FIG. 4

This and other 1950s-era advertisements for the psychotropic medication Serpasil showed women calmly suturing away their psychotic symptoms with the help of the new drug. (Source: American Journal of Psychiatry *112 (1955): xxxiii)* breakthrough medication rendered white women "clean, cooperative, and communicative," and thus able to calmly suture away their psychotic symptoms in unthreatening placidity with the help of new drugs. (As such, the ad forms a powerful point of contrast with the "assaultive and belligerent" Haldol image that appears in the preface of this book.)

This brief history in no way suggests that all people who suffered from a disease called schizophrenia in the 1920s through the 1940s were members of a category called white. Instead, many avenues of mainstream American culture marked schizophrenia, but not dementia praecox, as a disease of the familiar in ways that forced identification with certain groups of people while rendering other groups invisible. Such rhetorical strategies made it easy for America to identify white, middle-class housewives with split personalities or erstwhile philosophers with delusions of grandeur.

In an age of profound segregation, such rhetoric occluded recognition of the countless women and men diagnosed with schizophrenia who resided in segregated, southern "Negro hospitals" and suffered far below most realms of public awareness. For instance, medical researchers such as Betz, Fenichel, Martin, and others, conducted the majority of published clinical studies on white-only wards. One important counter example, R. E. L. Faris's notorious 1938 finding that schizophrenia spread like a virus through "urban slums," received surprisingly little attention in the popular press, even though sociology journals frequently cited Faris's work.[35]

Meanwhile, the popular media rarely mentioned the dismal conditions in black mental hospitals. Even in the aftermath of public outcry about mental asylums following the release of the film version of *The Snake Pit* in 1948, only one article in the entire American press made the obvious point that circumstances were far worse in those institutions than they were in hospitals that housed patients such as Virginia Cunningham. In April 1949, *Ebony* magazine reported that most private mental hospitals refused to admit African American patients ("fewer than three percent are accepted for treatment"), that only eight of the nation's 4,432 psychiatrists were African American, and that staff and funding shortages created a dire set of disparities. In the damning, heart-wrenching piece, *Ebony* wrote that "if for white patients, the result has been institutions that are more jails then hospitals, then for Negroes the situation approaches Nazi concentration-camp standards—especially in the South where three out of every five colored insane are confirmed. Georgia's Milledgeville State Hospital has been cited . . . as the worst in the nation and its Negro wards described as unbelievable 'this side of Dante's Inferno.'"[36]

■ ■ ■

WE DO NOT know whether Barry Leroy read the *New York Times,* books about Mary Todd Lincoln, or popular asylum exposés. But we do know that Dr. Leroy's beliefs about schizophrenia reflected the common knowledge of his era, and that this common knowledge impacted the ways he observed, understood and ultimately treated Alice Wilson during her first visit to the Ionia Hospital for the Criminally Insane.

Alice's case history contained numerous signposts of schizophrenia, as Dr. Leroy understood the disease. For instance, Alice was a model child who suffered early-life traumatic loss. She functioned well in the premorbid period, though she was socially isolated and something of a dreamer. Her first symptoms appeared long before the underpants episode, when she withdrew from home life and found no pleasure in her children. Her housework went undone and her family failed to command affection. Then came the textbook emotional splitting, a Bleulerian fissure between thought content and emotional expression. Recall, for instance, that when Leroy asked Alice about rejecting her family she laughed instead of cried. For Leroy, this was the moment of diagnostic certainty. Mothers should not laugh about their families.

In retrospect, maybe Dr. Leroy should have been more skeptical. Did Alice cry because her husband yelled too much? Did she drink moonshine? Was she hysterical? Had she suffered a concussion or head trauma? But retrospection also teaches us that Barry Leroy worked within the established guidelines of his profession and the beliefs of his era when he dictated "Schizophrenia" to his secretary before lighting another cigarette. Literally every doctor and every patient smoked. And his diagnostic options were limited. Depression and bipolar disorder were small and narrow categories, nowhere near what they are today. For instance, depression barely appeared in medical literature before the 1960s, and did not become a viable disease category until 1980. *Schizophrenia,* however, was a term as wide as the Grand River Valley. The term made room for the depressives, the too-neurotics, the paranoids, hallucinators, delusionals, and katatonics. Schizophrenia connoted emotions and personalities and intellects, and as such captured Alice, David Morris, Minnie Briggs, Milmouth Hunt, and many other split-minded patients housed at Ionia in the 1920s, 1930s, 1940s, and beyond.[37]

And so Alice, newly schizophrenic, met Dr. Leroy for weekly psychotherapy. Alice talked, and, after listening, Leroy suggested that Alice's psychotic feelings of disappointing her family resulted from early-life insecurities about taking care of her father. "Your personality is structured by the feeling that you let him down," he said. Alice worked hard to grasp the connection, and her understanding was no doubt aided by twenty-two electroconvulsive therapy treatments. After the final treatment, her nurses noted, without a hint of irony, that "the patient has limited recall about the events leading to her hospitalization." Alice also received fifteen sessions in "the tub," a maximum-security hydrotherapy bathtub that was something of a cross between a Jacuzzi and a porcelain pillory.[38]

There were rough moments, to be sure. According to the nurses' notes, Alice spent most of her time in her room during the first weeks of her stay at Ionia. She stared out the window, which looked out over the farm, and talked to herself on occasion. Her appetite was described as sporadic. At night, her crying spells could be heard all the way at the attendants' desk down the hall from her room.

After several weeks, however, Alice participated. She knitted and sewed, helped build the Ionia float for the county fair parade, worked in the bakery, and cut fresh flowers into floral arrangements. She taught piano to other patients and played as the accompanist for the women's traveling choral. "Improving," read the nurses' notes. "Becoming a citizen in ward activities." "Very good worker."

How did Alice feel about the diagnosis? Our best evidence comes from the recorded minutes of Ward Walk, a monthly all-staff meeting meant to assess patient progress and discuss disposition. The last meeting in which Alice was discussed took place six months after her admission to the hospital. All six Ionia psychiatrists attended, as did four nurses from the women's ward, three orderlies, an occupational therapist, a transcriptionist, and, of course, Alice herself. Ward Walk was something of a misnomer, since the staff sat comfortably in a large examination room while the patients, who were ward walkers anyway, came and went.

Dr. Richard McBride led the meeting. He was a serious man, known for his direct approach, parsimonious vocabulary, and occasional use of pince-nez glasses. "These are the members of the hospital staff," he explained as Alice was led into the room by Nurse Jones. "Please tell them why you came to the hospital."

Alice bordered on logorrhea. She felt comfortable in the midst of constant conversation, and often played speaker and listener both. It was not just a sign of illness: she spent too much time alone in her youth. "Well it would have to take quite a while to tell just what happened. I became confused on a trip this past summer. I had to go far south on a trip with my husband. That's what seemed to confuse me, how the heat bothered my head at the time. It was very hot, let me tell you—"

MCBRIDE (INTERRUPTS): How was your personality? Did you do things out of the ordinary?

ALICE: Probably my husband could tell you more about that because he was with me during that period of time. I wouldn't say that I was out of my mind. But things were confused at home even before the trip. My family and my husband's family were both living in my home at the time. When I'm just living with my own family in my home I feel real calm and capable and competent. . . .

MCBRIDE: Your husband tells us that you have periods where you get mixed up and do not dress properly?

ALICE (CALMLY): He's a businessman and I'm a housewife and he has many problems on his hands so perhaps he is not the best judge of how I dress or how I raise the family.

McBride, growing a light shade of scarlet, nodded toward Barry Leroy who sat nearby: "Do you know Dr. Leroy? He says he has in the past seen you in periods when you seem to think that people were against you."

ALICE: I don't know why he would say that because I have depended upon him very much in difficult times.

MCBRIDE: Are people against you?

ALICE: Oh no, not trying to harm me. My family is trying to work with me. I feel competent now.

Dr. Daniel Schriber then spoke: "Why does it take you so long to make up your mind to do something?"

ALICE: Probably because I am afraid of making a mistake. Don't you think that might be the case?

It was then Dr. Wilson Humphrey's turn: "Do you think that there is anything wrong with your mind?"

ALICE: I get worried about my family. I'm feeling fine now. Perhaps a little nervous.

"Were you hearing voices when you came here?" asked Dr. Royce Blunt.

ALICE (POLITELY): I don't think I was hearing voices that weren't really there. People talking sometimes disturbs me when I am in an unfamiliar places.

Finally, Dr. Robert Thompson, the senior member of the staff: "OK, that is all."

Alice smiled, rose, and left the room, accompanied by Nurse Vance.

A defiant streak courses through these transcripts. Perhaps Alice rebelled against a patriarchal system, and a patriarchal diagnosis, that allowed white male doctors and her white male husband to be the arbiters of her mental health. Perhaps Alice's alternative explanations for her actions were true— that the heat caused her confusion, that the voices were real. Or perhaps Alice's defiance was confabulation, a defensive method of hiding psychotic symptoms behind a steady flow of language that fooled no one but herself.

From the perspective of the history of schizophrenia in America, however, the most important aspect of the Ward Walk transcripts is that Alice's defiance was interpreted by her doctors as a symptom but not as a threat. Thus, the doctors unanimously recommended a predictable disposition.

DR. THOMPSON: She is evasive. From her history she seems to have had several attacks and her husband takes care of her. Her sentence has lapsed. I think we might consider letting her go.

DR. LEROY: I would agree.

DR. SCHRIBER: She is harmless. Let her go.

DR. HUMPHREY: I think I would let her go.

DR. BLUNT: I would agree with those who know her best.

DR. LEROY: It would seem to me that the husband knows how to handle her.

DR. THOMPSON: I suppose that her husband can see that she gets along.

DR. MCBRIDE: I think this woman is evasive. I think she is still psychotic, yet her husband clearly knows how to handle her so I would let him take her.

Alice Wilson was discharged to the care of her husband on March 20, 1942, six months and two weeks after admission to the Ionia State Hospital for the Criminally Insane. Her release form provided one last, tiny dagger into the heart of Emil Kraepelin's definition of dementia praecox as a fatal, deteriorating, biological illness. "Discharge Diagnosis: Paranoid Schizophrenia," it stated. "Condition: Personality is improved."

She would be back.

CHAPTER 5

Like a Family

ORAL HISTORY TRANSCRIPTION EXCERPTS
Former Employees of Ionia State Hospital
October 24–25, 2005
Interviewer: Jonathan Metzl
Location: Ionia Historical Society, Ionia, Michigan
Oral History #7: Retired Woman Attendant, Age 86

Q: *When did you start working at Ionia?*

A: I started [in] 1944.

Q: *I'm curious what it was like to come to work in the morning. What did it look like to drive up to Ionia Hospital in the 1940s?*

A: Well, they had a beautiful creek with a paddlewheel. Throughout the grounds were meticulously kept, I mean they were very, very beautiful at that point in time. Well landscaped. We had a wonderful landscaper. They had these old carts with the tall steel wheels that they . . . the patients—we'd have some patients that were allowed to work on the grounds, you know, men patients—and they'd push these carts around, and clean up things. It was interesting. Yes, the grounds were nice, very nice. They had their own laundry and their own bakery and of course they had a large herd of cattle and we always got milk and things from the dairy and bread from the bakery. Everything was right there. They had their own fire barn.

Q: *Were there any fires?*

A: No. (Laughs) Thank goodness, no. Beyond that I guess it really wasn't anything. I mean, you were coming to work, it was the thing to do. It was not that you thought, Oh dear, I'm going into a place with the criminally insane.

Q: *What was your job?*

A: I was an attendant. Five Building. I worked all three floors.

Q: *Five Building was the women's?*

A: Yes, it was for many years.

Q: *What was it like on the wards?*

A: Well, it was . . . what would I say, what was it like? In a way it was a little primitive. I'll have to tell you one experience I had the first day I was there. We always followed someone around who had more experience than you, to train you, and we had a patient, they called it the . . . I can't remember what they called it. . . . Anyway, that's where they put the dying patients. Just off the day room. And the poor lady was struggling to breathe and I picked up her pillow and was gonna fluff it and the pillows were made of horsehair and would've broke my fist. And this lady laughed, she said, "This surprised you, didn't it?" And I said it absolutely did. It was just as hard as it could be. And of course many of [the] mattresses were made of horsehair too. They were stiff.

Q: *When you say primitive do you mean that the conditions weren't very good?*

A: Well, I can't say that, because I think all the attendants tried very hard. But there were a lot of restrictions, you know, for the patients, many restrictions. When they came, they were isolated for about a week, for evaluation, you know.

Q: *Where were they isolated?*

A: In a room, in one hall, which was called the new addition. There was nothing in the room. Not a thing. Only maybe an indestructible mattress and a chamber pot, which was of metal, tin, you know. And I have to tell you—it's kind of humorous—they were all dented because they'd toss them around.

Q: *And so they'd take new patients and put them in a room for a week?*

A: Yes, for observation for a week. Usually for a week, but it lessened as time went on.

Q: *And what kinds of observations would they make over the course of the week?*

A: Behavior. The doctors of course made the observations. We charted everything but . . . they would consult us of course.

Q: *How much time during that week would the doctors spend with the patients?*

A: Maybe they might come in a couple, three times a week. But no more than that, I don't think.

Q: *And so they must have been very dependent on your observations?*

A: They were, they were. But you know, this is hard to understand but we would read of these, and hear on the news of these crimes these patients made, or did, but when we got them, somehow you accepted them as one of . . . it was like a family really. And these were some of the nicest people that committed the worst crimes. Really, they were just ill. It was very sad. It really was. And you felt bad about it, for them.

Q: *In what ways was it sad?*

A: You were seeing them at their worst . . . and seeing their regrets. Of course they had remorse. When they would get . . . when they recovered enough to know what they had done.

Q: *It sounds like you had a lot of compassion.*

A: Well, it was a hard job but, you know, I liked the job. I really did. It was an interesting job. Because as I say, you grew to like the people. And you wanted to help. And you saw them go from way down, to come up a bit, you know. And that was certainly compensating.

Q: *Do any particular cases stick in your mind?*

A: We had one patient from Five Building, which was the women's building. And she had drowned her children in the bathtub. But a really, I mean, a good worker. Very intelligent. We used to . . . after she was finally released . . . she was put on a program, and we would go down and have dinner with her after work. In fact, I've got doilies that she tatted for me when I got married. I still use them.

PART III

Octavius Greene

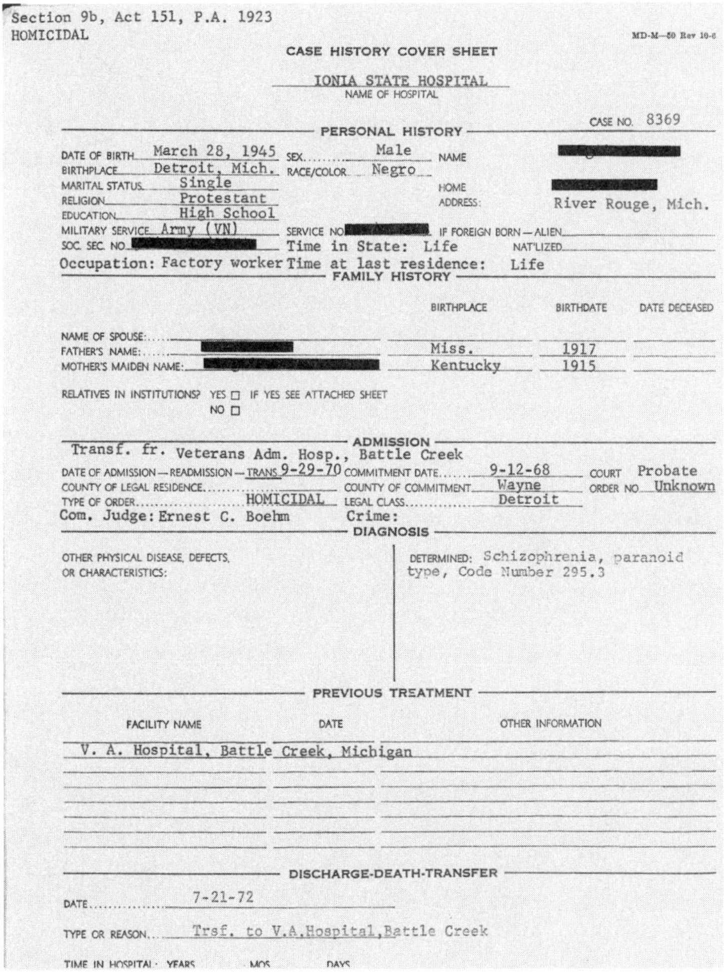

Section 9b, Act 151, P.A. 1923
HOMICIDAL

MD-M-50 Rev 10-6

CASE HISTORY COVER SHEET

IONIA STATE HOSPITAL
NAME OF HOSPITAL

CASE NO. 8369

PERSONAL HISTORY

DATE OF BIRTH March 28, 1945 SEX Male NAME [redacted]
BIRTHPLACE Detroit, Mich. RACE/COLOR Negro
MARITAL STATUS Single HOME ADDRESS: [redacted] River Rouge, Mich.
RELIGION Protestant
EDUCATION High School
MILITARY SERVICE Army (VN) SERVICE NO [redacted] IF FOREIGN BORN—ALIEN
SOC. SEC. NO. [redacted] Time in State: Life NAT'LIZED
Occupation: Factory worker Time at last residence: Life

FAMILY HISTORY

		BIRTHPLACE	BIRTHDATE	DATE DECEASED
NAME OF SPOUSE:				
FATHER'S NAME:	[redacted]	Miss.	1917	
MOTHER'S MAIDEN NAME:	[redacted]	Kentucky	1915	

RELATIVES IN INSTITUTIONS? YES ☐ IF YES SEE ATTACHED SHEET
NO ☐

ADMISSION

Transf. fr. Veterans Adm. Hosp., Battle Creek
DATE OF ADMISSION—READMISSION—TRANS 9-29-70 COMMITMENT DATE 9-12-68 COURT Probate
COUNTY OF LEGAL RESIDENCE COUNTY OF COMMITMENT Wayne ORDER NO. Unknown
TYPE OF ORDER HOMICIDAL LEGAL CLASS Detroit
Com. Judge: Ernest C. Boehm Crime:

DIAGNOSIS

OTHER PHYSICAL DISEASE, DEFECTS, OR CHARACTERISTICS:

DETERMINED: Schizophrenia, paranoid type, Code Number 295.3

PREVIOUS TREATMENT

FACILITY NAME	DATE	OTHER INFORMATION
V. A. Hospital, Battle Creek, Michigan		

DISCHARGE-DEATH-TRANSFER

DATE 7-21-72

TYPE OR REASON Trsf. to V.A.Hospital,Battle Creek

TIME IN HOSPITAL: YEARS MOS DAYS

FIG. 5 *The face sheet, a standard, thirty-item form, compiled basic information about each patient admitted to Ionia, including admission date, sex, age, date of birth, crime, race, and admission diagnosis. (Source: State Archives of Michigan)*

CHAPTER 6

The Other Direction[1]

ALICE WILSON NEATLY FOLDED HER belongings into a suitcase and left the women's ward to meet her waiting husband. The scene could not have been more unlike Olivia de Havilland's triumphant march away from Leo Genn and his Freudian snake pit into Mark Stevens's expectant, Freudian arms. Alice was tired—tired of the hospital, the patients, the food, and especially Dr. Leroy. George, for his part, was nervous and still a bit angry about everything Alice had put him through. Would she be different? Or still the same? Husband and wife shared a brief, functional embrace. George signed the requisite paperwork accepting responsibility for the patient, the prisoner, the spouse. The day was warm and bright. The couple walked silently past the manicured gardens, oblivious to the churning sounds of the ornamental water wheel, and into the parking lot.

George's car wound down the long driveway to freedom. Meanwhile, a police car drove hurriedly in the opposite direction. It is unlikely that, from the passenger's seat, Alice noticed the shackled man in the back of the passing car. But perhaps she did.

The man in chains was Octavius Greene, a forty-four-year-old convicted for "Uttering and Publishing." According to the transfer report, the police required tight security because of Mr. Greene's propensity for escaping ("ran away from the prison farm in Birmingham"), his volatility ("prone to fight"), and his unpredictability (". . . swallowed a large nail for no apparent reason. Nail in sigmoid colon for five years.").

The story of how Mr. Greene became Mr. Greene, how he came to be seated in the back of a police car speeding toward Ionia, and how a nail lodged in his sigmoid colon, began in Lumpkin, Georgia, in 1923. At that time, Mr. Greene was a twenty-year-old, recently married man named Rube Fleetwood. He had worked as a picker on a vegetable farm since the age of eight and largely kept out of trouble. But one summer night, after a bit of drinking, Mr. Greene qua Fleetwood became convinced that his neighbor was watching him through peepholes drilled into the thin walls of his house. Mr. Greene picked the wrong man to confront with his suspicions.

The neighbor was a light sleeper who in any case slept with a knife under his bed that was two inches longer than the knife Mr. Greene carried with him to the confrontation. Luckily, the wounds were superficial. Mr. Greene was the only one of the two African American combatants arrested—a rarity in the arrest-first, ask-questions-later segregated South—and sent to work off his paranoia on a chain gang in Birmingham, Alabama.

Two years into his sentence, Mr. Greene seized on a moment when Alabama prison security was more lax than advertised. He escaped. Combining the names of two prison bunkmates, Rube Fleetwood changed his name to Octavius Greene. He ran to Lumpkin, gathered his wife and his few belongings, and joined the great migration northward. The road was not lonesome. Roughly 114,000 African Americans from the South moved to Detroit between 1910 and 1929.[2]

Mr. Greene's family did not consider him a self-starter. This fact can largely be attributed to parts of his personality that would later be called symptoms. He felt as if he was constantly surveilled, which was perhaps not unreasonable for a man on the lam. He trusted no one and kept his monies in a burlap bag behind the kitchen cabinet. He worried that others could read his thoughts. He wondered whether his food was poisoned. He sometimes felt as if his body was not his own. So, according to records, he swallowed a nail to find out. Nail-swallowing could have been construed as malingering. And, while it is true that constant abdominal pain made it nearly impossible for Mr. Greene to hold steady employment, the act itself was likely genuine. The nail convinced Mr. Greene of his corporeal ownership, at least for the six years that it remained lodged inside of him, until it was dislodged and passed by a well-timed bout of tussance.

In June 1938, the police arrested Octavius Greene for cashing a bogus check made out to Octavius Greene. Searching for bail money, Mrs. Greene uncovered a trove of love letters penned by authors other than herself. She revealed the family secret in a fit of rage. The authorities continued to refer to Mr. Greene as Mr. Greene, even though they now knew he was also Mr. Fleetwood. After a prolonged detention, a judge sentenced Mr. Greene to two to ten years in the State Prison of Southern Michigan. Mrs. Greene moved in with her sister.

Prison is an unfortunate environment for the paranoid. Surveillance is a constant reality and intrusions into personal space are common. Mistrust is in many ways a healthy adaptation. But mistrust without limits becomes a pernicious anemia that deprives victims of oxygen necessary for hopes, dreams, and other requisite delusions of survival. Thus was the case with Octavius Greene.

Prison notes suggest that Mr. Greene simmered beneath the radar for the first four years of his confinement. He worked in the twine and textile mills and received no demerits for untoward behavior. This is not to say that he was well. Rather, he did not get into trouble and did not cause extra work for prison guards.

Sometime in early 1942, however, a fateful confrontation occurred. "Negro prisoner in heated argument with the Deputy Warden." "Shouting loudly." "Will not back down." Mr. Greene spent extended time in the "oo" ward—solitary confinement—followed by extended time with the chief medical officer. "Prisoner is full of abnormal ideas," the doctor wrote. "He claims he is able to interpret all news before it happens. He is noticeably paranoid and hostile in his attitude. He thinks someone is putting poison in his food. He rambles. Threatening." In the rigid vernacular of prison notes, this type of language bought you a one-way ticket to Ionia.

Thus did the car carrying Mr. Greene pass by the car carrying Alice Wilson on a winding Ionia driveway in March 1942. The interaction, as much as it was an interaction, involved the passing of two people going opposite directions. Alice Wilson headed away from the hospital toward a life where she would pass for normal, at least for a while. Octavius Greene's middle passage led him toward further incarceration, a series of locked rooms without escape. The two would not meet again. Alice Wilson later returned to Ionia. But Octavius Greene had long since passed.

Did the moment represent the crossing of two fates? Two races? Two diagnoses? Two social classes?

Up the road, attendants dressed in white met the car carrying Octavius Greene. After processing, they led Mr. Greene and his police escorts through the receiving hospital for evaluation by the staff psychiatrist, Dr. Leroy. Leroy noted that Mr. Greene was parched. He brought a glass of water. Dr. Leroy knew that patients, and particularly first-timers like Mr. Greene, felt disoriented and displaced upon arrival at Ionia. Kindness tended to ease anxiety, thereby reducing the chance for acting out. Dr. Leroy asked the officers to remove the Mr. Greene's handcuffs. Playing it safe, he also requested that the officers remain for the early part of his evaluation, and instructed the attendants to attend nearby as well.

Can you tell me, please, your full name? Can you tell me the date, month, and year? Say the alphabet. Count from 1 to 50. Name the months. Repeat the

Lord's Prayer. What is the largest river in America? What is the largest city in the world? What was the War of the Revolution? What was the Civil War? The questions were the same for every patient.

Dr. Leroy recorded his first observations of Octavius Greene in the evaluation section of the medical chart. The language was terse, stern, and wholly without the empathy that suffused Leroy's description of Alice Wilson. "The colored patient," as Mr. Greene would be known for the brief remainder of his life, "was admitted from the State Prison of Southern Michigan. He has in the past been very restless and disorderly and is considered a threat to others because of his strength. . . . He is considered dangerous and has been in numerous fights. . . . He thinks someone has been putting something in his food, and he has in the past swallowed some nails. He is clearly paranoid. . . . He talks about being framed for passing checks. . . . He gave a long, circumstantial explanation of the events surrounding his arrest . . . is always talking about 'they' and has fought with other prisoners and with the police . . . is very delusional and is sure that he has been the object of persecution for a long time . . . feels that there is nothing wrong with his mind and no reason for him being here."

Again, it is hard to not think diagnostically when reading such words. To our present-day eyes and our present-day minds, terms such as *paranoid, circumstantial,* and *delusional* connote the condition we know as schizophrenia. Phraseology such as *dangerous* and *disorderly* also taps into present-day stigmatizations of the disease. Moreover, from a historical perspective, aspects of Dr. Leroy's slanted description of Mr. Greene seem to come straight out of earlier media descriptions of dementia praecox. For instance, Leroy wrote in the personal history section of the evaluation that one of Mr. Greene's sons was "arrested on charges of assault and sent to the Reformatory. He had a mental age of 6 years, 10 months, I.Q. of 48—classified as a moron." So too, "the prison psychologist gave our patient a quick-score test which showed a mental age of seven years, seven months, I.Q. of 51."

It is all the more surprising, then, that Dr. Leroy did not diagnose Octavius Greene with schizophrenia. His differential diagnosis emphasized that Mr. Greene had a history of being "mean," "irritable," and "dangerous," and that he had committed numerous wrongs ("he has been a gambler . . . adulterous . . . frequently disorderly . . . he has many abnormal ideas . . .") for which he felt neither guilt not remorse. Leroy repeated on several occasions that Mr. Greene was "definitely resentful about being sent here, thinking that he has done no wrong."

For Dr. Leroy, this lack of regret was the sine qua non of a mental disorder, but that disorder was not schizophrenia. He instead believed that Mr. Greene suffered from the so-called moral insanity, a personality condition in which someone acted against others without a sense of morals. Such a condition was commonly known by the terms *psychopathic inferiority* or *moral imbecility,* but Barry Leroy's note employed the descriptor suggested by the 1942 *Statistical Manual for the Use of Institutions for the Insane:* psychopathic personality with amoral trends.[3]

CHAPTER 7

Categories

LET US THINK IN THIS chapter as if social scientists. A social scientist is someone who processes information categorically and demographically. The narratives of Alice Wilson and Octavius Greene help us understand individual experiences at Ionia during the 1930s and 1940s, such a person might say. But how representative are these narratives of the larger population of Ionia patients? What broader claims can be made?

To be sure, the Ionia stories derive power from their distinctiveness. Each chart discussed in this book, and the many, many charts left out, represents an individual tragedy, a life lost and then recorded by doctors' observations, nurses' and attendants' notes, commissary receipts, death notices, and other institutional documents that speak incompletely to the person as they were in the hospital and evanescently to the person as they were in real life.

Social scientists identify generalizable variables from individual cases in order to analyze aggregate groups. These scholars inhabit a "statistical universe," as the theorist Talal Asad describes it, in which individual experiences accrue meaning beyond the here and now only after these experiences are made to demonstrate connections to larger categorical trends.[1]

Gender, social class, crime, and geography come to mind as potential ways to categorize, and then compare, a lower-middle-class woman from Nashville, Michigan, with an often-impoverished man from Lumpkin, Georgia. Yet the different outcomes of the two cases ultimately resulted from differences in race and diagnosis, and the ways that the relationships between these two categories impacted prognostic perceptions of violence. Alice Wilson's chart lists her race as "White" and her diagnosis as "Schizophrenia." Doctors described her as harmless and set her free. Meanwhile, Octavius Greene's chart describes a "dangerous, Negro" man with sociopathy, whose stay at Ionia involved progressive detention in maximum security wards.

Here is a hypothesis (or, more aptly, a null hypothesis) that a social scientist might make based on the race differences between the charts of Alice Wilson and Octavius Greene: *Ionia charts from the 1930s, 1940s, and early 1950s do not associate schizophrenia with racial violence in ways that they would in later decades.* From the 1960s onward, patients described by doctors as African American, paranoid, delusional, and violent had disproportionately high chances of being diagnosed with schizophrenia. Patients described as white, tearful, sad, ruminative, and harmless, meanwhile, had disproportionately high chances of being diagnosed with mood disorders or anxiety states. But in the 1930s to the 1950s, at least at the Ionia State Hospital for the Criminally Insane, the combination of these variables led frequently to different results. Patients categorized as "Negro/Schizophrenia" were not inherently considered violent, and patients categorized as "White/Other Diagnosis" were not inherently considered safe.

Here is a way to test this hypothesis. First, take all of the charts from the Ionia State Hospital for the Criminally Insane housed at the State Archives of Michigan. This is a huge number of charts—enough to fill 624 large boxes in an archive, or an empty pool in someone's backyard, or several Winnebagos.[2]

Then, realize that there are too many charts for a small study, the kind of study described in a brief chapter in the middle of a book. The next task, therefore, is to narrow the sample size to a smaller number with the help of the face sheet. The face sheet is a standard, thirty-item form that compiled basic information about each patient admitted to the Ionia hospital. Admitting physicians filled out data, as they observed it, about each patient's admission date, sex, age, date of birth, crime, race, admission diagnosis, and other variables that were then amassed for the hospital census. By definition, the face sheet comprised the first page of each chart for each hospitalization. Patients admitted multiple times had multiple face sheets, a fact that becomes important later on.

Narrow first by admission date. Decide that you are primarily interested in charts of patients admitted between 1935, roughly the time that the term *schizophrenia* came into use in the hospital, and 1977, when the hospital closed. Narrow further by selecting charts from two comparable periods within this span, say 1935 to 1950 and 1960 to 1975. These decisions alone eliminate at least one of the Winnebagos.

Next, narrow by diagnosis and race. These are complex terms that should not be taken at face value. We know already, from the discussion of historical presentism, that disease definitions change over time. Ionia's early diagnostic categories roughly approximated those set forth in the *Statistical Manual for the Use of Institutions for the Insane*.[3] Schizophrenia became the most common admitting diagnosis in the mid-1930s, but it was just one in a long list of options. The category of psychosis alone asked doctors to choose from alcoholic psychosis, psychosis associated with organic changes of the nervous system, manic-depressive psychoses, psychoneurotic psychosis, paranoia and paranoid conditions, and psychoses with mental deficiency. Similarly, the criminal component of *criminal insanity* encompassed many complex modes of lawbreaking. Possible crimes ranged from acts against the person (26 percent) such as assault or homicide, to acts against property (28 percent) such as theft, larceny, arson, or forgery, to so-called sex crimes (26 percent) about which more is discussed below, to arson (4 percent), to "miscellaneous" minor offenses (16 percent) such as parole violations, public disturbances, or shoplifting.[4]

So too, meanings of race in the 1920s to the 1950s differed in important ways from those today. In today's parlance, we tend to define race in relation to such factors as biology, genetics, visible traits, or self-identification. However, at Ionia in the early twentieth century, race was a largely taxonomic category linked closely to what was called nativity, or the country of origin of a person's parents. For instance, *white* was not yet a racial descriptor that the sociologist George Lipsitz describes as a confederation of people of various European backgrounds based on skin color. Instead, Ionia charts used "White" or "Caucasian" almost exclusively to describe patients whose parents were born in the United States or, on exception, in England or Scandinavia. This language then differentiated such patients from the so-called nonwhites: the "U.S.-Negroes" comprised the largest category by far, but each year the hospital claimed that it admitted one or two people in each of twenty other seemingly random nativity categories such as Slavonics, Indians, Lithuanians, Nova Scotians, Jews, Italians, Scottish, Germans, and so on.[5]

Further complicating matters is the fact that doctors, nurses, and ward attendants marked a patient's race on the face sheet based largely on their own observations. No evidence exists that clinicians asked patients which race they considered themselves. Instead, mental-health professionals looked at patients, asked about their ancestries, and then categorized the patients in ways that conflated race, color, character, nativity, identity, and even citizenship. "We have in this case a colored male of 44 years who appears older than his stated age" was the opening sentence of the evaluation summary in Mr. Greene's chart. As if by echolalia, the face sheet qualified race by listing Mr. Greene's nativity as "Negro" and his citizenship as "American Negro." Meanwhile, charts listed Alice Wilson, David Morris, Milmouth Hunt, and many other Ionia patients as "U.S.-White" and their citizenship simply as "American."

Race theorists have successfully shown that connections between race and color represent cultural assumptions made by observers rather than innate biological properties of the observed. In his book *Race, Colour, and the Process of Racialization,* the psychoanalyst Farhad Dalal elegantly demonstrates how perceived racial differences change radically over space and time, and convey different meanings in different social or historical contexts. Dalal argues that shifting assumptions about who is black and who is white demonstrate how "people are not literally in any chromatic sense black or white," but, rather, that visual "discontinuities" between races represent "abstracted relationships embedded within other relationships." Researchers Jamie Brooks and Meredith King Ledford put it even more succinctly when they write that racial category-based research constructs "biological reality" out of "social reality."[6]

Associations between race, color, and nativity in the Ionia charts are important, as long as we remain clear that our study does not demonstrate anything about race or diagnosis per se. We can make no universalizing claims about African Americans, Caucasians, Mexicans, people with depression, kleptomaniacs, criminals, or other groups. Rather, we wish to learn about the hospital's way of categorizing people and to test for associations between categories.

According to its own classification system, it would seem that Ionia considered itself a largely white hospital in the 1920s, 1930s, and 1940s. This is because, even though it was a desegregated Northern hospital, the census counted the overwhelming majority of new admissions as U.S.-White. To recall chapter 2, the hospital averaged 150 admissions per year between 1920 and 1950. The average number of U.S.-White admits was 122. Most of these patients hailed from the rural Midwest—meaning that they had much in common with the hospital staff. In some years women comprised up to 25 percent of new admissions. Meanwhile, U.S.-Negro admissions averaged only 19 new admissions per year, which qualified for a distant second place.[7]

The 1939 census, for instance, portrayed a typical year (terms reproduced verbatim).

Patients	MALE	FEMALE	TOTAL
U.S. (WHITE)	113	29	142
U.S. (NEGROES)	18	3	21

Next, pull charts at random until you have at least twenty charts that meet the criteria in each of four categories:

Race: Black/Negro, Diagnosis: Schizophrenia, Admission Date: 1935 to 1950

Race: White/Caucasian, Diagnosis: Schizophrenia, Admission Date: 1935 to 1950

Race: Black/Negro, Diagnosis: Schizophrenia, Admission Date: 1960 to 1975

Race: White/Caucasian, Diagnosis: Schizophrenia, Admission Date: 1960 to 1975

As a comparison, compile at least ten charts for each category and from each time period whose diagnosis is "Other," i.e., anything other than schizophrenia.

You will quickly note that chart pulling for this particular study is anything but a rote exercise because the demographic categories are in a constant state of flux. Most important, for the group of patients categorized as "Black"/"Negro," schizophrenia is exceedingly small for the early time period. Black/Schizophrenia becomes far and away the dominant group in the 1960s, but the numbers of such patients are relatively small in the 1930s to the 1950s. Conversely, White/Schizophrenia cases grow fewer over time. For these reasons, you need to sample quite a few charts, nearly six hundred, to fill all the categories for analysis.

So too, "White" women comprise up to 20 percent of the earlier samples, particularly in the category of White/Schizophrenia, but disappear from the later time periods. Meanwhile, your sample uncovers only three women in the Black/Schizophrenia category. These gender trends are hugely important components of the overall story told in this book. As we will see, the disappearance of white women from the category of criminal/paranoid/schizophrenia resulted from a series of structural level shifts. Changing diagnostic language recast many of the women as depressed and as unthreatening to society. As a result, Ionia Hospital became an almost entirely male institution in the 1960s.

Meanwhile, the almost total invisibility of black women taps into vital feminist critiques that, to paraphrase a path-breaking book, *all the women are white, all the blacks are men, but some of us are brave.* To be sure, an extensive and important theoretical literature exists that addresses the invisibility of African American women's voices, not just in medical rhetorics, but also in the Black Power and Black Liberation texts I discuss in later chapters.

Similarly, scholars such as Melissa Harris-Lacewell and Susan Douglas[8] vitally examine the connections between assumptions about black women and psychiatric illness; though this literature demonstrates that most of the best-known associations, such as problematic representations of welfare queens or domineering black mothers, emerged in the 1980s in the context of Reagan-era reforms. Here, though, the absence of African American women in medical treatment narratives suggests that, for better and mostly for worse, these women suffered in silence. And, more to the point of this chapter, from a data perspective, the absence of white and black women in the later samples unfortunately means that you can make no change-over-time claims about gender.[9]

One hundred and twenty charts now fill two and a half file cabinet drawers. Thanks to random sampling, these drawers stand in for the Winnebagos by statistical metonymy. The key part of the study then involves developing a coding scheme. A coding scheme is a tool that helps quantify and analyze written contents of texts such as medical charts. Our particular study focuses on potential changes in associations between race, schizophrenia, and violence, over time. Since the variables of race and diagnosis have already been controlled for by the face sheet, the coding scheme should assess ways that doctors, and on rare occasion nurses and attendants, described patients as violent, criminal, aggressive, complacent, shy, quiet, or any number of other terms used to connote threats of volatility, or lack thereof, in the hospital notes.

The scheme developed for this study codes for items that include the following:

- List patient identifying information (gender/race-nativity/admitting diagnosis/listed crime)
- List specific descriptions/adjectives used to describe patient attitudes and behaviors
- How are symptoms characterized?
- If patient is described as hostile/violent/threatening,
  - Who is the threat made toward?
  - What is the context of the threat?
- List psychiatric treatments patient has received
- Is patient's home/family life/neighborhood mentioned?

Clearly, such questions assess much more than violence and aggression. But, for now, limit the analysis to whether doctors described patients as "hostile/

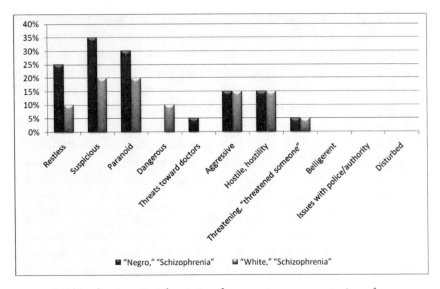

FIG. 6 *Schizophrenia patient descriptions from 1930 to 1950: a comparison of
key terms connoting action/aggression/distrust/violence toward others.
Data suggests that during the 1930s and 1940s Ionia doctors and nurses
did not consider patients with schizophrenia to be disproportionately
violent in relation to patients with other diagnoses.*

threatening," the contexts of these threats, and the types of adjectives used to describe attitudes and behaviors.

The next part of the study involves hiring researchers with expertise in coding methods. These researchers must remain blind to the aims of the study and must work independent of one another so that their results are not subliminally swayed. After several weeks of training to make sure that the coding scheme works, the next step involves asking the researchers to apply the scheme to the charts in the file cabinets. You instruct the researchers to focus on the initial evaluation section of each chart, since many of the charts are quite large. Data emerges. You plot the results. Then you look for trends.

Figures 6 and 7 compare "specific descriptions/adjectives used to describe patient attitudes and behaviors" in the charts of persons diagnosed with schizophrenia and categorized as White (n=20) versus persons diagnosed with schizophrenia and categorized as Negro/Black (n=20) between 1935 and 1950. (Findings from charts from 1960 to 1975 will appear in a later chapter.) To ease comparison with the later time periods, the most frequently used adjectives are divided into two charts, one that groups together adjectives that connote hostile intent or aggression toward others (figure 6) and one

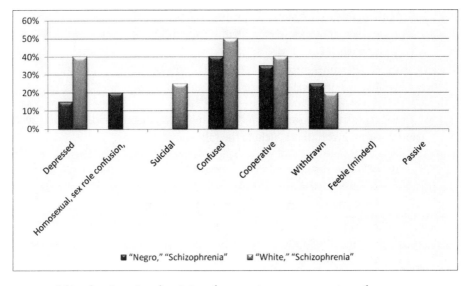

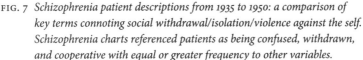

FIG. 7 *Schizophrenia patient descriptions from 1935 to 1950: a comparison of key terms connoting social withdrawal/isolation/violence against the self. Schizophrenia charts referenced patients as being confused, withdrawn, and cooperative with equal or greater frequency to other variables.*

that groups together adjectives that imply cooperation, confusion, social withdrawal, isolation, or violence against the self. As I will discuss further below, the difference between the adjectives used in Negro/Black charts and those used in White charts is not significantly large.

Some specific chart excerpts referring to Negro/Black men diagnosed with schizophrenia include the following:

1936: has no judgment, mental age of 12, not a deep thinker, attitude is not at all serious, stimulated by adolescent endocrine development, dull intelligence . . . restless, over talkative, confused, rambling speech

1941: would cry easily, hears voices

1945: could not carry on conversation . . . dull, listless, disinterested, slovenly appearance, takes no interest in ward or games, history of maladjustment

1947: tidy, autistic, disinterested, mumbled, confused . . . thinks slowly, unmotivated laughter, has never had insight, no affect

1948: seems he has his own philosophy about his place in society, indifferent, no friends on ward

1948: combative, smiles inappropriately, poor contact with reality, withdrawn, mute, evasive, sullen, dejected, full of resentment, smiling sarcastically

1949: delusional, incoherent, babbling, simple, childish, stereotyped behavior . . . possibly bisexual . . . neat and clean

Excerpts from the same period referring to White men and women diagnosed with schizophrenia include the following:

1937: White female, agitated, depressed, suicidal, confused, apprehensive, very self-assured, self-satisfied, self-pitying, cried constantly, argumentative, bizarre . . . quiet, irritable, sober, worried, unhappy

1946: White female, temporarily insane, hysteria, cooperative, anxious, accepts situation, confused, appears really happy, good wit, keen sense of humor

1948: White male, feeble minded, dejected . . . depressed, cried freely, suicidal . . . then, no facial expression, no emotional tone, manneristic, unmotivated laughter, restless, autistic, never does any work, mumbling

1948: White male, talking to himself . . . good speaking vocabulary . . . silly and flat affect . . . laughed without motivation

1949: White male . . . feels God talk to him daily, sees and hears angels singing . . . shallow affect, cooperative, friendly, sociable, overtalkative, freely verbalized

Meanwhile, excerpts from charts of patients diagnosed with conditions "Other" than schizophrenia (n=20), as divided by race, include the following:

1945: Negro male . . . withdrawn, anxious, agitated, paranoid ideas, pleaded for help and begged for reassurance that would become well, feelings of persecution, poor judgment, remorseful about crime, feels guilty

1941: White female . . . threatening attitude . . . coy, sexual difficulties . . . arrogant, aggressive

1946: White male . . . sexually threatening . . . never smiles, anxiety over charges . . . has shifty glance, questionable attitude, immature insight into problems, poor judgment, aggressive . . . homosexual

1949: White male, criminal sexual psychopath . . . would be very dan-

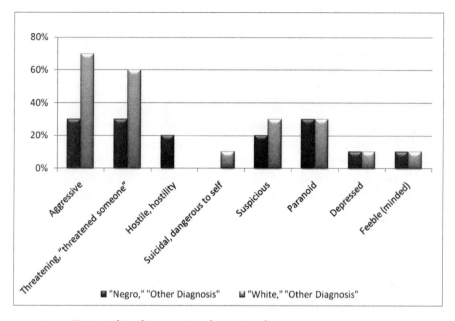

FIG. 8 *Key nonschizophrenia patient descriptions from 1935 to 1950. Data suggests that Ionia doctors considered patients with Other diagnoses to be the most volatile group.*

gerous outside of an institution . . . evasive, bizarre, aggressive, combative behavior toward wife and children, flat affect, tortured his children, attempted to rape children, difficulty in concentration, anxious, suspicious

Any social scientist will tell you to take these finding with a grain of salt because the sample size is small. The two and a half file cabinet drawers contain one hundred and twenty admit charts out of a hospital census that averaged over 120 admits per year, and the numbers above represent only 60 of the 120. Moreover, once again, the ratio of White patients to Negro patients in the hospital was not 1:1. Instead, for much of the 1930s, 1940s, and early 1950s, the hospital was as white as the town of Ionia. The reasons for these choices will become clear later on, when data from the 1930s to 1950s sample appears next to data from the 1960s and 1970s—decades when percentages and overall numbers of patients listed as Negro, Male, and Schizophrenia comprised the majority of the hospital census. For now, a 1:1 ratio enables comparison between the two time periods. Finally, of course, it would surely have helped the study to compare trends at Ionia to those at another comparable hospital.

Limitations acknowledged, we can rightly claim that the numbers support the hypothesis. Data suggests that during the 1930s and 1940s Ionia doctors and nurses did not consider patients with schizophrenia to be disproportionately violent in relation to patients with other diagnoses. Hostility, suspiciousness, and paranoia were frequent characteristics, but none of these terms approached even 50 percent of cases. Threatening, belligerent, aggressive, dangerous, and authority issues appeared hardly at all. Schizophrenia charts referenced patients as being confused, withdrawn, and cooperative with equal or greater frequency to other variables.

Differences between Negro and White schizophrenia groups were equally unimpressive. Patients in the former category were more likely to be suspicious, homosexual, and restless, while patients in the latter were more frequently suicidal. Put another way, doctors' descriptions of Ionia patients as Negro and violent did not correlate disproportionately with schizophrenia, and patients diagnosed as Negro and schizophrenic did not appear to be more violent than other groups. "Dull, listless, disinterested, slovenly appearance," read one such chart. Or, "Negro male, would cry easily." Or, "babbling, simple, childish, stereotyped behavior." Descriptions also frequently assumed that black schizophrenia manifest as sluggish intellect. "Has no judgment, mental age of 12, not a deep thinker, attitude is not at all serious," or, "Negro male, could not carry on conversation."

Meanwhile, charts described patients diagnosed as White/Schizophrenia more often as cooperative (40 percent) than threatening (5 percent). Adjectives used to describe these patients often included *depressed, suicidal, anxious,* and other signifiers that would be linked with mood disorders in later years. "White male, feeble minded, dejected . . . depressed, cried freely, suicidal."

Such findings raise the possibility that in the 1930s and 1940s, the category of schizophrenia at Ionia functioned in similar ways to the category of schizophrenia in American society. Definitions of the illness inflected Virginia Stuart Cunningham more than they did crazed, black schizophrenic killers on the loose. Or, more to the point, Octavius Greene's alleged aggression did not point reflexively to schizophrenia, and Alice Wilson's schizophrenia did not point automatically to crime.

Violence did function as an important mode of categorizing patients, particularly within an institution where every person who came through the door was already convicted of a crime. But the data suggests that Ionia considered patients with Other diagnoses to be the most volatile group. Doctors described Other patients of *both* races as suspicious, threatening, and, most of all, aggressive. Indeed, 70 percent of White/Other charts described patients as such: "Threatening attitude" or "Never smiles . . . has shifty glance, questionable attitude, immature insight into problems, poor judgment, aggressive."

Were these the charts of patients who, like Octavius Greene, suffered from psychopathic personality with amoral trends? The Ionia annual reports and superintendent's reports provide another, more likely explanation for such findings. Ionia housed convicted murderers, armed robbers, and other *hors-la-loi*. But the reports consistently voice concern about another subset of convicts, a subset assumed to be unduly aggressive and dangerous. These convicts were not, however, African Americans diagnosed with antisocial personality disorder, but were instead the largely white homosexuals, pedophiles, perverts, rapists, frotteurists, exhibitionists, voyeurs, nymphomaniacs, and other so-called criminal sexual psychopaths.

Sex criminals came to Ionia in the late 1930s in the aftermath of the notorious Goodrich Act (Public Act 165) of 1939, which revised sex laws in ways that permitted states to warehouse libidinally wayward individuals in mental asylums rather than in jails. The Goodrich Act, later known as the Criminal Sexual Psychopath Act, decried that "any person who is suffering from a mental disorder, and is not feeble-minded . . . coupled with criminal propensities to the commission of sex offenses" should be committed to the custody of the Department of Mental Health "for an indeterminate period of observation," with parole the sole responsibility of the department. The Goodrich Act further dictated that sexual psychopaths could not be "tried or sentenced on the original charge or conviction" after treatment in Ionia, but were instead to be returned to the population once restored to sanity or paroled.[10]

Hospital administrators greeted the appearance of such people with grave concern. For instance, in the debates leading up to the Goodrich Act, Ionia Superintendent P. C. Robertson argued that these offenders, most of whom were white men, were not so much mentally ill—"they are not insane, not epileptic, nor feeble minded"—as they were "deviant" and "violent." "Experience in the past has shown that these people should not be in the same institution that cares for the mentally ill," he wrote in his 1937–38 report to the state legislature. "The commitment of such persons to mental hospitals should be vigorously protested." In the 1940s, as numbers of these patients grew within the Ionia walls, Robertson argued that sexual deviants were unduly "dangerous," "aggressive," "combative," "threatening" criminals who posed particular threats to other patients.[11]

Of course, sexual psychopaths were far from the only patients considered violent by hospital staff. The 1940s alone saw vast expansion in use of the insanity defense in criminal trials, and a slow but steady flow of persons convicted of murder but found to be imbeciles, morons, or insane emerged as a result. But the sexual deviates made up the most significantly threatening group, so much so that, starting in the early 1940s, Ionia segregated these men in separate housing blocks and dining halls out of fear for their predatory natures.

We will return to the data from this study in a later chapter in order to help us understand how schizophrenia emerged as Ionia's most feared diagnosis in the 1960s and 1970s. For now, I mean merely to point out that charts from the 1930s and 1940s offer glimpses into a time when doctors, nurses, and the asylum system in which they worked propagated a different set of associations between race, mental illness, and threats of violence. During an era when Ionia was overwhelmingly "White," connections between sex and violence carried far more valence than did associations between race and violence. And the fear surrounding sexual deviants was not just that they would attack other patients, but also that they would molest or seduce them.

Social scientific analysis thus lays the foundation for exploring how the meanings of diagnostic categories changed even when the names of the categories remained the same. Again, this seemingly simple claim reads against work by scholars who believe that women in Salem had schizophrenia or that Emily Dickinson suffered from seasonal forms of bipolar disorder. Such easy transport of diagnostic categories, as if by time machines in which diagnoses never wrinkle or age, effaces the central reason why hypothesis-driven methods are potentially useful to historical claims: because the certainty of categorical data helps demonstrate the fluidity of the categories on which the data is based. Retrospective quantification thus helps us avoid retrospective presentism.

This brief exercise is in no way meant to minimize the impact of explicit racism against black patients at Ionia in the pre-1960s era. As the next chapters show, the hospital treated black patients terribly, leading to often-catastrophic results. Yet drawing connections between the treatment of such patients and current racial issues requires a delicate diagnostic touch, one that recognizes how the expert knowledge of today informs the ways we look back for answers, and the ways in which the act of looking back creates its own lapses, blind spots, and categorical assumptions.

CHAPTER 8

Octavius Greene
Had No Exit Interview

6–15–47. WARD NOTE.

PARANOID ATTITUDE. RESENTFUL. This Negro man is quite sure that someone is using their influence to make trouble for him. He says that "they framed me about passing checks." He tells a long circumstantial story about his experiences along that line.

10–18–47. WARD NOTE.

STILL VERY PARANOID. FEELS PERSECUTED. This patient feels that bad luck has trailed him since he came to Michigan. He says that it is not true that he passed out checks. He feels that he has been the object of persecution in Detroit and in prison and he is beginning to feel he is the object of persecution here. He promises better cooperation and admits he does not get anywhere by fighting.

1–17–48. WARD NOTE.

VERY DELUSIONAL. IDEAS OF PERSECUTION. This patient is still quite delusional. This morning he expressed some ideas about the whites and the blacks, saying that "my wife had a new white dress and they said I had a white wife and a black wife. I don't like that people are telling stories about me. They are telling lies on me. They persecute me." It is still necessary to keep him in his room.

3–9–48. MENTAL TEST.
Patient examined by Doctors Leroy, Humphrey, and Schriber on Ward Walk. Rambling, circumstantial, often incoherent.

> DR. LEROY: Do you know why you are here?
> OCTAVIUS GREENE: That spine test stirred me up. I've never had a nervous breakdown. They were messing with my food.
> DR. LEROY: Who was messing with your food?
> MR. GREENE: The others. They put filth and stuff on my tray in the dining room. They are trying to harm me. I don't get enough to eat.

DR. SCHRIBER: Are you happy?

MR. GREENE: No.

DR. SCHRIBER: Why not?

MR. GREENE: What you call happiness, I don't.

DR. HUMPHREY: Do you hear voices?

MR. GREENE: They tell me numbers. They do not bother me.

DR. HUMPHREY: That is all. You may be excused.

[AFTER MR. GREENE HAS LEFT THE ROOM.]

DR. HUMPHREY: I believe that his diagnosis should remain as psychopathic personality.

DR. LEROY: I agree. He is ignorant and he has misinterpreted many things. We might also consider paranoid condition or mental deficiency with psychosis.

DR. SCHRIBER: Agreed. He has no remorse. His lack of intelligence and his judgment and reasoning are definitely at a low level. He should continue to receive treatment at Ionia.

7–21–48. WARD NOTE.

POOR ATTITUDE. IDEAS OF PERSECUTION. DELUSIONAL. This colored patient is poorly accessible. He states that he is hungry all the time and his stomach is packed because his rectum won't turn for action. He said all the Bibles start frame-ups. He said they had messed him up in a frame-up since the First World War. He refuses to discuss his ideas. He has a resentful attitude. He has a sarcastic arrogant attitude toward the hospital in general.

10–14–48. WARD NOTE.

DELUSIONAL. ARROGANT. INCLINED TO BE TROUBLESOME. This patient has an arrogant attitude. He states he wants his freedom if he can get that. He states he was framed, that someone passed checks in order to buy some ham and coca-cola for a church picnic. His conversation is rambling and expansive. He has delusions about white paint on the wall like the white paint they use in the courtroom where he was convicted which he says stands in for the white race. A temperature check was taken on this patient for ten days and it was normal throughout that period. He does nothing to pass away the leisure time.

11–21–48. WARD WALK.

This patient is not suitable for transfer.

2–15–49. WARD NOTE.

FIGHTING WITH OTHER PATIENTS. SUPERIOR ATTITUDE. SURLY. This patient is a poor worker. He tries to get out of all the work he possibly can. On the ward he has a superior attitude and a surly disagreeable disposition. He is difficult to get along with. He is reasonably clean about his person and room. His general health is good. He denies hallucinations and states that he feels alright. On February 9, he had trouble with another patient in the dining room over the matter of passing some water. The patient sloshed his hand around in the water pitcher before passing it and the men tied into each other on the ward later. The patient was definitely the aggressor. He grabbed a chair and hit the other man with a chair but the other man stopped the blow with his arm and then retaliated causing several bruises before the trouble was forcibly stopped by attendants. Physical Examination: Weight, 175. Blood Pressure, 146/92. Pulse, 74, regular. Heart and lungs negative.

3–4–49. TRANSFER.

This patient was transferred to Ward 7–2 due to illness.

3–11–49. DEATH NOTE.

The patient Octavius Greene died at 2:55 P.M. Cause of death was myocardial degeneration and his paranoid state. This Negro male with a history of a resolved pneumatic process had been in poor health since February of this year, at which time it was discovered that the patient suffered from heart failure. At the time of death he had purple edema, as well as considerable congestion in both lungs. His death was attributed to his medical condition and the contributing cause, of course, was his paranoia. Because of his mental state he was combative and refused medical treatment and this undoubtedly accelerated his exodus. He was released at 5:00 p.m. to William Diggs, mortician.

CHAPTER 9

The Persistence of Memory

ORAL HISTORY TRANSCRIPTION EXCERPTS
Former Employees of Ionia State Hospital
October 24–25, 2005
Interviewer: Jonathan Metzl
Location: Ionia Historical Society, Ionia, Michigan
Oral History #16: Retired Male Attendant, Age 87

Q: *When did you start working at Ionia?*

A: In 1936.

Q: *What year did you retire?*

A: 1976.

Q: *What was the hospital like in 1936?*

A: . . . We called it all kinds of names back then.

Q: *What did you call it?*

A: Bug house. (Laughs) I mean, that's ridiculous. I shouldn't even use that; I shouldn't even bring it up. But it was commonly known among us, not by the State of Michigan, I'm sure. But . . . you take how many of these things that happened in these institutions where patients did something, they had been convicted and also had a hearing and all of this sort of thing. I don't know. I'll tell you about a black man during those days, but I can't give you dates, that's the trouble.

Q: *What happened?*

A: Well, the inside of the institution was riot-like, and this black man attacked another patient on his ward. And he also, before he got done with the attendants he had him pretty good.

Q: *Attendants went at a patient?*

A: The patient, yeah, big black guy. Subdued him. Roughed him up pretty good.

Q: *So there was a fight?*

A: Yeah.

Q: *The patient he attacked was a white guy?*

A: Yeah.

Q: *And when was this?*

A: I should have the dates, but I don't. I regret a lot of that . . . how important it is for dates, for your own satisfaction, you know. In the '30s or '40s? . . .

Q: *Was there a lot of violence on the wards?*

A: Um, not as a rule. There'd be a riot, and then fights, you know . . . just scuffling, then separate them, then lock them in the room for a while.

Q: *Did your job feel dangerous?*

A: Oh no, not very often. . . . You had a white coat on . . . you were an attendant with a white coat. And the patients knew who the attendants were. . . . We also had keys with a chain on it. . . .

Q: *And they respected your authority?*

A: As a rule, yeah. 'Cause we were . . . I wouldn't say that we was ever unfair. Though sometimes it was tough going.

Q: *In what ways was it tough going?*

A: Well, like, they have a lot of trouble, some of them. 'Cause they have . . . a lot of trouble . . . as to how far do you go? Sometimes I think maybe probably went too far.

Q: *In what way?*

A: Well, we had to fight . . . to try to subdue 'em, and give 'em a thump or two.

Q: *You'd give them a thump . . . so there was actually . . .*

A: But . . . as a rule, overall, I think we got along real well for the conditions. This was before medications.

Q: *Over all those years, any particular patients stand out in your mind?*

A: Just that man. He brought his prison credentials with him, and everybody was aware of him. But then, I know that they wouldn't do him any harm but apparently they did. The attendants had a big job on their hands.

PART IV

Caeser Williams

FIG. 9 *A riot in the Southern Michigan Prison in 1952 garnered international attention and sparked revolts at prisons throughout the United States. (Source:* Life, *May 5, 1952. Used with permission.)*

CHAPTER 10

Too Close for Comfort

ANXIETY SPREAD LIKE SMOKE THROUGH Ionia's narrow corridors in the 1950s. In many ways, the anxiety resulted from prosperity. More patients meant more business. But more business did not necessarily mean more doctors, nurses, or state funds. Instead, the growing census created growing tensions and growing needs. Thus, the anxiety was also a manifestation of propinquity, volatility, and potential combustion.

"This institution is becoming dangerously overcrowded and on January 1, 1951, the resident population was 1,095 patients," Ionia Superintendent Perry C. Robertson wrote in his *Report for the Fiscal Year 1950–1951*. "The architectural normal capacity is 926." Robertson attributed overcrowding to a lack of building expansion, along with the fact that "according to law, the Medical Superintendent of this hospital must receive all patients committed by the criminal courts of Michigan." The report also noted that several key buildings violated fire codes, and had been condemned by the county fire marshall.[1]

Robertson's *1954–1955 Report* sounded an even more urgent refrain. That fiscal year saw extensive maintenance to many of the older hospital buildings and the installment of a new, dry-pipe sprinkler system. Ionia also added a new, 200-bed building for male patients, at a cost of $1,225,318.31. However, according to the superintendent, the new structure created problems rather than treating them. "The opening of a new 200 bed building for male patients has increased the work required to adequately care for the patient load," he wrote. "The building did not in any way relieve the overcrowdedness of this hospital. With inadequate facilities available, the steadily increasing population, and the lack of technical employees," he added with politically astute reticence, "one can only comment that everything possible is being done to better the psychiatric care and treatment for patients."[2]

By August 1955, the census rose to 1,416, or nearly 200 patients in excess of the hospital's maximum capacity of 1,221. By December 1958, the number of patients was 1,475. Incredibly, only six physicians covered the entire hospital—the medical superintendent and five staff psychiatrists. In a master stroke of understatement, the *1957–58 Report* explained that "it is necessary to assign up to 350 patients to one doctor. Under these circumstances, psychotherapy for individual patients is greatly hampered."[3]

Psychoanalysis teaches us that anxiety is a complex process because external symptoms function as metaphors for deeper, psychical conflicts. For all the world, our worries about jobs, finances, or relationships seem ends in and of themselves. Yet, from an analytic perspective, these concerns are objective correlatives, window dressings for unconscious uncertainties about who we are and how we got there.[4]

Thus was the case at Ionia in the 1950s. Manifest concerns about the census belied latent inquietude about the very function of the hospital, and the relationships there within. Unease emerged from somewhere and nowhere at the same time. Rhetorical earth shifted underneath the definitions of seemingly stable terms, such as *patient, treatment, doctor,* or *asylum.* Somatic symptoms of institutional change were the result.

A good part of the heightened tension resulted from transformations not just in the numbers of patient bodies, but in the bodies themselves. Petty larcenists, shoplifters, perverts, women, and small-time criminals who had long served as the hospital's rank-and-file were quietly shunted to less restrictive environments. Patients with reputations for uncontrolled violence appeared in their stead.

For instance, in his *1954–1955 Report,* Superintendent Robertson wrote that "*the over-crowdedness in the institution has increased to the point of being dangerous, not only to the patients, but to the employees. It must be appreciated that the aggressive type of individual that is cared for at this hospital requires more room as close contact causes arguments that start fights and may even grow into a serious riot.*" (italics added)[5]

In previous years, language warning of an aggressive type of individual would have connoted criminal sexual psychopaths (CSPs). Ionia considered CSPs its most dangerous inmates for much of the 1930s and 1940s, and the numbers of these patients swelled throughout the 1950s as well. But Robertson clearly referenced a new set of individuals, one volatile enough to cause arguments that start fights and, in extreme cases, a serious riot. As the superintendent well knew, riots were particularly serious concerns in the Michigan penal system in the aftermath of the infamous 1952 riot at the Southern Michigan Prison in Jackson. The uprising, which garnered international attention and sparked revolts at prisons throughout the United States, began when prisoners seized control of the disciplinary cell block and took eleven guards hostage. Protesters quickly overran the prison's central control station, opened most of the cells, took over the public address system, and urged mutiny. According to the *Washington Post,* over one thousand prisoners soon rampaged, "throwing plates, cups, and other utensils in a wild demonstration. They knocked out hundreds of panes of glass and threw burning papers out the windows." Buildings soon burned. Michigan police restored order after four days of destruction and over two million dollars of damage.[6]

Newspapers later reported that overcrowding lay behind the Jackson riot—and indeed behind a host of similar riots nationwide. For instance, the journalist Ira Freeman sounded much like Superintendent Robertson when he wrote in the *Times* on April 27, 1952, that prison revolts resulted when human needs superseded structural capacities.

> Big as it is, the prison is usually overcrowded. Two and sometimes three men must share a cell 11 by 6 by 8 feet. The United States prison population has been rising from a wartime low of 134,669 in 1945 to more than 167,000 last year, and new building has not kept pace.
>
> These thousands of desperately unhappy, frustrated men have plenty of time to dream hateful, destructive dreams. There is not enough work to go around, largely because of restrictive legislation, increasingly adopted since 1929 at the behest of manufacturers, against prison-made goods, according to Austin H. MacCormick, executive director of the Osborne Association, penal reform society.
>
> IDLENESS AS A FACTOR
> "Idleness is the biggest single factor in prison unrest," he asserts. "Many hundreds of men in numerous prisons languish in complete idleness, without work, educational or recreational programs. They just mope in their cells or mill around undirected in the yards."
>
> Even so, the great majority of the prisoners are not planning to escape or revolt. Most of them are too defeated and apathetic to take an active part in, much less organize, such an undertaking. It is a few "hard guys," young men, intelligent but unstable, with impressive records of bloody crimes, who have been plotting a "show" for many weeks. Facing life imprisonment or unbearably long terms, these desperadoes have nothing to lose.

Freeman added that these tensions worsened because of the dramatic lengthening of prison sentences to then-shocking periods of time: "more than 25 per cent [of inmates] are now sentenced to ten years or more."[7]

Associations between the prison riots and mental illness circulated widely in the aftermath of the revolt. National newspapers reported that the leader of the uprising was a man named "Crazy Jack" Hyatt, and the press frequently portrayed the rioters as if mental patients gone wild. *Life* magazine decried the decision to place mentally ill prisoners within the general prison population. And *Reader's Digest* described the "sudden flare-up of violent rebellion, seizing of hostages, setting fire to buildings, looting of food supplies, hordes of prisoners running through the cell blocks and yards like madmen."[8]

Lesser known, however, was that fact that, after guards restored order, prison officials reclassified inmates it deemed particularly problematic as psychotic, and transferred them to hospitals for the criminally insane. Ionia State Hospital became a primary receiving site. As Robertson noted in his *1954–1955 Report,*

> . . . since the time of the riot at the State Prison of Southern Michigan in the Spring of 1952, although we were extremely overcrowded at that time, 90 patients were admitted from that institution up to February 1955, causing increased over-crowdedness, and in addition to this 90, 150 psychotic patients have been received in 1955. . . . This makes a total of 240 patients that have been received from the Department of Corrections. There still remains a long waiting list of psychotic patients in the Corrections Department. . . . It is rather obvious that if additional buildings are not furnished in the very near future, the same problem of caring for the inmates of the prison will continue to grow and become more serious.[9]

Robertson did not describe the new patients, but the census overwhelmingly categorized these people by crime, race, and gender in similar ways. For instance, in 1951, several years before the riot, the most common convictions among Ionia's 220 new patients were "Indecent Liberties" (26), "Indecent Exposure" (25), "Felonious Assault" (23), "Miscellaneous Sex Crimes" (23), and "Miscellaneous Minor Crimes" (22). Continuing longstanding trends, the report classified the majority of these cases as "U.S. White" (terms reproduced verbatim).

Patients	MALE	FEMALE	TOTAL
U.S. WHITE	156	10	166
U.S. NEGRO	31	3	34
U.S. INDIAN	1	0	1

Admissions from the Southern Michigan Prison radically altered the hospital census. In 1954–55, the sex crime of "Indecent Liberties" remained atop the list, with 59 cases among the 411 new admits. But it was closely followed by a host of violent crimes including "Felonious Assault" (54), "Murder" (42), and "Breaking and Entering" (41). Meanwhile, nativity demographics showed significant increases of many groups of male patients, but most significantly in admissions of "U.S. Negro" men.

Patients	MALE	FEMALE	TOTAL
U.S. WHITE	243	20	263
U.S. NEGRO	115	3	118
U.S. INDIAN	1	0	1

By 1956, "U.S. Negro" men comprised 40 percent of the overall census, up from 16 percent only six years earlier, and by 1958, the percentage increased to nearly half.

Thus, Superintendent Robertson meant something specific when he worried about the *aggressive type of individual* at Ionia. His concern about the overall census was also a concern about the new enemy within. The criminal. The murderer. The rioter. The Negro.

Shifting taxonomies of mental illness were another source of tension in the 1950s. Through much of the first part of the twentieth century, Ionia psychiatrists diagnosed patients using terminology from the *Statistical Manual for the Use of Institutions for the Insane*. Published initially by the American Medico-Psychological Association in conjunction with the National Committee for Mental Hygiene, the *Manual* codified the prevailing belief that insanity resulted mainly from somatic etiologies. The first edition, in 1918, divided mental disorders into twenty-two principal groups, of which twenty attributed causality to disturbances in a person's biological functions. Not surprisingly, this list included dementia praecox. The tenth and final version, published in 1942 and widely used at Ionia throughout the 1940s, accommodated for psychoneurotic and behavioral disorders but continued to emphasize the "constitutional basis" of psychiatric disease.[10]

Psychiatric diagnosis underwent major revision in the aftermath of World War II. As many historians of psychiatry note, psychoanalysts dominated the American Psychiatric Association's 1951 Committee on Nomenclature and Statistics. The analytic presence helped shape the first postwar classification of psychopathology, *Mental Disorders: Diagnostic and Statis-*

tical Manual published in 1952. The manual, which became known as the DSM-I, retained a good amount of diagnostic language from earlier classification systems. But the new text brought to the fore the belief that mental disease resulted, not only from biological lesions, but from early life conflicts as well. DSM-I promoted the notion that such "nonorganic" conditions as "psychoneurosis," "conversion," and "displacement" represented underlying psychological conflicts or maladaptive reactions to life stressors. The DSM-I also qualified many disorders with the postpositive word *reaction*—such as *schizophrenic reaction* or *manic-depressive reaction*. The term came from the work of the German psychiatrist Adolf Meyer, who viewed mental disorders as individualized personality reactions to a combination of psychological, social, and biological factors.[11]

The DSM-I must have seemed an uncomfortable sea change for Ionia psychiatrists. State hospital clinicians, often referred to as "directive-organic" psychiatrists, oversaw huge patient populations and had little time for individual therapy. These so-called D-O psychiatrists, increasingly graduates of foreign medical schools, had uneven exposure to psychoanalysis in their training, and psychoanalysis was in any case associated with a world of ivory-towered privilege and wealth far removed from state mental institutions. Yet, the DSM quickly became the mandatory means of classifying all state patients. The state required Ionia doctors to diagnose all hospital admissions using the new criteria starting in 1953, and to rediagnose all long-term patients via DSM-I categories soon thereafter.[12]

Finally, the 1950s saw the advent and expanded use of important chemical treatments for mental illness. Most notably, the major tranquilizer chlorpromazine was approved for wide use in the United States in 1955—coincidentally the same year that the flow of men from the Southern Michigan riots reached its peak. The new treatments inexorably altered the practice of psychiatry and, more important, the treatment of patients at state hospitals such as Ionia. As the historian David Healy describes it, "State mental hospital doctors were so eager to use the new drug that when chlorpromazine was finally launched as Thorazine, in 1955 . . . the take-up in psychiatry was astonishing—[drug maker] SK&F reportedly took in $75 million the first year the drug was sold . . . some of the American state asylums, such as Pilgrim State in New York, had up to 15,000 residents. Everyone got the new drug."[13]

Chlorpromazine and other antipsychotic medications have widely been credited with emptying American psychiatric hospitals by rendering calm seemingly uncontrollable patients, thereby eliminating the need for such hospital-based treatments as electroshock therapy, insulin coma, and psychosurgery. But at Ionia, the opposite dynamic occurred. State administrators used the medication to justify a vast expansion in the hospital census, even while the number of doctors, nurses, and attendants remained the same. The hospital employed only four psychiatrists at the height of overcrowding in the mid-1950s, and on some units, the ratio of patients to staff grew to an incredible 282:1. Given such ratios, it is little wonder that the rhetoric in the hospital's annual reports, doctors' notes, and ward transcripts shifted from restoration—*our goal is to return this patient to normal functioning*—to containment—*we used chemical therapies to control this patient's violent tendencies.*[14]

It must be remembered that life at Ionia likely appeared calm from the outside. Michiganders who drove by the hospital in the 1950s could not have helped but notice that the grounds remained meticulously groomed. Flowers lined the winding driveway in the springtime. Deer frequented the sloping lawns. Crops grew in the expansive fields, and livestock reproduced in the barns. In short, Ionia looked like many other rural Michigan properties in the 1950s, save the small matter of the heavily guarded 2,000-bed mental hospital that dominated the landscape.

The calm was a mirage. The census surged, and the patients grew ever more unlike the Michigan community from which they were partitioned. Long-employed diagnoses and treatments collided with new modes of intervention. Tradition abutted revolution, and revolution abutted revolt. The outside may have conveyed the message of peaceful reassurance. Yet the hospital's placid exterior could not entirely contain the anxiety that rumbled from within. The full impact of the inquietude would not be fully realized for another decade. But change, to paraphrase the singer Sam Cooke, was gonna come.[15]

CHAPTER 11

His Actions Are Determined Largely by His Emotions

CAESER WILLIAMS WAS BORN INTO a life of violence. And violent he did become.

Mr. Williams was born in Redding, California, in December 1919. His father, Aaron, died in a fight over a gambling debt three weeks later. His mother, Birdie, was a thoughtful, kind person who had a thing for volatile men. She met Walter David one year after Aaron's death. David was a self-described "rolling stone," and Birdie and Caeser rolled with him from small town to small town in Northern California. Birdie later recounted that she "carried a gun" on her person at all times to protect herself and Caeser from Walter's abuse. Caeser attended seven different schools by the time he was eleven. His eighth school was in San Jose, a sleepy California outpost that Birdie moved to after Walter's anger became too much for her to bear.

Birdie cared deeply for Caeser. She fed and clothed him even when she could not afford for herself, and her proudest moments were the Sunday mornings when she attended church with her handsome young son. But Birdie was Caeser's primary caretaker during difficult times, a reality that forced her absence from his life more often than she desired. Most days, she left for work before Caeser awoke and returned after he went to sleep.

Caeser was a bright child who missed school with regularity. His mother's excuse letters demonstrated penmanship strikingly similar to his own. He fought and smoked cigarettes and spent his lunch money on movies and pinball machines. At the age of fifteen he quit school and worked briefly at a local country club.

The first episode occurred when Caeser was eighteen. One day, seemingly out of the blue, he emptied his bank account of its modest savings and traveled spontaneously to San Francisco. Caeser rented a hotel room near North Beach and spent three sleepless nights awakening to the pleasures of city life. As his mother later explained to a medical examiner, Mr. Williams returned from that trip "with his first dose of gonorrhea and a badly shaken faith in women."

Another surprise came when Caeser was twenty-two. He later admitted that he ran with a "fast crowd" and was "no angel" during this period of his life. He lived beyond his means and had a bad habit of spending sprees. In other words, Mr. Williams was not the marrying type. Yet marry he did, in a fit of passion, to a woman he had met only two weeks prior.

Susie was a deeply religious woman. Caeser respected her sense of propriety, and Susie saw in Caeser a soul to be saved. She took him to church, just like his mother once had, and tried to organize his life. And she succeeded, at least for the first year of their marriage. Caeser went to work each morning at a property management company and came home promptly at six each evening. Susie had dinner waiting.

The term *stressor* comes to mind when describing the negative impact that an otherwise positive event had on Caeser Williams's state of mind. One night in late 1948, Susie told Caeser that she was pregnant. She sensed in him a tinge of resentment. But the worst was yet to come. Susie looked for him to be a partner, but Caeser instead became a stranger, someone frightening.

Caeser lost control in the weeks before Susie's delivery. He spoke streams of pressurized nonsense and stayed up for days on end. He described himself as "royalty." He threatened Susie, and then he threatened everyone else. The police investigated him for armed robbery. Two weeks later, officers picked him up on suspicion of breaking and entering. Charges of "Larceny from a Person" hung in the air. Susie bailed him out of jail twice. But the third call came collect from a lockup unit in Detroit, a city to which Caeser inexplicably traveled on a bus ride of fancy. According to police reports, Caeser shot a man in the leg after an argument. This time Susie did not bail him out. This time she filed for divorce. On March 15, 1951, a jury convicted Caeser Williams of attempted murder, and a judge sentenced him to ten to twenty years at the Jackson State Prison in southern Michigan.

Prison life was exceedingly difficult for Mr. Williams. He fought often with guards and other inmates. A prison psychologist attributed his unrest to an "inadequate personality." More likely, Caeser Williams lacked the soul for confinement. He was, after all, a child of wanderers, and wandering guided his perceptual proclivities. He wanted to be elsewhere, anywhere but in prison, anywhere but stuck in a routine.

Perhaps wandering lust helps explain why Mr. Williams participated in the prison riots of 1952. "MUTINY . . . A force of 200 state troopers, throwing tear-gas bombs and firing submachine guns, restored a measure of order in Jackson State Prison today after 20 hours of rioting by mutinous convicts," the *New York Times* reported on April 22. "The rioting began last evening when three convicts in the disciplinary cellblock overpowered four guards."

News of the protest quickly spread to the nearly 2,600 prisoners who were out of their cells at the time, including Mr. Williams. Soon, according to the *Times*, "convicts raced through the prison smashing windows and furniture, raiding the commissary and kitchen and creating a tumult of noise with musical instruments taken from the recreation rooms. They set fire to several buildings, including the prison print shop, library, laundry, and greenhouse." The rioters took eleven guards hostage and demanded to speak to newspapermen about dire conditions in the prison. But troopers came instead.[1]

Mr. Williams was not a leader, a hostage taker, or an impromptu musician. Instead, he was a happenstance participant who misread chaos as an opening, when in fact the doors were always closed. He raced through the halls looking for a way out. Mr. Williams was still searching when the state police arrived. The twitch of freedom proved a greater pull than the interpolating voice of the trooper. "Put your hands behind your head," the voice called. "Kneel down. Now lie on the ground." Mr. Williams could not comply. His ears surely heard the commands. But his eyes, and his spirit, and perhaps even his feet continued to search for a breach. Even if he had complied, it was unlikely that he would have avoided the club to the stomach or the kicks to the head.

Solitary confinement proved anything but solitary. Perhaps the voice of the Lord in Mr. Williams's head was the sound of an opportunity. More likely, being kicked in the skull and spending one year alone in a small cell facilitated Jesus's participation in Mr. Williams's interior dialogue. Either way, the prison reclassified Caeser Williams as a psychiatric inmate. A prolonged period of observation ensued. When the Virgin Mary and several angels joined the chorus, prison officials transported Mr. Williams to the Ionia State Hospital for the Criminally Insane. The transport face sheet warned that "this man is belligerant [*sic*], threatening, and assaultive."

Victor Murrows was the evaluating psychiatrist. A graduate of the University of Michigan Medical School, Ionia was his first job after his service in the Army medical corps. Dr. Murrows considered himself an expert in diagnosis. During his military years he championed use of new terminology from the American Psychiatric Association's Committee on Nomenclature and Statistics. When the APA published *Mental Disorders: Diagnostic and Statistical Manual* in 1952, Murrows quickly mastered the text.

According to archived documents, Dr. Murrows met with Caeser Williams five times over the course of the one-month evaluation. Notes suggest that the interactions did not go well. Mr. Williams was by that point an exceedingly angry man who mistrusted most forms of authority. The first words attributed to Mr. Williams in his medical chart were "Everyone here is crazy. I will kill them if they mess with me. I will kill you if you mess with me. I want to go home." Dr. Murrows, meanwhile, reflexively read mistrust of medical authority as a symptom of mental illness.

Murrows spoke twice with Birdie in person and twice with Susie on the phone. He then reviewed extensive records detailing Mr. Williams's participation in the riot and his subsequent "psychological" treatments in prison. The documents explicitly reveal that Dr. Murrow knew about Mr. Williams's unstable upbringing, flights of fancy, prolonged solitary confinement, and the kicks to his head.

Dr. Murrows performed a physical examination, which found no abnormalities save a random X-ray finding that "there is a .38 calibre bullet lying just within the chest wall just above the angle of the diaphragm." On Wechsler-Bellevue psychological testing, Mr. Williams reportedly attained "a full scale score of 113, which indicates intellectual functioning in the bright normal level" and "a verbal score of 110, which is in the average range."

Dr. Murrows began his report as follows.

We have here a large Negro man of 37 years of age who loathes authority and is very defiant. He participated in the prison riot and allegedly destroyed property and fought with guards. He gave a history of hallucinatory experiences at prison and said he started to hallucinate several years ago. He now claims that he will attack those that stand in his way, and it is quite evident that he intends to do so. He says in our first meeting that the Lord "commands" him to attack a ward attendant, Mr. Wright. . . .

It was this examiner's feeling that he was withholding information. On the next part of the examination he was more verbose and rambling. . . . He claimed that he hears the voice of Jesus and that he has certain powers. He claimed that he can make teeth grow. . . . He talked about his philosophy of life, yet he knows very little about philosophy and has formulated his own beliefs in a type of pseudophilosophical jargon. On each interview he will tend to ventilate this type of thinking. It is a type of ruminating, loosely connected wishful thinking that certainly is not too factual. . . . On one interview he talked about his color and he implied he had been subordinated because of that. . . . He is keenly aware of his lack of social status and wealth. Yet he continues to hallucinate and he is often grandiose in his ruminations. . . . He denies that he is mentally ill.

The patient has never shown much affect and is rather indifferent. . . . He has not made friends on the ward. He does what he is told in a resentful manner. At no time does the examiner feel that he has established rapport with the patient, who remains either overtly hostile or else cool and distant and frequently evasive. On the ward he is given to hostile behavior. At other times he is found sitting alone in a corner in an autistic mood. He attempts to manipulate others despite his confused state. His actions are determined largely by his emotions rather than by critical, accurate thinking.

The inconsistencies are dreadful. How could a person be both autistic and antagonistic? Or isolated and manipulative? Or philosophical, verbose, and indifferent? Worst of all, how could one person demonstrate a detachment from reality such that he believed that he could make teeth grow, and at the same time demonstrate the volition required to act in a resentful manner?

To be fair, Dr. Murrows likely sought to help Mr. Williams by diagnosing him. Prisoners often felt, rightly, that a trip to Ionia meant detention without end. But from Murrows's perspective, a psychiatric diagnosis meant entry into the hospital system and a course of treatment that included promising new medications and even a potential cure.

To this end, Murrows had several options from the new *Mental Disorders: Diagnostic and Statistical Manual* that helped explain the constellation of symptoms. For instance, should Dr. Murrows have decided that hallucinations and delusions were the most important aspects of Mr. Williams's presentation, he might have settled on a diagnosis of schizophrenic reaction, "a group of psychotic reactions characterized by fundamental disturbances in reality relationships" as well as "emotional disharmony, unpredictable disturbances in stream of thought," and "regressive behavior." The paranoid type was perhaps particularly salient to Mr. Williams's case because it included "delusions of persecution and/or of grandeur, ideas of reference, and often hallucinations" accompanied by "excessive religiosity."[2]

Dr. Murrows might also have considered spontaneous trips and spur of the moment spending sprees to be the central aspects of Mr. Williams's complex history, and might therefore have chosen a diagnosis of manic-depressive reaction, manic type. The 1952 definition of manic-depressive reaction was only a speck of what it would become in later years, when terms such as *grandiosity, pressured speech,* or *excessive involvement in pleasurable activities* entered the lexicon and formed the core of a diagnosis now known as bipolar disorder. But the early text's description of a condition marked by "severe mood swings" and periods of "elation or irritability with over-talkativeness, flight of ideas, and increased motor activity" aptly explained North Beach, Detroit, marriage, and many other instances where the course of Caeser Williams's life was worsened by his periodic inability to sit still. The 1952 definition also allowed for "accessory symptoms such as illusions, delusions, and hallucinations," some of the very words Murrows used in his evaluation.[3]

Acute brain syndrome associated with trauma was another alternative if Murrows thought the abuse Mr. Williams suffered in the aftermath of the riot caused a subsequently organic affect. The diagnostic manual defined that condition as a set of impairments of orientation, memory, intellectual functions, affect, or judgment following "head injury produced by external trauma of a gross, physical nature."[4]

Hypochondriacal reaction was another possibility. That not-yet-standardized diagnosis raised the possibility that Mr. Williams's symptoms represented conscious or unconscious attempts to feign illness for secondary gain, such as one might get by escaping prison through becoming insane. Were he so inclined, Dr. Murrows might also have considered the possibility that mental illness did not reside in Mr. Williams at all. Terms such as *dissocial reaction* attributed untoward personality traits to the effects of living in an "abnormal moral environment." The terminology clearly pathologized the urban poor, whose mental symptoms arose from "allegiance to the codes of their own predatory, criminal, or social group."[5]

As you might have guessed, Victor Murrows eschewed these new diagnostic formulations. Instead he chose the well-worn option. He took Mr. Williams at face value and decided that hostility, a lack of guilt, and a propensity to blame others were the pathognomonic features of the case. "This patient is a Negro man of 37 years of age who loathes authority and is very defiant" were his opening words. Dr. Murrows located this defiance not in society, history, or an insane prison system. Instead, he located illness solely in the black man who stood before him, through a logic that connected the color of Caeser Williams's skin to the moral workings of his psyche.

"This patient is unable to conform to the norms of society," Murrows dictated. "He is frequently in trouble, and learns little from experience or from punishment. He is callous and shows emotional immaturity, with lack of sense of responsibility, lack of judgment, and an ability to rationalize his behavior so that it appears warranted and justified. [Author's emphasis] *The diagnosis is Psychopathic Personality with Psychosis.*"

By "unable to conform to the norms of society," Murrows meant that, like Octavius Greene, Caeser Williams suffered from a form of sociopathic personality. But something was askew. On page 38, the 1952 DSM described a personality disturbance marked by continuous legal trouble, callousness, hedonism, immaturity, and rationalization. But the disorder described was specifically *not* psychopathic personality. Instead, according to the DSM-I, the term *psychopathic personality* was passé. The manual instructed clinicians to use a new descriptor it deemed to be more precise. "Cases previously classified as 'psychopathic personality,'" the manual explained, were to be defined by a new term called *antisocial reaction.*

It is of course possible that the otherwise au courant Victor Murrows made a mistake. Maybe there were gaps in his expertise. Maybe page 38 fell out of his edition of the DSM. Maybe the error was caused by the transcriptionist instead.

A more likely explanation is that Dr. Murrows's use of the outdated term reveals something important about relationships between white doctors and black patients at Ionia in 1956. It suggests that, at least in the case of Caeser Williams, the structure of old race relationships trumped the structure of new clinical relationships. Dr. Murrows may have championed new descriptive language, but his assumptions about race were firmly rooted in the past. According to this past, black defiance to white medical authority was psychopathic. But schizophrenic it was not—at least not yet.

As we now turn to explore, the case of Caeser Williams was more than merely a symbol of the past: it was also a beacon of the future. That is because the diagnostic narrative did not end when Victor Murrows diagnosed Caeser Williams with *psychopathic personality* in 1956. Instead, that interaction was just the beginning.

CHAPTER 12

Revisionist Mystery

IONIA DOCTORS, NURSES, AND ATTENDANTS compulsively charted daily life on men's ward 9–1. From these notes, we know that Caeser Williams took 100 milligrams of Thorazine and one multivitamin capsule per day. We also know that Mr. Williams averaged twenty-five electroconvulsive therapy sessions in each of the first five years of his confinement. We know that Mr. Williams developed a rash on his right forearm in October 1959, which doctors treated with topical nitrogen mustard. We also know that Mr. Williams ordered items from the regular food menu, drank coffee and fruit juice each morning, and purchased chewing tobacco from the commissary. We even know that he mailed three "Xmas cards" on December 17, 1962, penned perhaps to Birdie, Susie, and his son.

Mr. Williams's own voice is largely missing from these documents. Unlike Alice Wilson, his statements were not recorded in Ward Walk transcripts. Instead, the voice of Caeser Williams appears indirectly at two important sites in his extensive chart. First, between 1957 and 1965, Birdie exchanged a series of poignant, heartbreaking letters with the Ionia medical superintendent. In each letter, she inquired about the conditions of her son's incarceration and plans for his release. The correspondence was archived in its own section at the back of Mr. Williams's file. "Dear Dr. Robertson," she wrote in January 1957. "My son tells me in letters that he is not well. This news troubles me a great deal. Although he is a man, in my eye-sight he is still my child. Please let me know when I may see him." In March 1960, Birdie again appealed to the superintendent's sense of family. "Dear Doctor, thank you for your answer to my letters and phone calls. It gave me a little more hope to also hear from my son that he is feeling better. However I am still very much concerned. When things like this strike home, I know as I believe you are a family man you too would be concerned. I am so far from Caeser and I would like nothing more than to be at his side." By June 1962, her requests became more direct. "Dear Dr., I realize that with so many patients one can not expect too much personal attention," she wrote. "But can you see about transferring Caeser to a facility closer to his home? He longs to be closer to family. Please keep us informed and if anything develops that we as his people should know, do not hold back and tell us." "My son has not responded to my letters," read Birdie's resigned, desperate letter of March 1964. "I would like very much to hear something about him."

A voice attributed to Mr. Williams also appears in numerous incident reports documenting altercations with staff or other patients. Here, attendants quote threats allegedly made by Mr. Williams in order to justify their reactions. For instance, on April 4, 1958, a note claimed that Mr. Williams "refused to take his medications." "He says 'I ain't stone crazy,' " read the report. "He says he hears the Lord talking to him." On June 17, 1959, a report explained that "the patient became very demanding and threatened to leave and take this employee's keys, stating the Lord told him the attendants were to let him out. He picked up a chair and demanded the keys. He had to be put in seclusion." On February 22, 1962, "he had to be kept in seclusion for 115 hours because he was belligerant [sic], threatening, and assaultive. He claims that 'the attendants always beat me up.' He is considered a menace to those about him because of his strength." "Patient says 'I want to go home,' " Caeser Williams's chart read on July 10, 1966. "He threatened to hit another patient and an attendant with a chair."

We learn little about Caeser Williams's sense of himself from these two sites, save to say that he shared his mother's feelings of anger and helplessness about his confinement. But we do learn something important about the ways that the institution viewed its progress—or rather, its lack of progress—in treating Mr. Williams's so-called mental illness. Both sites suggest that Mr. Williams's symptoms did not change despite Thorazine, ECT, art therapy, milieu therapy, psychotherapy, or any other therapy. In practically each reply over their eight-year correspondence, the superintendent claimed to Birdie that her son's condition remained the same. "There is no reason why one should worry about your son's physical condition," read a 1962 letter in a familiar refrain. "Mentally there is very little change in his condition as he continues to be hallucinated [sic]. Rest assured that everything possible is being done for your son." Meanwhile, incident report after incident report described Mr. Williams as "unchanged," "guarded," "still hostile," and "without insight."

However, the chart reveals that something important *did* change about Caeser Williams over the first decade of his stay at Ionia: his diagnosis. In the mid-1960s, the institution decided that Mr. Williams no longer suffered from a sociopathic personality. For the remainder of his stay at the hospital, Ionia classified Caeser Williams as suffering from schizophrenia instead.

Mr. Williams was not alone: in the 1960s, a number of African American men at Ionia saw their diagnoses shift from personality disorders to various forms of schizophrenia. We know this in part because transcriptionists of the 1950s and 1960s did not have the luxury of computers, word processors, or electronic medical records. When a doctor revised a patient's diagnosis, a clerk mined the chart and literally crossed out the former condition with a pen or typewriter. The clerk would cross out mentions of personality disturbance from each summary list and progress note, even though the old diagnosis often remained legible underneath. Ever the revisionist historian, the clerk then added a new diagnosis in its stead.

How did these men *become* schizophrenic?

The most likely answer to this question is also the answer directly disproved by the evidence. That answer: the men's symptoms worsened over time. By this logic, the men at Ionia regressed, decompensated, or suffered so-called schizophrenic breaks during their time at Ionia to the point where they met criteria for schizophrenic illness. The problem with this explanation is that practically every chart contains text suggesting that the men's symptoms did not change. Caeser Williams hallucinated and threatened staff on the first day of his stay at Ionia, much like he did in the final days before he was transferred to another state institution and then lost to follow-up. "Con-

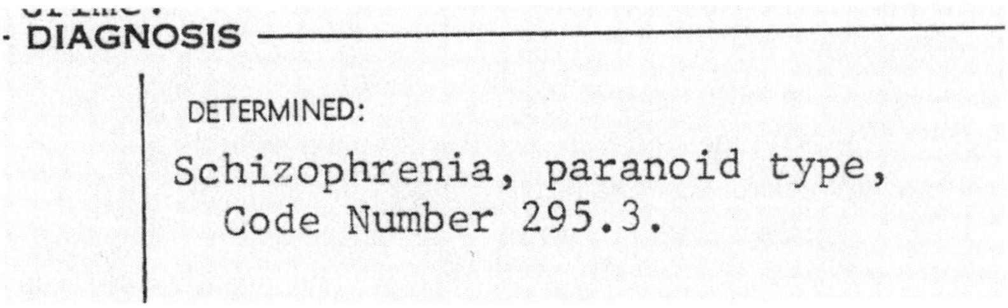
DIAGNOSIS

DETERMINED:
Schizophrenia, paranoid type,
Code Number 295.3.

10A

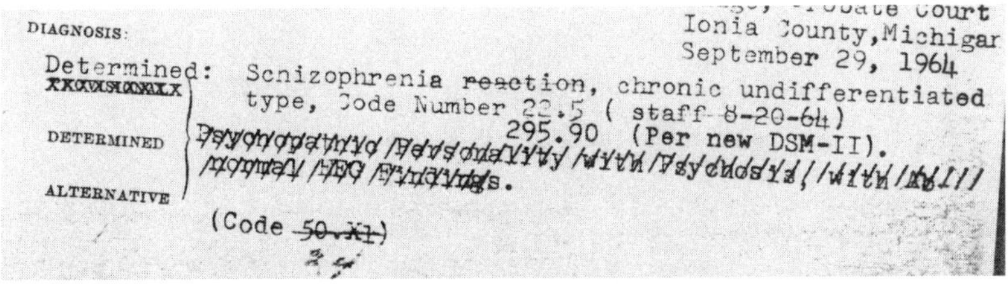
Ionia County, Michigan
September 29, 1964

DIAGNOSIS:
Determined: Schizophrenia ~~reaction~~, chronic undifferentiated type, Code Number 22.5 (staff 8-20-64)
295.90 (Per new DSM-II).
DETERMINED
ALTERNATIVE
(Code ~~50.X1~~)

10B

FIGS. 10A AND 10B *In the 1960s, the official diagnosis in Caesar Williams's chart shifted from psychopathic personality to schizophrenia (10a). The face sheets of other African American male patients showed this transformation more clearly (10b). (Source: State Archives of Michigan)* tinues to deny that he is mentally ill," read one of the final reports from 1968, before Mr. Williams's chart and records abruptly end. "Resentful. *He has not changed during his hospitalization.* Frequently evasive."

Neither did these men develop schizophrenia because of the punitive actions of their doctors, at least not explicitly so. Evidence also refutes theories of the 1960s, which raised the possibility that the men caught schizophrenia like a virus, developed schizophrenia because of early-life interactions with cold, dominant, rejecting mothers, contracted schizophrenia as a result of *double-bind* situations in prison, faked schizophrenia like a game of charades, or mimicked schizophrenia because of the power of suggestion from other patients.[1]

At the end of the day, the fact that these men became schizophrenic had relatively little to do with the men's actions, their doctors' intentions, or any other variable linked to daily life at Ionia. Instead, African American men at Ionia developed schizophrenia because of changes in the interpretive structures surrounding their actions.

This is not to suggest that many of the men did not suffer from debilitating mental anguish—indeed, the men lost lives and dreams and loved ones, and were often deeply in need of treatment and care. But the associations implied by that anguish changed over time. In institutional terms, "Negro symptoms" such as hallucinations, delusions, and violent projections came to mean different things. African American men who looked for all the world like sociopaths in the 1950s then appeared to doctors, nurses, attendants, and even perhaps to the men themselves, as if schizophrenics in the 1960s.

Thus did African American men at Ionia develop schizophrenia, not because of changes in their clinical presentations, but because of changes in the connections between their clinical presentations and larger, national conversations about race, violence, and insanity. And thus did the men develop schizophrenia not just because of symptoms, but because of civil rights.

CHAPTER 13

A Racialized Disease

TWO HISTORICAL REASONS EXPLAIN WHY the diagnosis of schizophrenia captured African American men at Ionia in the 1960s. And why, soon thereafter, schizophrenia disproportionately captured African American men throughout the United States. And why, as a result of that capturing, schizophrenia became violent at the same moment in time that it became black. The first reason is as follows: schizophrenia became a racialized disease in the 1960s in ways that preferentially selected black male bodies.

Ironically, the 1960s were the decade in which American psychiatry began a sustained attempt to eliminate bias from its diagnostic criteria. After fifteen years and twenty printings, the *Mental Disorders: Diagnostic and Statistical Manual* was set for revision. Though the first version of the diagnostic bible had enjoyed surprisingly extensive use, an increasing chorus of psychiatrists criticized the first DSM edition for containing vague and unspecific diagnostic guidelines. In response, the American Psychiatric Association's Committee on Nomenclature and Statistics met through the 1960s in an effort to produce a new manual that would "facilitate maximum communication within the profession and reduce confusion and ambiguity." The committee sent drafts of updated criteria to 120 of the nation's leading psychiatrists starting in the mid-1960s, and as a result, psychiatrists in places such as Ionia employed the new diagnostic terminology several years prior to the publication of the second edition of the *Diagnostic and Statistical Manual of Mental Disorders* (DSM-II) in 1968.[1]

Authors of the DSM-II believed that the revised manual defined mental illness in ways that were less culturally specific to the United States, and more in line with the World Health Organization's *International Classification of Diseases.* "This second edition of the *Diagnostic and Statistical Manual of Mental Disorders* (DSM-II) reflects the growth of the concept that people of all nations live in one world," read the opening sentence of the first page of the text, a sentence that echoed Margaret Mead's belief that human survival depended on recognition that "we all live in one world."[2]

The new definition of schizophrenia appeared to be the hallmark of such uniformity—so much so that the introduction to the DSM-II cited schizophrenia as the primary example of a diagnosis that had been broadened and simplified in order to account for disparate international understandings of the illness. To recall, DSM-I defined mental disorders as a series of "reactions" between individual personalities and external events. Schizophrenic reaction was an emotional disharmony that manifested through "unpredictable disturbances in stream of thought" and "regressive behavior."

The DSM-II eliminated the word *reaction* from disease descriptors. Its modified criteria encouraged doctors to disarticulate symptoms from the axis of essence, and to begin to think of mental disorders as distinct groups of illnesses rather than as individual extensions of normal personality. Schizophrenic reaction became schizophrenia, a change that asked doctors to understand the illness not as the result of early-life development issues, but as the result of exogenous disease. The effects of this transition would not be fully realized until the 1980s, with the advent of the third edition of the DSM. But, as with the civil rights movement, the fits and starts of earlier decades lay the groundwork for the revolution.

Here is how the DSM-II defined schizophrenia.

295 SCHIZOPHRENIA

This large category includes a group of disorders manifested by characteristic disturbances in thinking, mood, and behavior. Disturbances in mood are marked by alterations of concept formation which may lead to misinterpretation of reality and sometimes to delusions and hallucinations, which frequently appear psychologically self-protective. Corollary mood changes include ambivalent, constricted and inappropriate emotional responsiveness and lack of empathy with others. Behavior may be withdrawn, regressive, and bizarre. The schizophrenias, in which the mental status is attributable primarily to a *thought disorder,* are to be distinguished from the *Major affective illnesses* which are dominated by a *mood* disorder. The *Paranoid states* are distinguished from schizophrenia by the narrowness of their distortions of reality and by the absence of other psychotic symptoms.

The manual further defined the paranoid type as follows.

295.3 SCHIZOPHRENIA, PARANOID TYPE

This type of schizophrenia is characterized primarily by the presence of persecutory or grandiose delusions, often associated with hallucinations. Excessive religiosity is sometimes seen. The patient's attitude is frequently hostile and aggressive, and his behavior tends to be consistent with his delusions. In general the disorder does not manifest gross personality disorganization of the hebephrenic and catatonic types, perhaps because the patient manifests the mechanism of projection, which attributes to others characteristics he cannot accept in himself. Three subtypes of the disorder may sometimes be differentiated, depending on the predominant symptoms: hostile, grandiose, and hallucinatory.

It is important to recall that the DSM-II represented progress. In the years following its publication, the manual was maligned, critiqued, and ultimately revised due to its inclusion of homosexuality as a mental disorder. But schizophrenia was not central to that conflict, and in any case automatic dismissal of the DSM-II overlooks the ways in which the 1968 text radically improved upon its predecessors.[3]

However, the DSM-II was far from the objective, universal text that its authors envisioned. In unintentional and unexpected ways, the manual's diagnostic criteria—and the criteria for schizophrenia most centrally— reflected the social tensions of 1960s America. A diagnostic text meant to shift focus away from the specifics of culture instead became inexorably intertwined with the cultural politics, and above all the race politics, of a particular nation and a particular moment in time.

For instance, in a vital step, the DSM-II criteria for schizophrenia, paranoid type, foregrounded masculinized hostility, violence, and aggression as key components of the illness. Earlier, the DSM-I had described schizophrenia and most other disorders in a gender-neutral, passive-voice without sex-specific pronouns. ("This type of reaction is characterized by autistic, unrealistic thinking. . . . It is often characterized by unpredictable behavior.") DSM-II added male actors, described through universal male pronouns, who translated hostile and aggressive male feelings into stereotypically male behaviors. "The patient's attitude is frequently hostile and aggressive, and his behavior tends to be consistent with his delusions." Masculinized hostility was so central to the revised diagnosis that it formed its own subtype of paranoid schizophrenia. Of course, such language reflected linguistic conventions; but, in the case of schizophrenia at least, a subtle shift in linguistic conventions had enormous unintended implications.[4]

Another important characteristic was that persons with paranoid schizophrenia rationalized hostility through a mechanism previously associated with antisocial reaction: by blaming other people for their problems. DSM-I schizophrenia mentioned nothing of projection. Yet there it was in the

DSM-II: "the patient manifests the mechanism of projection, which attributes to others characteristics he cannot accept in himself." Projection still appeared under antisocial personality as well (though it was not called projection—simply "they tend to blame others or offer plausible rationalizations for their behavior"). But now, diagnosticians had another option when encountering the defense mechanism deemed so essential to Octavius Greene, Caeser Williams, and other patients.

Finally, the new definition of schizophrenia excluded persons such as Alice Wilson, whose feminized insanity resulted from instability of mood rather than of intellect. Authors of the DSM-II removed terms such as *emotional disharmony*, since emotions were no longer thought to be the roots of the problem. In a major blow to gender-inflected, psychoanalytic definitions of schizophrenia, the new text instructed clinicians to "distinguish" real schizophrenic illness from that caused by "major affective illnesses" such as melancholia and manic-depression.

The DSM-II was not an explicitly racist text. The drive for revision was almost certainly grounded in a desire for diagnostic accuracy, and the revisers likely felt little connection between their task at hand and the politics of civil rights. "We did the best we could at the time and under the circumstances," academic psychiatrist and DSM-II author Robert Spitzer explained to me in a recent conversation. "We felt we were being objective."[5]

Yet, the DSM-II functioned as an *implicitly* racist text because it mirrored the social context of its origins in ways that enabled users to knowingly or unknowingly pathologize protest as mental illness. This was because the 1960s was an era when the notion that large groups of people acted in hostile ways while rationalizing their aggression as a justifiable response to the attitudes of others was a tremendously powerful social message. But that group was not people with schizophrenia; it was people who were black.

Scholars of the civil rights era have shown that the mid-1960s was a time of important transformation in the Unites States in general, and in the civil rights movement in particular. Mass protests based in nonviolent resistance and civil disobedience, championed by the National Association for the Advancement of Colored People (NAACP), the Southern Christian Leadership Conference (SCLC), and Dr. Martin Luther King Jr., led to a series of key victories following the U.S. Supreme Court's *Brown v. the Board of Education of Topeka* decision of 1954. Sit-ins, boycotts, freedom rides, and other direct-action tactics resulted in major, if painful steps toward stated goals of desegregation, racial integration, and ultimate equality. Legislation such as the civil rights acts of 1957, 1964, and 1968 and the Voting Rights Act of 1965 promised equity, on paper at least, in workplaces, public spaces, and voting booths.

However, in the aftermath of the Watts riots of 1965, voices from within and beyond the movement argued that equality would never be attained in racist America. Black Power became the rallying cry of Stokely Carmichael (later Kwame Toure), Willie Ricks (later Mukasa Dada), Eldridge Cleaver, and others. Black Power advocates rejected what they held to be the "accommodationist" strategies of mainstream civil rights leaders. Their goal was not so much equality as independence, and as such they believed that African Americans needed to seize power rather than to seek compromise. Carmichael advocated revolutionary violence to overthrow oppression, while denouncing even sympathetic whites. His successor as leader of the Student Nonviolent Coordinating Committee (later the Student National Coordinating Committee), H. Rap Brown (later Jamil Abdullah al-Amin), famously described violence "as American as cherry pie." In 1966, Huey Newton and Bobby Seale formed the Black Panther Party, an organization that espoused a doctrine of armed resistance in the interest of African American justice. Meanwhile, Pan-Africanists and African nationalists such as Malcolm X described a "global African community" connecting "native" and "diaspora" Africans, or argued, as did Elijah Muhammad, that "the white devil's day is over." In 1968, a pair of brothers from Detroit named Milton and Richard Henry (later Gaidi and Imari Abubakari Obadele) argued that African Americans in the United States should form their own independent nation-state, the Republic of New Afrika, in the so-called Black Belt South.[6]

These two 1960s-era trajectories—psychiatric diagnostic revision and increasingly confrontational civil rights protests—merged in the pages of leading professional psychiatric journals, where authors suddenly rediscovered African American research subjects. To recall chapter three, race was rarely a category of comparative analysis in psychiatric research in the 1950s. At that time, the *American Journal of Psychiatry* contained few comparison studies of "black" versus "white" groups of patients, and many key articles described research done on segregated, white-only wards. One of the infrequent authors who wrote on the topic, the sociologist R. A. Schermerhorn, bemoaned the fact that "full-scale comparison of Negro and white mental patients is not possible today because the federal statistics take no account of race," and that the most "accurate comparison of mental disorders by race" remained Benjamin Malzberg's research from the mid-1930s.[7]

This disparity changed in the 1960s when, for better and worse, civil rights messages of political and social recognition catalyzed research subject recognition. Growing numbers of psychiatric studies described research conducted in newly desegregated hospitals, and as such compared and contrasted "white" and "Negro" forms of particular diseases. Such comparisons did not focus solely on schizophrenia, but schizophrenia was far and away atop the list. Researchers used DSM-II criteria to uncover *hostile* aspects of black schizophrenia, such as paranoia, delusions, or rage, or to associate schizophrenia with civil rights remonstrations. Meanwhile, studies conflated black schizophrenia with Black Power in order to illustrate evolving understandings of the illness as hostile or violent, or used long-standing stereotypes about manic, crazy black men to demonstrate "new" forms of schizophrenic illness.

Again, the most egregious practitioners of such an approach were the New York psychiatrists Walter Bromberg and Franck Simon, who in 1968 described a new form of what they called *protest psychosis*, a condition in which the rhetoric of the Black Power movement drove "Negro men" to insanity. According to Bromberg and Simon, the connection between Black Power and psychosis was neither metaphorical nor allegorical. Rather, black liberation movements literally caused delusions, hallucinations, and violent projections in black men.

"The stress of asserting civil rights in the United States these past ten years and the corresponding nationalistic fervor of Afro-American nations during the same time period has stimulated specific reactive psychoses in American Negroes," Bromberg and Simon wrote in a research article in the prestigious *Archives of General Psychiatry* in August 1968. "The particular symptomatology we have observed, for which the term 'protest psychosis' is suggested, is influenced by social pressures (the Civil Rights Movement), dips into religious doctrine (the Black Muslim Group), is guided in content by African subcultural ideologies and is colored by a denial of Caucasian values and hostility thereto. This protest psychosis among prisoners is virtually a repudiation of 'white civilization.'"

Bromberg and Simon described afflicted "Negro men . . . under the pressure of a criminal charge or the stress of awaiting criminal trial," whose case studies read as if Ionia case files. "This Negro, age 38, charged with robbery and assault was admitted with complaints of severe headaches which did not yield any physical basis. A month or two later, he spoke about being tricked by his father." Or, "A Negro male . . . alias Allah Allbuckbar, was referred because of rigid, mute, uncommunicative attitudes in the house of detention.

His charge was assault." The authors debated whether these cases met criteria for schizophrenia or were signs of a new disorder entirely. Yet, tellingly, Bromberg and Simon described each case, and the syndrome as a whole, using DSM-II terminology such as *delusions, anger, hostility,* and *projection*: "The delusions are clearly paranoid projections of racial antagonism of the Negroes to the Caucasian group. Since the patients had already committed aggressive acts, their persecutory delusions were of destruction at the hands of hospital doctors or correction officers."

Bromberg and Simon argued that themes of Africa and Islam, so central to the ideologies of Elijah Muhammad, Malcolm X, and other leaders, were causal agents in the path to insanity. "Careful investigation of the mental content," they wrote, "demonstrates antiwhite productions and attitudes. . . . It becomes apparent that the intellectual dissociation represents in part a refusal to accept the syntactical language of standard English. . . . Often the prisoners draw pictures or write material of an Islamic nature, elaborating their ideas in the direction of African ideology with a decided 'primitive' accent. . . . The language used may be borrowed from the ancient 'Veve.' . . . Islamic names are adopted or they change them in such a way so as to deny the previous anglicization of their names. . . . Bizarre religious ideas are Moslem in character, either directly from Mohammedan practice or improvised."

Since mind symptoms often led to bodily acts—and, particularly, acts of terrorist aggression against white people—Bromberg and Simon suggested that it was "sometimes necessary" for "Negro psychiatrists and psychologists" to conduct clinical examinations, since these "Negro professionals" were less likely to incur the wrath of the men's "antiwhite productions and attitudes."[8]

Bromberg and Simon's central contention, that participation in civil rights protests *caused* violent schizophrenic symptoms in "Negro populations" in ways that threatened "white" civilization, appeared in various forms in many other mainstream psychiatric research articles in the 1960s and 1970s. In an article titled "Six Years of Sit-Ins: Psychodynamic Causes and Effects" in the *International Journal of Social Psychiatry,* Drs. Pierce and West argued that Negroes developed delusions, grandiosity, magical thinking, and "dangerous aggressive feelings" when they participated in civil rights sit-ins. Drs. Raskin, Crook, and Herman wrote in the *Journal of Consulting & Clinical Psychology* that "blacks" with schizophrenia rated higher than "whites" on a set of "hostility variables" due to delusional beliefs that "their civil rights were being compromised or violated." In a series of high-profile articles in *Psychiatry: Journal for the Study of Interpersonal Processes* titled "Social Conflict and

Schizophrenic Behavior in Young Adult Negro Males," the social psychiatrist Eugene Brody argued that black culture was itself a risk factor for becoming schizophrenic.

> Many, if not all, American Negroes appear to suffer from a series of problems in identification, stemming from culture conflict, caste restrictions, and minority status, mediated in part through the family structure. Ultimately their developing unification around common aspirations may determine certain changes in the forms of psychiatric illnesses which are exhibited . . . these considerations suggest that growing up as a Negro in America may produce distortions or impairments in the capacity to participate in the surrounding culture which will facilitate the development of schizophrenic types of behavior.

North Carolina psychiatrists Vitols, Waters, and Keeler sounded a similar refrain in their *American Journal of Psychiatry* study, "Hallucinations and Delusions in White and Negro Schizophrenics." The authors linked the finding that "incidence of hallucinations was significantly higher among Negro schizophrenics than among white schizophrenics first admitted to the state hospital system" to the possibility that "there are factors in the Negro culture that predispose to more severe schizophrenic illness." [9]

Nowhere was the racialized resonance between emerging definitions of schizophrenia and emerging anxieties about black protest seen more clearly than in pharmaceutical advertisements for new antipsychotic medications that appeared in the pages of leading American psychiatric journals. The preface of this book contains an advertisement for the major tranquilizer Haldol from the *Archives of General Psychiatry* showing an angry, hostile African American man with a clenched, inverted, Black Power fist. The James Brown-like figure literally shakes his fist at the assumed physician viewer, while the orange, burning, urban setting appears to directly reference civil unrest in cities such as Los Angeles, Detroit, and Newark. Like the "Protest Psychosis" article, the ad compels psychiatrists to diagnose masculinized black anger and unrest as explicit threats not to patients, but to the social order represented by "white" doctors. The ad gives phantasmagoric illustration to Bromberg and Simon's contention that black anger corporeally threatened white authority. Indeed, the high-profile ad works by asking doctors to identify with their own projected fears—it asks its assumed white viewers to be scared. And the ad goes a step further by suggesting that a doctor's racial anxiety could be assuaged by chemically subduing the threats represented by unruly black men. "Assaultive and belligerent?" the ad asks before answering its own, racially charged question. "Cooperation often begins with Haldol."

The Haldol ad was far from the marketing campaign that played on doctors' racial anxieties in order to promote antipsychotic medications as treatments for clinical *and* social pathologies. High-profile advertisements for the neuroleptic medication Stelazine in the *American Journal of Psychiatry* from the 1960s and 1970s unsubtly portrayed tribal masks and artwork during the precise moment in time that Malcolm X described a global African community, and Bromberg and Simon connected "African themes" with black psychotic symptoms.

Thorazine advertisements from the 1970s shockingly depicted the tool of the "Primitive" to illustrate the claim that psychiatric medications controlled psychotic agitation. Initial ads from the Thorazine series visualized primitivity through war staffs, walking sticks, and other phallic forms. At the end of the series, advertisers appallingly replaced the masculinized images with Ghanaian "fertility protective statues" that again literalized black bodies in the selling of antipsychotic medications, while completing a racialized transformation from the white women who appeared in antipsychotic ads two decades before. (Of course, the 1970s were the heyday of the mother's little helper era, when pharmaceutical advertisers promoted antidepressant drugs to white, middle-class women. Stelazine ads make clear, however, how deeply antipsychotic discourse was made to function as the racial abject of the mother's littler helper phenomenon.)

Thorazine advertisers surely knew that the term *primitive* connoted racist assumptions. For instance, in the early twentieth century, the eminent American psychiatrist William Alanson White equated western mental illness with the "primitive" thought patterns of "uncivilized" black people when developing evolutionary theories of mental illness. Similar assumptions coursed through 1930s-era research articles in the *American Journal of Psychiatry*, where the terms *primitive* and *civilized* functioned as code words for "black/insane" and "white/sane," and made their way into 1960s-era articles such as "Protest Psychosis" by Bromberg and Simon (who defined black psychosis as a demonstration of "ideas in the direction of African ideology with a decided 'primitive' accent"). Pharmaceutical advertisements shamelessly called on these long-held racist tropes to promote the message that social "problems" raised by angry black men could be treated, at the clinical level, with antipsychotic medications.[10]

A small but vocal set of voices from within psychiatry protested what they held to be the profession's emerging racism. Researchers including

Robert Simon, Joseph Fleiss, and Arturo and Genevieve de Hoyos published data suggesting that people of different racial and ethnic backgrounds expressed schizophrenia in similar ways, and that race was not a predictor of schizophrenic violence. Meanwhile, evolving networks of politically active African American psychiatrists and psychologists decried the psychiatric codification of threats to "white norms" as mental illness, or picked up claims, first made by the journalist and historian of psychiatry Albert Deutsch in the 1940s, that racism itself was a form of schizophrenic illness.[11] Dr. Alvin Poussaint became southern field director of the Medical Committee for Human Rights. Dr. Charles Wilkinson organized a group of leading clinicians and researchers whose aim was to investigate the psychological ramifications of civil rights for black Americans. His efforts led to the formation of the Black Psychiatrists of America (BPA). Meanwhile, emerging coalitions of clinicians and activists published research articles and essays that explored topics ranging from racism and mental health to the psychological impact on black doctors of training in white residency programs.[12]

FIG. 11 *During the early to mid-1970s, psychiatric journal advertisements for the antipsychotic medication Stelazine depicted tribal artifacts or masks. (Source:* Archives of General Psychiatry 33, *nos. 2 and 9 (1976): back cover)*

Though vital, such protests were in the minority, and were unable to stem a larger tide that codified connections between blackness, protest, aggression, and schizophrenia. At the time, it likely appeared to many mainstream psychiatrists that an epidemic of schizophrenia spread among angry black men. In fact, research articles, pharmaceutical advertisements, and the DSM suggest that psychiatry's focus on angry black bodies *produced* new categories of schizophrenic illness.

Once again, summative data enriches this historical claim. For instance, most American psychiatric journals are now archived electronically in ways that allow researchers to perform quick searches of historical articles. One such database, maintained by the American Psychiatric Association's publishing arm, American Psychiatric Publishing, Inc. (APPI), contains psychiatric research articles from eight leading journals from the past one hundred years. This format allows for a relatively simple comparison of two groups of articles. The first group contains articles from the 1950s, 1960s, and 1970s that mention the word *schizophrenia* in their titles or abstracts, but that do not

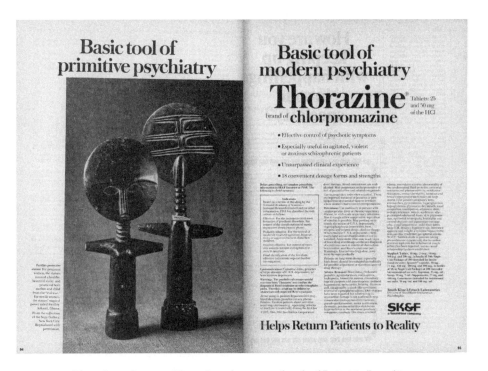

FIG. 12 *Throughout the 1970s, Thorazine ads portrayed tools of "primitive" psychiatry. (Source:* Archives of General Psychiatry *35, no. 1 (1978): 94–95)*

categorize patients according to race. This serves as a list of general/random articles about schizophrenia. The second group contains articles that mention the words *schizophrenia* and *Negro* in their titles or abstracts, and that in some way describe "schizophrenic" patients of color. This list emphasizes the growing number of articles that grappled with the definition of schizophrenia once race was added to the mix, such as those by Bromberg and Simon, Brody, Pierce and West, and others.[13]

As with the charts, narrow the two lists using random sampling, and then devise a coding scheme that compares use of DSM-II terms such as *aggression, hostility,* or *projection,* related terms such as *criminality* or *violence,* and opposite terms such as *cooperative, depressed,* or *apathetic,* between the two sets of articles.

Our study[14] of over three hundred research articles from eight leading psychiatric journals from 1950 to 1980 found several significant trends: (1) articles that did not explicitly mention race (termed the "Random" group in our study) overwhelmingly assumed white research subjects, or described research conducted in white-only wards; (2) articles described patients in this Random grouping as generally cooperative, anxious, or apathetic; and (3) research authors used descriptive language connoting aggression or hostility overwhelmingly to describe patients in the race-specified group (termed "Test" in our analysis). Not surprisingly, such racialized usage of diagnostic terms reached its zenith in the 1960s and 1970s, in the era surrounding release of the DSM-II. Trends from this period are illustrated strikingly in Figure 13.

Put another way, data analysis suggests that authors of research articles in leading psychiatric journals preferentially applied language connoting aggression and hostility to African Americans during the 1960s and 1970s. The spike in such associations raises the specter that the DSM-II codified ways of talking about blackness in addition to talking about mental illness. To be sure, the DSM claimed to seek neutrality. But, in the real world, doctors and researchers used the manual's charged language to modify, describe, and ultimately diagnose the category of black under the rubric of the category of schizophrenia.

Psychiatric diagnostic criteria, research articles, advertisements, and other medical sources from the 1960s and 1970s, then, provide one possible explanation for the mystery of why Caeser Williams and other African American men at Ionia *became* paranoid schizophrenics in the 1960s, even though the men's symptoms did not change. At an institutional level, particular aspects of the new definition of paranoid schizophrenia preferentially selected African American men, including men whose antiestablishment projections and aggressions previously connoted antisocial personality disorder. As we will see, the new definition also explicitly shunted other groups of patients into other subtypes of schizophrenia, or into mood disorders such as bipolar disorder or depression.

Again, the political construction of the diagnosis of paranoid schizophrenia in the 1960s and 1970s exists in constant tension with the ontological reality of a disease called schizophrenia, particularly at the level of individual patients. People of all different races, ethnicities, genders, and social classes undoubtedly suffered from symptoms of mental illness in the 1960s and 1970s, much as they do in the present day. The pain and anguish these people experienced was undoubtedly real. Moreover, the cultural milieu of the era undoubtedly made the symptoms worse. As Frantz Fanon and other scholars prove, racism, poverty, frustration, helplessness, and political upheaval generate social traumas that become embedded in real, material ways in individual minds. The result is indeed a form of mental illness; and the response, as Fanon realized, needs to alleviate the suffering of individuals even as it critiques the oppressive systems in which these individuals fought and died.[15]

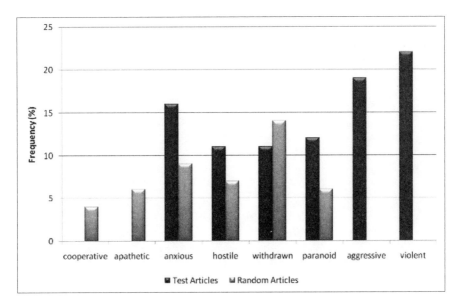

FIG. 13 *Adjectives used to describe patients with schizophrenia in leading psychiatric journals from 1960 to 1979. (Random=race unspecified/assumed white. Test=race identified as Negro or black. N=341.)*

Yet medical sources from the 1960s and 1970s suggest that the reality of schizophrenia was also, and at times primarily, shaped by a dynamic whereby the project of helping certain groups of people merged all too easily with the project of controlling them. Whether intended or not, psychiatric discourse co-opted the protesting voices of social others, and then encoded the protest rhetoric into new definitions of schizophrenia. In a host of explicit and subtle ways, psychiatry thereby *positioned itself as an authority that made sense of the crisis posed by angry, protesting black men during the civil rights era.* And the moment of crisis bolstered psychiatry as an authority that treated cultural "pathologies" in addition to individual illnesses for decades to come.

Perhaps the Ionia doctors should have recognized the political nature of schizophrenia. Perhaps they should have refused to participate. Or perhaps the diagnostic changes allowed doctors to intellectualize racist feelings. At the end of the day, we have no way of knowing the doctors' intentions. We do know, however, that the notion that Ionia doctors changed Mr. Williams's diagnosis out of volitional racism is complicated by the fact that, much like Barry Leroy in the 1930s, doctors of the 1960s followed state-of-the-art professional standards. These standards defined anger, hostility, and projection as known symptoms of a known symptom cluster. In this sense, angry, hostile, projecting black men like Caeser Williams likely appeared schizophrenic because, by the book, they were.

CHAPTER 14

A Metaphor for Race

THE FACT THAT SCHIZOPHRENIA BECAME a racialized diagnosis explains why a doctor in Ionia, Michigan, looked differently at a man from Redding, California, in the 1960s, and then looked down to change the diagnosis in that man's medical chart. But it is only part of the answer, the part derived from medical sources. The second part comes from the next level outward, beyond the walls of the hospital and beyond the boundaries of the profession, in the realms of American popular culture. During the civil rights era, the terms *schizophrenia* and *schizophrenic* powerfully entered the American vernacular. Here, at the same time that schizophrenia became a racialized diagnosis, it also became a complex metaphor for race.

Of course, psychiatric terminology enters everyday parlance for a host of complex reasons. Sometimes a diagnosis becomes a topic of consternation or debate. *Why are so many children diagnosed with attention deficit disorder?* More often, people use psychiatric terminology for its derogatory tinges, its implicit transport of the abnormal into realms of the quotidian. *Don't get hysterical!* was one such use at an earlier time, much as *Why are you so obsessive-compulsive?* is today.

History teaches us that particular psychiatric words become everyday intonations at particular moments in time. Their entry into speech is neither happenstance nor random. Rather, the process whereby psychiatric terms enter popular speech reveals as much about the historical moments of entry as it does about the words themselves. The historian Elaine Showalter has shown that the term *hysteria* entered the English vernacular during a cultural moment intimately concerned with feminist protests against patriarchal society. Cultural critic Christopher Lane describes how the notion of *social phobia* appeared in the American lexicon at the precise moment in time when American psychiatry and pharmaceutical companies tapped into anxieties about social relations in order to expand markets for new diagnoses and new drugs. Historians of the future will undoubtedly look at present-day American society and attribute the wide use of words such as *depression* or *obsession* to fixations with productivity, betterment, or chemical selfhood.[1]

Schizophrenia and *schizophrenic* were the psychiatric terms du jour in the

1950s, 1960s, and 1970s. Popular use of these terms increased beginning in the late 1950s and rose dramatically in the mid-1960s. For example, the word *schizophrenia* appeared in 605 articles in three U.S. papers—the *New York Times,* the *Chicago Tribune,* and the *Los Angeles Times*—between 1930 and 1955, and the word *schizophrenic* appeared in 422 articles over this same time period. However, between 1955 and 1979, *schizophrenia* appeared in 2,759 articles, and *schizophrenic* in a full 3,162.[2]

Schizophrenia and *schizophrenic* are not the same word, although the division is more complicated than a mere noun-versus-adjective, clinical-versus-cultural comparison (recall, for instance, that *schizophrenic reaction* was the clinical descriptor in the DSM-I). Suffice to say that both terms rose not only in overall usage, but also in what might be considered racialized usage. For instance, an electronic newspaper archive search for articles with the terms *schizophrenia* and *schizophrenic* in combination with terms such as *Negro, racial, civil rights,* and, by comparison, with *Caucasian, feminism,* and *Equal Rights Amendment,* reveals a series of significant numeric trends starting in the late 1950s. As but a few examples, the electronic archives of the *New York Times, Los Angeles Times*, and *Chicago Tribune* show the terms *Negro* plus *schizophrenia* or *schizophrenic* returned 36 results dated 1930 to 1955 and a staggering 259 results dated 1956 to 1979. A search for *Negro* plus *paranoid* or *paranoia* similarly returned 12 results dated 1930 to 1955 versus 358 results dated 1956 to 1979. *Caucasian* or *white* plus *schizophrenic* or *schizophrenia* returned no results from 1930 to 1955 and only 1 from 1956 to 1979, and *feminism* or *women's rights* plus *schizophrenia* or *schizophrenic* returned no results from 1930 to 1955 and 10 results dated 1956 to 1979.

Findings are equally impressive within time periods and specific publications. The word *schizophrenia* appeared in 372 articles in the *New York Times* between January 1, 1930, and January 1, 1955, but only 3 of those articles contained the word *Negro* (and none used the terms *African American* or *Black American*). Similarly, only two of the 274 *New York Times* articles with the word *schizophrenic* during this time period contained the word *Negro.* Related trends appear in a host of other electronic archives, including the *Time* magazine electronic archive or the *Reader's Guide to Periodical Literature Archive.*[3]

Complicating matters further, similar trends appeared in historically black newspapers, such as the *Chicago Defender,* as well as in other "Black Press" papers.[4] For example, a search for the terms *Negro* or *the Race*[5] plus *schizophrenia* or *schizophrenic* returned 4 results dated 1930 to 1955 versus 26 results dated 1956 to 1979, and *Negro* or *the Race* plus *paranoid* or *paranoia* returned 6 results dated 1930 to 1955 versus 25 results dated 1956 to 1979. Related searches for the terms *Caucasian,* or *white, feminism* or *women's rights,* and *schizophrenic* or *schizophrenia* returned no results from either period.

Why did the terms *Negro* and *schizophrenia* keep increasing company over time? One obvious answer is that cultural usage reflected psychiatric usage. Post-1956 articles reveal no shortage of violent black male bodies with schizophrenia. Such depictions appeared with increasing frequency in American newspapers and magazines starting in the late 1950s and early 1960s, much as they did in psychiatric journals. In some instances, popular print culture connected race, violence, and schizophrenia prior to the publication of the DSM-II, complicating the notion that new psychiatric definitions trickled down into popular domains. Clearly the opposite dynamic took place as well.

Previously, to recall the 1920s, 1930s, and 1940s, the public image of schizophrenia was that of a white housewife whose schizophrenic mood swings resulted from domestic strife or emotional isolation. But in the late 1950s, the new face of schizophrenia shifted to that of William Earl Fikes a "schizophrenic . . . 30-year-old Alabama Negro" who, as *Time* magazine reported on January 28, 1957, lived "under sentence of death for burglary with intent to rape the daughter of Selma, Alabama's mayor."[6] Or, the new face was that of Eddie Machen, a "strong, lithe Negro" who, like Caeser Williams, hailed from Redding, California. Machen was a one-time World Heavyweight title contender until Ingemar Johansson defeated him in a stunning first-round knockout. Machen's life went into a downward spiral after the fight, and on December 28, 1962, *Time* reported,

> Fortnight ago, on a highway near Vallejo, Calif., a state policeman found Machen in a parked car with a loaded gun, muttering about committing suicide. Bundled off to Napa State Hospital, he went berserk, knocked out two attendants. Last week, described by doctors as an "acute schizophrenic," his boxing career apparently at an end, Eddie Machen, 30, was committed to a mental hospital.[7]

Or, it was the face of one of two "Negro boys" arrested for the "robbery and slaying" of a seventy-two-year-old Brooklyn woman on September 28, 1964. The *New York Times* described how the "disturbed and maladjusted" boys, one of whom was "schizophrenic . . . with a warm personality and an uncontrollable desire to steal," broke into a Brooklyn mansion shortly before dawn, and went up to the top floor where they said they strangled Miss Louise Schultz in her bed. They allegedly took $20 from her, then went to the adjoining bedroom where they beat Miss Delia Walsh, the maid, and robbed her of $2.03 which was in her suitcase.[8]

Or, the new face was that of Leroy Ambrosia Frazier, the notorious "Negro Mental Patient" added to the FBI's 10 Most Wanted list. As the *Chicago Tribune* reported on July 6, 1966,

> Leroy Ambrosia Frazier, an extremely dangerous and mentally unbalanced schizophrenic escapee from a mental institution, who has a lengthy criminal record and history of violent assaults, has been added to the FBI's list of "Ten Most Wanted Fugitives." He has made many threats to kill and has vowed not to be taken alive.

Frazier's story was even more graphically described in a UPI wire story published in the *Chicago Defender* and the *New Pittsburgh Courier,* among other sources, which wrote:

> When last arrested on a narcotics charge in 1959, Frazier savagely bit a policeman on the leg and tried to shove him out of a second-story window. While in prison . . . he was found with a knife, threatening to kill any inmate or guard who stepped on his toes. According to the FBI, Frazier is a schizophrenic who has a persecution complex and hates law enforcement officers. Relatives and former friends fear him for his cunning and viciousness. Despite his small stature, the fugitive is known as extremely strong and brutal . . . The FBI said Frazier also had a history as a sex pervert.[9]

These and other articles likely reported real events, but they did so by demonstrating the same associations seen in psychiatric journal articles. Schizophrenia was a disorder of black, male hostility, and black, male hostility was by extension schizophrenic. As in the protest psychosis article by Bromberg and Simon, black schizophrenia was thought to lead to crimes in which perpetrators were described as "Negro" and victims were assumed to be "white," or to represent the white authority of doctors, mansion owners, or law-enforcement officers. Meanwhile, the American press never described other forms of violence as schizophrenic, such as black-on-black crime or, more gallingly, anti–civil rights violence by whites *against* African Americans.[10]

Clearly, the media did much more than simply reproduce the DSM. Mainstream American newspapers and magazines propagated schizophrenia's complex, contested, and highly connotative meanings as well. Again, denotative (*I suffer from a disease called schizophrenia*) and connotative (*Our nation suffers from political schizophrenia*) use differs. One use implies a clinical diagnosis, the other a mode of rhetorical embellishment. However, in the 1960s and 1970s, American news media freely mixed these two uses when boycotts, marches, Black Power, and Black Liberation forced mainstream America to confront the frustrations and aspirations of African Americans.

For example, the *New York Times* frequently used phrases such as "our national racial schizophrenia" or "the schizophrenia of race in America" to suggest not a Bleulerian mind split by mental illness, but a country split by racial strife. More often than not, such usage linked schizophrenia to violent civil rights protests. On October 11, 1964, an article titled "More is Called For Than Social Protest and Desegregation" reviewed a series of books that analyzed the increasingly "violent and irrational" language of the civil rights movement, and particularly Black Power, which often caused the "average American" to feel "worried and bewildered."

> Written by men who hold solid credentials for discussing the Negro revolution, these works contain no magic formulas for instant racial peace . . . chilling analyses of this country's racial agony—of the shameful past, of the explosive present, and, if steps are not taken, of the calamitous future for white man and black man. The warnings are all here. But some hardheaded suggestions for coming to grips with our national schizophrenia are here too . . .[11]

In June 1965, the *Times* similarly used schizophrenia to describe the political scientist Samuel Lubell's contention that the United States was split between poles of "White and Black" in the aftermath of the Black Power movement. The paper wrote that Lubell's book, *White and Black: Test of a Nation,* told "a history of our racial schizophrenia. Treatment prescribed: strong doses of realism for us all."[12]

In May 1967, a front-page article titled "Integration in South: Erratic Pattern" described a "pattern of racial progress and recalcitrance [that] covers the South like a crazy quilt now that the civil rights movement has collapsed in the region." The result was "a patchwork of integrated and racially segregated towns, hotels, restaurants, nightspots, movie theaters," leading to a

state-of-affairs where "among whites, there is both noticeable change in racial attitudes and a conspicuous lack of it. States and towns and even individuals seem torn by a sort of racial schizophrenia in which Negro equality
is simultaneously accepted and rejected."[13]

These articles deployed schizophrenia as a metaphor for fissured notions
of American unity. Perhaps that unity was an illusion before civil rights, the
logic implied, when two races lived next to each other much like two hemi-
spheres of the brain. But the movement explosively pulled apart the very notion of "our" national unity or "our" mental health—and particularly mental
health for whites. Desegregation broke down the natural order, and the civil
rights movement disrupted the psychical equilibrium in its wake.

Other mass-circulation articles used schizophrenia to illustrate a split
of the black mind. In these cases, the term almost always implied an uneasy
divide between love and hate, or between trying to succeed in white society
while at the same time seeking to destroy it. For instance, on October 6, 1967,
a *Time* article titled "Black Pride" described how, "After a summer of race
riots, Negro students are returning to college campuses with a new and aggressive pride." On one hand, according to the article, black students enjoyed
lives of privilege afforded by higher education. These students learned new
ways of "thinking" and became "assimilated" into college life and "white values" on campuses such as Yale and Harvard. But on the other hand, students
who had participated in race protests felt a "new mood" that ranged

> from angry militancy to a brotherly desire for mutual improvement—
> and it does not reject violence as one way to make the black presence
> felt. . . . Graduate Student Brown McGhee scoffs: "Let me tell you how it
> is, baby. When I get out, I have two choices—to exterminate the white
> man or to prostitute myself to the white man. I haven't decided what
> I'll do."
>   . . . College Negroes nonetheless feel schizophrenic about their climb
> out of the ghettos into the white world. . . . Although Negro students by
> and large reject Detroit-style rioting as deplorable, they are willing to use
> the threat of violence to gain their campus goals. . . . Sociology Teacher
> Harry Edwards, a towering (6 ft. 8 in.) former San Jose basketball star,
> contended that Negro students could not find decent housing in San
> Jose. . . . "The first step is rational debate," explained the triumphant Ed-
> wards, "but the biggest single lever we had is the threat of violence." The
> new Negro mood means that few college administrators can be confident
> that the new academic year will be nonviolent.[14]

A 1965 *Time* exposé titled "The Negro After Watts" imposed a similar binary between forward-lookers and slum-dwellers in the aftermath of the Watts riots.

> The mood of many Negroes in the late summer of 1965 ranges from let-down to rage. Many secretly or openly think that "violence is valuable" because "now people care about Watts." "I'm as full of hate as a rattlesnake is of poison," hisses a Negro in Montgomery. "There's people walking around mad all over here," an unemployed Memphis janitor says. A rich Harlem lawyer finds it reasonable that "anybody could get caught up in rioting like that." The Rev. Albert B. Cleage Jr., one of Detroit's most mili-tant Negro leaders, reports that Negroes there "had a tremendous sense of sympathy and identity." Across the U.S., more moderate Negroes, re-jecting such words as hatred and anger, admit at least to bitterness.
>
> Whether he likes to be reminded of it or not, the Negro has made spectacular progress in the past decade; if he angrily refuses to look back over his shoulder to see how far he has come, he has nevertheless ad-vanced along the road to full equality in U.S. society. . . . All of this adds up to a great deal of political, social and economic advancement, and a great many Negroes know it and take pride in it. But more than ever, af-ter the overriding duty of thinking of all human beings as individuals, the U.S. must look upon Negroes as divided into two groups: a prosper-ing level, committed to integration and possessed of a stake in society; and a slum level, mired in deepening ignorance, immorality and irrespon-sibility, and growingly enamored of a chauvinistic, equal-but-separate kind of segregation. This schizophrenia visibly affects Negro leadership. Understandable compassion for the poor leads even the most moderate leaders to play down Negro duties, play up white guilt; the extremists of Negro hatred get by unchided. Understandable embarrassment on be-half of the law-abiding middle classes leads the same leaders—generally after a riot has got out of control—to declarations that "violence must be deplored, but . . ."[15]

Similarly, a *New York Times* article on February 9, 1969, described New York's African American newspaper, the *Amsterdam News*, as demonstrating a "schizophrenia" that

> expresses, unconsciously, that part of the black psyche which admires so much of the white world and has subtly come to take on so many white

standards as its own; and yet, at the same time, it expresses the black man's fear and distrust of that white world and really relaxes only in an atmosphere of black standards.[16]

In September of that same year, the *Times* described Roy Wilkins, executive director of the NAACP, as living a life of political "schizophrenia," trying to please "white politicians" on the one hand and "black militants" on the other.[17]

In a different vein, on September 12, 1963, the *Times* published film critic Bosley Crowther's review of Samuel Fuller's B-movie classic *Shock Corridor,* a film touted as the 1960s follow-up to the *Snake Pit.* Crowther detailed the "hard driving and realistic" plot in which a previously sane journalist, played by Peter Breck, has himself committed to a chaotic mental hospital in order to solve a murder. The review, and indeed ads for the film itself, referenced ways in which, like the *Snake Pit,* Fuller's new film exposed conditions in overcrowded asylums and connected those conditions to larger social issues. (Fuller's hospital ward is thus aptly named "The Street.") However, the 1963 film vitally departed from Anatole Litvak's 1948 masterwork. As the review explained, the patients in Fuller's asylum were predominantly men. And the main "schizophrenic" character was not an Olivia de Havilland housewife, but instead an African American, former civil rights protester named Trent (Hari Rhodes), whose black mind had been torn asunder by his attempts to desegregate white society. Rhodes's character was once a desegregation pioneer who internalized and then enacted the hatred directed toward him. Unlike Olivia de Havilland's Virginia, who ultimately conformed to societal expectations, Rhodes's Trent tried to change the system but instead became infected by it. Desegregation and its violent discontents literally drove Trent insane. As a result, according to Crowther, the former protester became self-hating, "schizophrenic," and "violently anti-negro." In the film's key scene, Trent starts a race riot on the ward.[18]

These and other media associations between schizophrenia and civil rights reflected prevailing debates about the scarring psychological impact of segregation and poverty—debates in which the psyche became the battleground for equality as much as schools or lunch counters. The work of the psychiatrist Frederic Wertham and the psychologists Kenneth and Mamie Clark, among others, gained prominence during the *Brown v. the Board of Education of Topeka* ruling in 1954. The Clarks provided expert testimony about the results of their infamous doll studies in *Briggs v. Elliott,* one of the cases later combined into *Brown v. Board,* in which children's preference for playing with dolls of lighter skin color provided evidence of internalized psychological racism. Wertham similarly called on clinical research to testify that segregation caused "unsolvable emotional conflicts" in the minds of segregated children. Meanwhile, Kenneth Clark's 1965 text, *Dark Ghetto,* described a "ghetto pathology" that led to "some Negroes having a complex and debilitating prejudice against themselves."[19]

Like psychiatric journals, the popular media also explicitly suggested that mental illness resulted not just from conditions of poverty, prejudice, and segregation, but from political attempts to change them. Schizophrenia in this context was a split between regress and progress, or between the part of the black psyche that wished to build and the part that plotted to burn. "Negro students" went to college to assimilate and ascend, but even at Yale these students threatened to immolate the school. Black leaders deplored violence even while they admired its political benefits. Hari Rhodes's character Trent in *Shock Corridor* sought to improve the system, but in the end he fell back on primal, ghetto brutality and self-loathing. The message was that each step forward carried the threat of two steps back. The mind wished to advance in a civilized manner, but the body aggressively defended the old ways of doing business. Or, as Plato might have put it, the enlightened leaders of the polis were constitutionally connected to, and dragged back into violence by, the unruly hoi polloi.[20]

In this sense, the American press cast the insanity of the marginalized through the projected anxieties of the mainstream. In the aftermath of Watts, Detroit, and other internal and internalized moments of chaos, mass-circulation newspapers and magazines defined schizophrenia as a condition that divided "good" blacks from their "bad" selves. One part wished to lead, the other hissed in the streets. One part sought to build, the other to destroy. This division unsubtly collapsed class struggle into race struggle, and then collapsed both into a struggle for sanity. Schizophrenia also provided a framework for dividing civilized blacks from unruly ones, the Martin Luther Kings and Jackie Robinsons[21] who espoused nonviolence from the LeRoi Joneses, Stokely Carmichaels, and Rap Browns who did not. As the *Time* article "The Negro After Watts" described it,

> In LeRoi Jones's *The Toilet,* eight Negroes abuse a white boy and then beat him up. . . . Love and nonviolence, by contrast, is the overriding message of Martin Luther King, yet after the riot in the Watts section of Los Angeles, Governor Brown thought it prudent to discourage even King from visiting California. King went anyway—and thus inadvertently re-

vealed that though he may be heeded and respected by Southern Negroes and Northern middle-class Negroes, he has little standing among slum dwellers. [22]

However, it would be an oversimplification to conclude that the American media employed the term *schizophrenia* solely to pathologize protest or the prospect of radical social change. To be sure, such undercurrents suffused the *New York Times, Chicago Tribune, Los Angeles Times,* and *Time* magazine. But historically, African American newspapers such as the *Chicago Defender, New Pittsburgh Courier,* Memphis's *Tri-State Defender, Oakland Post, Amsterdam News,* and *Sacramento Observer* told a different story. Or, rather, these tabloids told the same story with a difference. In their pages, schizophrenia also became a rhetorically black disease. But, instead of a condition caused by civil rights, schizophrenia resulted from the conditions that made civil rights necessary. Civil rights did not make people crazy, racism did. Instead of a mark of stigma, schizophrenia functioned as a protest identity and an internalized, projected form of defiance.

For instance, the *Tri-State Defender* described college student protests well in advance of stories in *Time.* "U. S. Students In 1st Fight for Freedom," read a headline on April 16, 1960, above an article that described organizing efforts that connected students in the southern United States with those in the North. Here, schizophrenia did not result from internal conflict, and thus did not reside in the protesters themselves. Instead, America itself enacted and demonstrated schizophrenia. According to the article, America "preached equal rights abroad while neglecting them at home." Referencing Vernon A. Eagle, executive director of the New World Foundation in Chicago, the article explained that

> this nation, which is called upon to provide world leadership, particularly to new emerging nations of Asia and Africa, can ill afford the schizophrenic standards prevalent at this time. The responsibilities that are inherent in freedom demand a strong sense of moral, ethical and spiritual values. One can not expect respect for our recent official condemnation of South African race relations when we ignore our own. [23]

Other articles assumed that schizophrenia was a condition that existed in American cities and towns well before civil rights. A 1961 article about the singer Leontyne Price described the long-standing "etiquette of race relations" as follows:

White people in the South are afraid to give public expression to their admiration, respect, and affection for Negro acquaintances and friends. They don't want to appear to be "N—r-lovers." Negroes don't want to appear to be "Uncle Tom's." The result is a cotton-pickin' mess of mixed emotions, which give the South a schizophrenic personality that baffles the world.[24]

An article titled "U.S. Music Taste Jim Crow, Says Jerry Butler," the *Oakland Post* described a similar situation faced by the singer Jerry Butler.

Butler is in 9th place on Billboard's annual list of top male singers . . . but it doesn't exactly relieve Butler's worries about being classified, because he's a Negro, as a R&B singer only, and being largely ignored by white music lovers. Butler is a victim of what he calls "Chicago schizophrenia," which is characteristic of many cities, New York and Los Angeles perhaps excluded. Negro Chicago and the rest of the town for performers like Butler, Ramsey Lewis, Ahmad Jamal, Junior Wells, Muddy Waters, and Howlin Wolf are like two separate towns. Every once in a while, performers like these will get rave notices from an appearance at something like the Newport Festival and the rest of Chicago or White Mansville, U.S.A. will "discover" them, and they will enjoy a vogue. But that's not usually the way it goes.[25]

The threat of schizophrenic segregation also appeared in a 1963 *Chicago Defender* article titled "Chicago's Growing Racial Crisis," which decried growing racial tensions on par with those seen in the southern United States. The article led with a quote by Edwin Berry, executive director of the Chicago Urban League, proclaiming "Chicago must integrate its neighborhoods or it will become 'as racially schizophrenic as any city of the Old South.'"[26] [27] Writing in the *Sacramento Observer,* the African American congressman Augustus Hawkins decried "America's schizophrenic character, often described as double standard,"[28] while the legal reporter Harold Sims described a "disturbing schizophrenia in the [U.S.] Supreme Court's attitude towards the problems of minorities."[29] [30]

The subtle distinction between a schizophrenia caused by protest against racism and a schizophrenia that reflected existing structural racism extended to the internal body as well. Like the mainstream press, black-press articles assumed a split in the black mind. But in the black press, such a split signified the adaptations necessary for survival in racist societies rather than the symptoms that arose when trying to disrupt them. Schizophrenia here func-tioned as a way of debating the implications of violence in response to injus-tice—a debate that split the leadership of the movement itself.

Thus, as the *New Pittsburgh Courier* reported, Dr. Martin Luther King's address before the eleventh constitutional convention of the Transport Work-ers Union of America in October 1961 used the examples of "schizophrenia" and "madness" to urge workers to psychologically "maladjust" themselves in the name of nonviolent protest. The paper cited King's remarks that

> It is no longer a choice between violence and non-violence. It is now either non-violence or non-existence.... And so I call upon you to be maladjusted and continue in the maladjustment that you have already demonstrated, for it may well be that the salvation of our world lies in the hands of the maladjusted. And so, let us be maladjusted.[31]

Such language was not unusual for King, a thinker and rhetorician who of-ten used psychological binaries to preach nonviolence. In his book *Where Do We Go from Here: Chaos or Community?* King relied heavily on psychologi-cal language to outline the philosophical binary of "nonviolent coexistence" on one hand and "violent coannihilation" on the other.[32] And in his famous "Unfulfilled Dreams" sermon, his soaring, elegant, final address at Ebenezer Baptist Church, King described the psychic split as follows.

> There is a tension at the heart of the universe between good and evil. It's there: a tension at the heart of the universe between good and evil.... Now not only is that struggle structured out somewhere in the external forces of the universe, it's structured in our own lives. Psychologists have tried to grapple with it in their way, and so they say various things. Sig-mund Freud used to say that this tension is a tension between what he called the id and the superego.
>
> But you know, some of us feel that it's a tension between God and man. And in every one of us this morning, there's a war going on. It's a civil war. I don't care who you are, I don't care where you live, there is a civil war going on in your life. And every time you set out to be good, there's something pulling on you, telling you to be evil. It's going on in your life. Every time you set out to love, something keeps pulling on you, trying to get you to hate. Every time you set out to be kind and say nice things about people, something is pulling on you to be jealous and envi-ous and to spread evil gossip about them. There's a civil war going on.

There is a schizophrenia, as the psychologists or the psychiatrists would call it, going on within all of us. And there are times that all of us know somehow that there is a Mr. Hyde and a Dr. Jekyll in us. . . . There's a tension at the heart of human nature. And whenever we set out to dream our dreams and to build our temples, we must be honest enough to recognize it. . . .

In the final analysis, what God requires is that your heart is right. Salvation isn't reaching the destination of absolute morality, but it's being in the process and on the right road.[33]

In these and other instances, King's use of the term *schizophrenia* implied an ethical, spiritual divide that was at once universal to mankind and particular to the African American experience. As a universal archetype, the split mind signified the timeless tension between good and evil, chaos and community, that humans faced since the beginning of time. Those who wished to find salvation were to resist the allure of Satan, the pull of hate, the anger of the body, and to instead walk the path of Christ, who turned the other cheek. As a specifically black term, *schizophrenia* functioned as a powerful metaphor for King's articulation of the conflict at hand. In his formulation of civil rights, African Americans were always and already divided, their minds split both because of racism and segregation and because of the choices they faced in their attempts to change the system. "There are times that all of us know somehow that there is a Mr. Hyde and a Dr. Jekyll in us." People who acted with anger or violence—rioters, Black Panthers, Black Power agitators, Malcolm X, Huey P. Newton—lived on the side of the unbridled id. But those who felt the allure of anger yet reacted with the measured, civilizing response of the superego walked down the "right road."

Conversely, in the rhetorical circles of Malcolm X, Stokely Carmichael, Robert F. Williams, or H. Rap Brown, schizophrenia was an ethical response to racism in which violence was the only sane treatment for an otherwise insane problem. In this context, the language of paranoia, psychosis, and schizophrenia became a means of pathologizing white society while justifying aggressive self-defense.

Schizophrenia was a particularly complex term for Black Power, Black Nationalism, Nation of Islam, and other movements advocating nonpassive resistance or armed self-defense. Many of the movements' leaders had been spuriously diagnosed with the illness by the FBI as a way of highlighting the insanity of their allegedly militant revolt against the United States. According to declassified documents, the FBI diagnosed Malcolm X with "pre-psychotic paranoid schizophrenia," and with membership in the Communist Party and the "Muslim Cult of Islam," in the 1950s.[34] In the early 1960s, the same agency diagnosed Robert Williams, the controversial head of the Monroe, North Carolina, chapter of the NAACP, as schizophrenic, armed, and dangerous during his flight from trumped-up kidnapping charges. As the *Amsterdam News* reported in September 1961 in an article titled "FBI Hunts NAACP Leader," "Agents for the Federal Bureau of Investigation were searching many areas of Harlem this week as part of a nation-wide hunt for bearded Robert F. Williams, Monroe, N.C., NAACP leader. . . . 'Williams allegedly has possession of a large quantity of firearms, including a .45 caliber pistol . . . He has previously been diagnosed as schizophrenic and has advocated and threatened violence.' " The FBI distributed 250,000 posters to the same effect.[35]

Perhaps it is not surprising, then, that leaders of Black Power and other movements located insanity not within the minds and bodies of people who fought back against unjust social systems, but within racists who perpetuated them. In his influential text, *Negroes with Guns,* Williams turned his alleged schizophrenia diagnosis against his white oppressors. ("In describing me as schizophrenic they do not say who had psychoanalyzed me. Do they mean I was analyzed as being schizophrenic by Monroe's semi-illiterate chief of police?") In a section of the book titled "Minds Warped by Racism," Williams sets up his argument for the creation of a "Black Militancy" by arguing that

> We have come to comprehend the nature of racism. It is a mass psychosis. . . . Extreme examples of the racist mentality only appear comic when looked upon as isolated phenomena. In truth they are perfectly logical applications of the racist mentality. Look at the phenomena this way and they are the thoroughly diseased mind. The racist is a man crazed by hysteria at the idea of coming into equal human contact with Negroes. And this mass mental illness called racism is very much a part of the "American Way of Life." . . . When Afro-American liberation is finally achieved in the U.S.A., one of the many new developments in such a society will be some sort of institution that will correct those Americans whose minds are thoroughly warped by racism. Somehow a way will be found so that these insane people will be made whole and well again.

(Activist Angela Davis makes a similar argument in her autobiography in recounting the behavior of a white woman who occupied the cell next to hers in the days after she was arrested in New York City.)[36]

Psychological claims were not altogether atypical within the context of

Black Power, black nationalism, or what Williams described as "Black Inter-nationalism." These rhetorics frequently used psychological language, and specifically the notion of psychological conflict between blacks and whites, to justify calls for social transformation. For instance, in a landmark 1966 Mis-sissippi speech that predated King's "Unfulfilled Dreams" by two years and yet profoundly anticipated its rhetoric, Stokely Carmichael critiqued King and other Southern Christian Leadership Committee (SCLC) leaders for their nonviolent stance by contending,

> There is a psychological war going on in this country and it's whether or not Black people are going to be able to use the terms they want about their movement without white peoples' blessing. We have to tell them we are going to use the term "Black Power" and we are going to define it because Black Power speaks to us. We can't let them project Black Power because they can only project it from white power and we know what white power has done to us. . . . We are going to build a movement in this country based on the color of our skins that is going to free us from our oppressors and we have to do that ourselves. . . . Everybody in this country is for "Freedom Now" but not everybody is for Black Power because we have got to get rid of some of the people who have white power. We have got to get us some Black Power.[37]

Other voices argued that African American violence reflected the natural psychological consequences of violent American racism—an argument that tracked back to mid-century at least, when Langston Hughes described the "Jim Crow shock" of black soldiers whose insanity resulted not from battle fa-tigue, but from the internalized impact of American racism and segregation. The leading 1960s-era advocates of this position were the African Ameri-can psychiatrists William Grier and Price Cobbs, whose Malcolm X–inspired book, *Black Rage,* became a national bestseller in 1968. Numerous black-press articles detailed how the book used mental-health principles to address the question of "Why are blacks in America so angry that they are impelled to burn, loot, kill, in a rage against white society?" as an article in the *Bay State Banner* put it in July 1968. The answer, according to Grier and Cobbs, was ongoing "emotional trauma" to the black mind, and particularly the black male mind, caused by the legacy of slavery and the "psychic stresses" brought about by segregation and discrimination.[38]

In *Black Rage,* Grier and Cobbs depicted schizophrenia as a condition of survival for black Americans. Paranoid schizophrenia, they wrote, was a potentially violent state that emerged when black men were pushed into a split between adhering to the mores of white society and fighting back against them in order to stay alive. "If blacks are frightened," the authors warned white America, "consider what frightens them and consider what happens when they feel cornered, when there is no further lie one can believe, when one finally sees he is permanently cast as a victim, and when finally the sleeping giant wakes and turns upon his tormentors."

Like King, Grier and Cobbs believed that schizophrenia was a healthy adaptation in addition to a mental illness, even if in their formulation it potentially resulted in hostility. They wrote that "for a black man survival in America depends in large measure on the development of a healthy 'cultural paranoia.' He must maintain a high degree of suspicion toward the motives of every white man." Expanding on this point, Grier later explained to the *Amsterdam News* that "the heroic psychological maneuvering of the Black man in America has enabled him not only to survive but to maintain a sense of dignity."[39]

Meanwhile, in interviews surrounding the premier of his one-act play *Dutchman,* the poet, playwright, and second-nation activist LeRoi Jones famously likened "the whole situation of the Negro in America" to a form of playacting, in which activist intellectuals were forced into a split between a "Negro self" and an "American self." Jones articulated this split as necessary for social transformation, in contradistinction to King, mainstream America, and indeed to psychiatry.

> To see this schizophrenia between being American and being alienated from America, well, that alienation has reached a point where a lot of people value it . . . a lot of young Negro intellectuals are not interested in integration in the sense of making a head-long flight of disappearing into white America. It's like being asked to take up residence in a burning building. They're interested in having society transformed so it's a better thing.[40]

Readers familiar with African American philosophical thought will recognize that definitions of *schizophrenia* in the black press, and in civil rights rhetoric more broadly, complicate the notion that psychiatric definitions of the term trickled down into American society as if by force of gravity. To be sure, King, Grier and Cobbs, Jones, and others knowingly or unintentionally referenced the DSM's assertion that schizophrenia was a disease of projection, anger, and hostility. But their usage also invoked much earlier intellectual formulations.

For instance, as is well known, W.E.B Du Bois described an African American double consciousness in ways that presaged King's call for an internal civil war on one hand and Carmichael's survive-at-any-cost mentality on the other. In an infamous 1897 *Atlantic* magazine essay and later in his 1903 masterwork, *The Souls of Black Folk,* Du Bois described double consciousness as a requisite "two-ness" of being "an American, a Negro; two warring ideals in one dark body, whose dogged strength alone keeps it from being torn asunder." As he wrote,

> The history of the American Negro is the history of this strife,—this longing to attain self-conscious manhood, to merge his double self into a better and truer self. In this merging he wishes neither of the older selves to be lost. He would not Africanize America, for America has too much to teach the world and Africa. He would not bleach his Negro soul in a flood of white Americanism, for he knows that Negro blood has a message for the world. He simply wishes to make it possible for a man to be both a Negro and an American, without being cursed and spit upon by his fellows, without having the doors of Opportunity closed roughly in his face . . . Here in America, in the few days since Emancipation, the black man's turning hither and thither in hesitant and doubtful striving has often made his very strength to lose effectiveness, to seem like absence of power, like weakness. And yet it is not weakness—it is the contradiction of double aims.[41]

Present-day scholars locate the inspiration for double consciousness in European Romanticism, American Transcendentalism, and indeed in early psychiatry. The literary scholar Bruce Dickson cites as an influence the published 1817 case of Mary Reynolds, a patient reported in psychiatric literature as "A Double Consciousness, or Duality of Person in the Same Individual." Du Bois, though, understood the divide as emanating primarily from internalized racism, and from a "contradiction of double aims" in the African American individual between "African" and "American" components. He argued that black Americans were able to split, and in splitting adapt, because they contained African souls, psychical connections with African spirituality, folklore, and faith.[42]

Of course, an African soul was precisely what the protest psychosis article and antipsychotic advertisements pathologized. In Bromberg and Simon's article, men like Allah Allbuckbar spoke in Veve languages and planned the overthrow of white civilization. Ads showed primitive symbols and African masks as points of differentiation from civilization, representing primitive symptoms that needed to be controlled to ensure the smooth running of white society.

Du Bois and other intellectuals instead celebrated the link to Africa precisely because they believed that it helped African Americans reject the pathology that resided not in the black psyche, but in the materialistic white civilization in which it was forced to reside. Debunking the common myth that African slaves brought to the New World were godless heathens, Du Bois argued that the newly American Africans disguised their religious beliefs, and specifically those that encouraged a "spirit of revolt and revenge" against the institution of slavery, beneath a thin "veneer" of Christianity.[43]

The notion of a structural, psychical split forged in adaptive response to white society coursed through black political thought for much of the next century. Double consciousness also figured prominently in the work of 1940s and 1950s intellectuals such as Richard Wright and Ralph Ellison. In her brilliant essay "The Lunatic's Fancy and the Work of Art," the literary critic Shelly Eversley details connections between Du Bois's ideas and Ellison's 1945 claim that the United States was a nation of "ethical schizophrenics" whose pathology, once again, resided in "the sickness of the social order" rather than in the pathologized black body. Eversley writes that Ellison believed that "black people had become 'confused' by a paradox: the reality of racist social inequality in the US and the nation's postwar reputation as a champion of democracy had exposed the 'psychological character' of 'the Negro's perpetual alienation from the land of his birth.'" Such alienation dominates the final scene of Ellison's classic text, *Invisible Man,* in which the recognition of being a "*part of them* as well as apart from them," or of being "'for' society and then 'against' it," pushes the Invisible Man into a form of insanity that, ultimately, begets clarity.[44]

Reflectively similar splits also appeared in debates about the psychological impact of racist segregation beyond the United States. In the colonial context, the psychiatrist Frantz Fanon, whose ideas extensively influenced Black Power activists, defiantly described an "internal divide" that resulted when "the Negro" entered a white symbolic order. "The black man has two dimensions," Fanon wrote in *Black Skins, White Masks.* "One is with his fellows, the other with the white man . . . That this self-division is a result of colonial subjugation is beyond question."[45]

When read through black philosophical thought, King, Grier and Cobbs, Jones, and other civil rights–era activists can be seen to call on traditions distinct from psychiatric ones. This lineage allowed civil rights thinkers to signify the adaptive importance of, rather than the pathologization of, defiance to "Caucasian values." And this lineage helps explain why schizophrenia became a potent metaphor within and between black rhetorics in the 1960s. For King, Grier and Cobbs, Jones, and others, schizophrenia was more than a mental illness; it was also a critique of white society, and an identity forged through time and experience and then worn as a mark not of stigma, but of strength and survival.

Connections between schizophrenia, the mental illness, and what might be called schizophrenia *agonistes* help explain why, when fifty leading rabbis and clergymen met in New York in January 1969, Rev. Wyatt Tee Walker claimed the disease moniker as constitutive of black identity. The highly publicized meeting was meant to heal rifts between black and Jewish communities that emerged during later phases of the civil rights era. But tension emerged when Albert Vorspan of the Union of American Hebrew Congregations spoke in psychiatric terms about the effects of anti-Semitism and Nazism: "I see an anxiety [in the Jewish community]," Vorspan explained in a set of transcripts later reproduced in the *New York Times,* " . . . which borders on hysteria . . . a profound visceral reaction . . . a kind of trauma . . . Jews have come by their paranoia honestly . . ." In response, the Reverend Walker, once a top aide to Dr. King, claimed a different mantle: "It was heartening for me to hear of your paranoia," he trumpeted,

> because it allows me to admit to the black community of our schizophrenia . . . we are desperately trying to survive in a racist society . . . I confess to having some anti-white feelings. If I didn't have anti-white feelings there's something wrong with me and I should be put in an institution.[46]

For the Reverend Walker, schizophrenia was a communal condition of the black community, and the black community was uniquely schizophrenic. In a Du Boisian sense, schizophrenia constituted a response to racist society, rather than a psychotic break from it. And, in direct opposition to Bromberg and Simon, schizophrenia marked the marginalized but pathologized the mainstream.

Connections between schizophrenia, black claims of identity, and double consciousness raise the radical possibility that psychiatry's own definition of the illness reflected black culture as much as the other way around. To be sure, 1960s psychiatric journals pathologized black militancy, while pharmaceutical advertisements shamelessly peddled drug treatments for African rage. But history suggests that such associations were not invented by psychiatrists or pharmaceutical companies. Instead, the condition singer Mamie Smith described in 1920 as the "crazy blues," in which going crazy functioned as a means of fighting back against racial injustice, clearly predated the protest psychosis by a century, if not more.[47]

In this sense, far from discovering a "new" form of illness, as Bromberg and Simon claimed, the protest psychosis mimicked a conversation that was already well underway. The notion of a schizophrenic, divided African soul that revolted against Caucasian values circulated in nuanced, complex ways in black thought long before the DSM came into existence. And associations between blackness, madness, and violence functioned as forms of black autobiography long before they became tools of white projective identification.

If this theory is in any way correct, and if denotative and connotative schizophrenia are in any way related, then the fact that schizophrenia became overly diagnosed in African American men at Ionia—and indeed nationwide—in the late 1960s can be partially attributed to a selection bias that seems paradoxical indeed. In this scenario, psychiatry's anything-but-new DSM criteria circumscribed a preexisting condition. Here, patients came to doctors, not merely as blank slates on which to be diagnosed, but also as complex African souls who were already torn asunder. Doctors, new criteria in hand, simply followed the lead.

PART V

Rasheed Karim

FIG. 14 *Ionia Building #10, the Men's Building, housed male*
patients deemed hostile or threatening by hospital staff.
(Source: Michigan State Archive. Printed with permission.)

CHAPTER 15

Turned Loose[1]

ORAL HISTORY TRANSCRIPTION EXCERPTS
Former Employees of Ionia State Hospital
October 24–25, 2005
Interviewer: Jonathan Metzl
Location: Ionia Historical Society, Ionia, Michigan
Oral History #11: Retired Male Attendant, Garage Supervisor, Age 71

Q: *I'm interested in the atmosphere at Ionia in the 1960s. What was that like for you?*

A: Um, to me it was great because I only worked inside one year then. And then I went into the garage and was garage supervisor, and that's outside. But I had patients working for me. One night, just before I went home, they called out in the supervisors' room and said, "Tomorrow morning we want you to go to Detroit. Take the flat rack truck and go to Detroit and get a load of cabbage for the kitchen." Well, this one—the garage always had to haul coal cause they heat that place up there with coal furnaces—and we had a couple patient drivers that did that. And I told this one driver that was from Detroit, I said, "You bring a jacket or something with you tomorrow—kind of chilly—cause we gonna go to Detroit." Well, when we got down to Detroit it was right down on the waterfront. And here comes a cop on a motorcycle, to escort us—it happened to be this guy's brother, this patient's brother. And he said, "This is no place for you guys down here alone." After we got loaded he escorted us clear to the city limits.

Q: *Why did he say that?*

A: 'Cause they had trouble down there I guess.

Q: *Detroit was considered a pretty dangerous place?*

A: Um hm.

Q: *Was there any difference in the patients who were brought from Detroit?*

A: You never knew. You did know that in 1968 our Congress came out with a law that said, "If you can't cure 'em, turn 'em loose." You knew that, didn't you?

Q: *Right . . .*

A: And of course all of us that worked there knew, you couldn't turn them loose. Well, little by little in the next couple of years, they did it for many of 'em, but not all. And the people that worked there—well, I'm getting ahead of myself—you'd read in the Detroit paper: such-and-such killed somebody or did this-or-that, former patient of the Ionia State Hospital. Well then they came out and said you can't use the Ionia State Hospital's name. You can put the person that did the crime name but you can't use the Ionia State Hospital. So then, only the people that worked there would recognize these names . . . a former patient.

Q: *The patients who would kill people were patients from Detroit?*

A: Yes.

Q: *What were the patients like—the ones who were turned loose?*

A: Uh, occasionally I would see them, the local ones at least. There was —when they was turning these people loose there, after '68—there was two CSPs [criminal sexual psychopaths] that was turned loose and one afternoon they was coming back to the hospital to report for something. And they dropped their girlfriends off at my house. They dropped their girlfriends off there and wondered if they could stay until they went up there, reported in, and came back. So they did. And we talked for probably half hour. Then they left. But about nine o'clock here they come—the two guys come back in—they'd run out of gas. And they didn't have enough money to buy any, they said. So I had a five-gallon gas for the lawn mower and I took 'em back out there. They had hitchhiked over there—so they said. And I took 'em back out there and the girlfriends are still in the car. And we put the gas in and I gave 'em five dollars and let 'em go on. I suppose I coulda got knocked in the head and car taken and everything else. But I didn't. One of them I used to play cards with a lot, up there. And, but, I always kind of liked him, so I helped him. Who knows?

CHAPTER 16

Deinstitutionalization

THERE IS SOMETHING ELSE YOU should know about the 1960s and 1970s in order to understand why schizophrenia became a violent disease. The era saw protest not just against American society, but against American psychiatry as well.

"The notion of mental illness has outlived whatever usefulness it might have had and now functions merely as a convenient myth," psychiatrist and critic Thomas Szasz famously argued in his erstwhile opus, "The Myth of Mental Illness." "The belief in mental illness as something other than man's trouble in getting along with his fellow man is the proper heir to the belief in demonology and witchcraft. Mental illness exists or is 'real' in exactly the same sense in which witches existed or were 'real.'"[1]

Such claims anthemed a wide-ranging social movement called anti-psychiatry, whose casus belli was the critique of psychiatric authority. Anti-psychiatry practitioners and activists argued that psychiatry passed ideology as science, or enforced state-sanctioned mind and body control in the guise of treatment. Szasz, R. D. Laing, David Cooper, and other scholars contended that psychiatry policed societal norms by pathologizing and controlling deviance—a notion that achieved wide resonance through Ken Kesey's novel *One Flew Over the Cuckoo's Nest*. Though he rejected the anti-psychiatry label, the philosopher Michel Foucault similarly argued that psychiatry and psychology enforced power relations rather than treating actual clinical conditions.

Given this theoretical framework, it is not surprising that schizophrenia became a topic that connected anti-psychiatry with civil rights. In his seminal text, *Psychiatry and Anti-Psychiatry*, Cooper sounded very much like Grier, Cobbs, or the case-study patients from "The 'Protest Psychosis'" in arguing that schizophrenia was a product of society whose only solution was revolution. For Cooper, the minimal violence perpetuated by people dubiously labeled as schizophrenic paled in comparison to "the violence *of* psychiatry in so far as the discipline chooses to refract and condense on to its identified patients the subtle violence of the society it only too often represents."[2]

Meanwhile, Stokely Carmichael participated in at least two projects organized by the anti-psychiatrists Cooper, Laing, Joseph Berke, and Leon Redler under the rubric of studying "that predominant form of socially stigmatized madness that is called schizophrenia." In the multiauthored publication that emerged from the Congress on the Dialectics of Liberation in July 1967, Carmichael used Cooper's notion that "doctors . . . attach the label 'schizophrenia' to the diseased object and then systematically set about the destruction of that object by the physical and social processes that are termed 'psychiatric treatment'" as a jumping-off point for discussing the destructive psychological effects of racism.[3]

Philosophers such as Theodore Lidz, Silvano Arieti, Gilles Deleuze, and Félix Guattari similarly theorized schizophrenia as an attempt to cope with, or check out from, a capitalistic, "sick society." Laing sounded downright Du Boisian when he described a (here deracialized) divided self who turned to schizophrenia as an adaptive response to societies or families that failed to address their needs. Meanwhile, novelists such as Joseph Heller popularized the theories of ethnographer Gregory Bateson, who famously argued that schizophrenia was a communication disorder that had its origins in children's early-life relations with their parents. In the 1950s, Bateson presented the influential "double-bind" theory of schizophrenia, in which children pressured into impossible situations by the ambivalent commands of their parents were literally driven crazy. In Heller's *Catch-22*, the double-bind became parodically constitutive of American military life, a theme that also appeared, in more serious form, in psychiatrist Robert Jay Lifton's arguments that American engagement in Vietnam represented "our country's moral and psychological schizophrenia."[4]

Anti-psychiatry went hand in hand with an international movement called deinstitutionalization that pushed for the liberation of people warehoused in psychiatric hospitals. In the United States, the movement's crowning achievement was the Community Mental Health Act. Signed by President John F. Kennedy in October 1963, the act, whose full title was the Mental Retardation Facilities and Community Mental Health Centers Construction Act (PL 88–164), represented the combined efforts of politicians, community psychiatrists, and patient activists, who successfully cast state politicians and hospital administrators as responsible for squalor in long-term "custodial care" asylums. The result was nothing short of a mass exodus. Over the next fifteen years, the census of state and county mental hospitals declined by about two-thirds.[5]

Deinstitutionalization is often associated with general psychiatric hospitals, but institutions that housed the criminally insane felt its effects as well.

Like most state hospitals, the impetus for closure of criminal hospitals began with public outcries about treatment. As with other hospitals, this dynamic was propagated by sensationalistic press reporting that mixed concern for patients with thinly veiled bias against them. And, as with other institutions, the state ultimately used the situation to find cheaper ways to care for people it cared little about.

Ionia's deinstitutionalization story began in the early 1960s, when a series of local news stories exposed disconcerting aspects of daily life at the hospital. Two patients committed suicide within weeks of each other. Reports uncovered abuse of patients by hospital staff. A local newspaper reported the inconvenient fact that the hospital employed not a single trained pharmacist. Dr. Woodward, one of only four trained psychiatrists on staff, passed out drunk on the lawn in the middle of the day and was relieved of his duties soon thereafter. A hospital administrator appropriated funds to bolster his collection of antique furniture. And the hospital placed ninety-five men into isolation after a well-publicized gonorrhea outbreak that spread like an anomeric virus through one of the male locked wards.[6]

Citizens groups protested, and the governor of Michigan convened several high-profile investigative commissions. The Mental Health Inquiry Board examined treatment plans of over 3,000 hospitalized patients. The Special Committee on Mental Health Legislation for Criminal Cases pushed for revision of the definition of criminal insanity. And the Ionia State Hospital Medical Audit Committee dropped the ultimate Szaszian bomb when they concluded that "the Ionia State Hospital should be phased out insofar as its present function is concerned," and that "the responsibility for treating mentally ill offenders should be decentralized to the regional state mental hospitals."[7]

An outpouring is one way to read the changes that ensued, if one reads these changes through the standard narrative of deinstitutionalization. For instance, the inquiry board found that Ionia housed 987 patients in excess of their sentences without valid rationale. As a result of that board's actions alone, the census dropped from nearly 3,000 patients in 1960 to 1,501 in 1965. In 1968, the Special Committee on Mental Health Legislation repealed the infamous Public Act 165, also known as the Criminal Sexual Psychopath Act. Most of Ionia's 350 convicted "sexual psychopaths" transferred to community treatment centers, and a new law decreed that "persons who commit sex offenses and are found competent to stand trial are sentenced" to prison instead. And Michigan House bills 3344, 3342, and 3343 effectively released or transferred many remaining patients. The census fell to 752 patients in June 1969, to 409 patients by September 30, 1972, and to 343 patients by June 1, 1973.[8]

Thus, the outpouring was one of patients who walked the streets, congregated at bus stops, slept on park benches, and, by so doing, helped shape American notions of deinstitutionalization through its most visible manifestations. Deinstitutionalization liberated these people, these others, and set them free on public space.

But deinstitutionalization's additional effects were less known because they were less evident: the process did not only dictate which patients the state set free, it also determined which patients it held onto.

Ionia administrators argued that this latter and much smaller group— most all of whom were men—suffered from a particularly violent form of schizophrenia, one that required their continued incarceration. As a result, these men became the institutionalized bodies that deinstitutionalization left behind. Or, they became the embodied sites of institutional memory. Which is to say that the men witnessed first-hand how a hospital for insane criminals became something else instead.

CHAPTER 17

Raised in a Slum Ghetto

IONIA MUST HAVE SEEMED LIKE the Alamo in May 1976. Grand buildings stood battered and empty. Wind swept through vacant dining halls. Recreation yards hosted no recreation. Weeds overwhelmed promenades and gardens. Most treatment rooms lay dormant, save the wilted leather straps that swung like numb appendages from empty examination tables. Even the name was gone: earlier that year, state legislators renamed the Ionia State Hospital for the Criminally Insane the Riverside Psychiatric Center in a failed attempt at salvation.

Meanwhile, the defiant awaited the inevitable. At its peak in the early 1960s, Ionia housed nearly 3,000 patients and employed over 500 staff. But by the fateful spring of 1976, 250 of the most hardened attendants, nurses, and doctors stood final guard over fewer than 200 of the most dangerous patients. "The future of our hospital hangs like a cloud over patients and employees," acting director Robert G. Kilpatrick wrote in a hospital-wide memo on May 2, 1976. "The threat of closing is ominous, and our future is uncertain. In the event that the move is approved by the Legislature, plans have to be formulated."[1]

New fortifications surrounded the hospital complex and contributed to the sense of siege. Activists of the era had framed deinstitutionalization as a move to tear down asylum walls. Ionia built moats and barbed-wire-topped hurricane fences instead. Perhaps the walled-in staff fantasized that the new barriers kept out the army of bureaucrats massed on the horizon. In reality, the enclosures were meant to contain the remaining patients who were too volatile or too black to be set free on Ionia streets.

Abdul-Rasheed Karim was one of those patients. Mr. Karim was a twenty-eight-year-old African American man whose chart described him as "possibly one of the most hostile inmates in this institution." "He has been in numerous fights with staff," the chart expanded. "He claims to hate all authority figures and all white people." The chart also described an "angry," "belligerent," and "massive" young man. Mr. Karim spent most of his time at Ionia locked in seclusion on the men's ward.

Mr. Karim had lived most of his life as Otis James. Otis James was the name listed on his birth certificate. Otis James was also the name by which he was known to his family, his few friends, the U.S. Army, and even, in the unlikely event that he read protest letters sent on Mr. Karim's behalf, to President Richard Nixon. But after a prison conversion to the Black Muslims, Otis James answered only to the name of Mr. Karim, Abdul-Rasheed, or, to those few people he trusted, Sheed.

Mr. Karim grew up in the Brewster-Douglass housing projects of Detroit. Dedicated by Eleanor Roosevelt in 1935, the projects initially functioned as successful experiments in affordable public housing, but they soon became excuses for segregation. Brewster was the only public housing open to African Americans, and the projects' overwhelmingly black population became the target of the Detroit race riots of 1943. By the time Mr. Karim came of age in the 1960s, high-rises replaced the neat row houses, and drug deals, gunshots, and police raids shattered heroic attempts by many residents to live lives of normalcy in the midst of chaos.[2]

Mr. Karim was the third of five children born to Quincy and Evelyn James. Quincy worked for the Detroit Street Railway until he was forced to retire due to an on-the-job accident. Evelyn worked for twenty-one years as a saleswoman at the S. S. Kresge store on Woodward Avenue. According to an evaluation by the Detroit Recorder's Court, Quincy was a "fair but strict disciplinarian," and Evelyn was "a proud woman, warm, who always kept the apartment neat and clean." "She is always talking and laughing on the telephone and playing cards with her friends, and she is real active," a neighbor said. Quincy and Evelyn tried to instill in their children the importance of work, education, and community. They took the children to music lessons, enforced study time on school nights, and had little patience for truancy.

Mr. Karim was a bright child who did well in school. But he also had a knack for trouble. He stole bicycles and took money from cash registers when he was ten years old. He stole cars when he was thirteen. He joined a gang called the Brewsters when he was fourteen and ended up briefly in a juvenile reformatory, the Detroit Training School for Boys. Mr. Karim's family recognized trouble long before psychiatrists or the police did. Quincy and Evelyn fought with him about the company he kept. They sensed that something was wrong in their son. Danger too easily found him. He seemed guarded and aloof. Sometimes he was alone in a room full of people. At other times he appeared to speak to other people when no one was around. They worried about his anger, his suspicion, and his mistrust.

Quincy and Evelyn were not pleased when the U.S. Army drafted their son in November 1966. The war was a world away, and they had lost one child to the military already. At the same time, they felt a measure of pride that their family stood to be counted. And perhaps discipline might be a good thing for their wayward third son?

The army assigned Mr. Karim to Fort Knox, Kentucky, for basic training. Mr. Karim had difficulty following orders at first, but he soon discovered a talent for soldiering. He was a large man, and full of rage. His abilities impressed his superiors. They sent him to Fort Cordon, Georgia, for advanced combat training, and then to Fort Leonard Wood, Missouri, for additional infantry.

Mr. Karim's ship-out orders came on March 5, 1967. He was given three days' leave and took a Greyhound bus home to Detroit to show off his uniform and his newfound pride. The bus dropped Mr. Karim in downtown Detroit at four o'clock in the afternoon, and he decided to walk the two miles to Brewster-Douglass. But Mr. Karim never made it home. And he never made it to Vietnam.

Mr. Karim was not the instigator of the fight. He had just a short time in Detroit, and he wanted to see his family. But the three white boys on the corner would not let it rest. They saw a black man in uniform and they projected their anger and their disappointment. "Just 'cause you got a uniform don't mean that you can glare at me" was what Mr. Karim recalls the first one saying. "You are no better than me." Then the second one threw a can and the third one spit. Mr. Karim could take no more.

Police who rushed to the scene belonged to tac squads, four-officer units that roamed the streets looking for trouble. Tac squad officers notoriously harassed black citizens under the pretense of identity checks. Police brutality, and even death, sometimes ensued. In his book *Violence in the Model City*, Sidney Fine details the high-profile cases of Shirley Scott, an African American woman shot in the back while fleeing from a patrol car, and Howard King, an African American teenager who was severely beaten in front of numerous witnesses for "disturbing the peace"—or, as locals called it, "disturbing the police." A *Detroit Free Press* survey of Detroit residents in 1968 listed police brutality as far and away the leading cause of the Detroit riots that occurred only a few months after the altercation between Mr. Karim and the three white men.[3]

The officers fixed their gaze on the large black man with the upper hand who refused their efforts of interpolation. "He ignored cease and desist commands," read a direct report of arrest that slipped eerily into passive voice when describing police brutality, "and clubs had to be used." The report did not mention Mr. Karim's contention that the police continued to beat him after they released the white men. Instead, the official record detailed how "the perpetrator hit one of the officers in the eye . . . from that point on a struggle occurred until the perpetrator was subdued, resulting in tenderness and swelling over one officer's left eye and tenderness in the right arm . . . the injuries resulted in the officer being treated at Detroit General Hospital . . . at the precinct the perpetrator refused to be fingerprinted and attempted to walk out, and was again subdued."

A court arraigned Mr. Karim on the charge of "bodily injury to a police officer" on March 7, 1967, and he pleaded not guilty. At the hearing, Mr. Karim shouted that he was the victim of attack by the white officers—"they called me nigger and boy"—but to no avail. The judge set bail at $1,000, which Mr. Karim was unable to pay. Upon arrival to the Wayne County Jail for pretrial holding, the physician noted that Mr. Karim had two broken ribs, a cracked tooth, and a skull laceration that required eleven stitches.

It was not much of a trial. Mr. Karim had accrued "17 misconduct tickets" in the four months he sat in Wayne awaiting the proceedings. Prison staff testified to his "belligerent, uncooperative nature," "poor adjustment," and "need to learn control." Mr. Karim refused to participate in the process. Said the court report, "Otis James refused to raise his hand in oath and refused to answer questions. He periodically grimaced, remained silent for long minutes, looked up to the ceiling with his eyes rolling in all directions." Quincy and Evelyn cried quietly in the back of the courtroom.

The court found Mr. Karim neither guilty nor innocent. Rather, it read his actions and his attitude as indicative of the need for further evaluation. The court remanded him to the Marquette Prison in northern Michigan for "close supervision." The date was July 22, 1967. Adding insult to injury, the transfer order was accompanied by a detainer from the office of the 68th Military Police attachment from Detroit: "MP office is to be notified immediately when any form of release is contemplated." In spite of the circumstances, the military wished to charge Mr. Karim for going AWOL. As the bailiff led Mr. Karim out of court, he muttered again and again, "I am a political prisoner."

Mr. Karim's expansive chart contains no documents describing the transfer to Marquette. The process likely occurred without incident. But perhaps Mr. Karim looked back on Gomorrah from the back of the squad car that drove him out of town. And perhaps, from that vantage point, he saw the glow, and the smoke, and the anger of the Detroit riots that followed a vice squad raid on a welcome home party for two African American soldiers on July 23, 1967. The police attempted to arrest all eighty-two people in attendance. A crowd grew around the arrested. Someone broke a window, and then another. Looting and fires quickly spread through Detroit. The police could not contain the rage. The National Guard arrived, and then the 82nd Airborne Division. Rampage met rampage, and Detroit was forever burned. After five days of what the historian Thomas Sugrue rightly describes as "cataclysmic violence," the numbers were as follows: 43 dead, 1,189 injured, and over 7,000 arrested.[4]

REVELATION CAME IN whispers, and shards of paper, and smuggled books. "Elijah Muhammad understands your plight," said the voice in the night at the maximum security block. "He knows that you have been wronged. He wants to help you fight back." It was not a hallucination, or if it was, then so were the scraps of cardboard passed from cell to cell. "Allah is God and the blue-eyed white man is the devil," they read. Or, "Love and unity of self and kind is the key to salvation." "The entire creation of Allah is of peace, not including the devils who are not the creation of Allah." "Fight back. The enemies of Allah are the European race." "The black man, who is by nature divine and good, must separate from the white man as soon as possible, lest he share the white man's hour of total destruction." The handwritten messages conveyed immense power in the context of a maximum security block where white guards ruled through intimidation, and where iron bars and empty hours imprisoned hopes, desires, and dreams.

Prisons served as major recruiting grounds for African American protest groups long before Mr. Karim's arrival at Marquette. For instance, in the early 1930s, word spread throughout Michigan prisons about the "new prophet" Wali Farad (or Wallace Fard Muhammad). Farad preached that he had come from the holy city of Mecca with a mission to "teach blacks the truth about whites" and help "prepare for the battle of Armageddon . . . the final confrontation between blacks and whites." Farad attracted nearly 10,000 followers in Detroit between 1930 and 1933, many of whom were prisoners or unemployed autoworkers. When the prophet mysteriously vanished in 1934, his leadership position was taken up by an unemployed autoworker named Elijah Muhammad (née Elijah Poole). Muhammad, who autocratically led the Black Muslims for much of the next forty years, similarly viewed prisons as major support centers for his claims that salvation for African Americans lay in withdrawal into an autonomous state.[5]

Prisons were important for secular protest groups as well. Prisons served as important sites of resistance in the writings of activist leaders such as Eldridge Cleaver (*Soul on Ice*) and George Jackson (*Blood in My Eye*). Most inmates knew of the tragic prison experiences of mainstream civil rights pro-testers, such as the Freedom Riders incarcerated at the Mississippi State Peni-tentiary at Parchman, aka, Parchman Farm. H. Rap Brown had a particularly strong following in Michigan prisons in the aftermath of his speech at a De-troit Black Power rally in July 1967, where he is famously claimed to have said, "Motown, if you don't come around, we are going to burn you down." The Black Panthers enlisted supporters in Michigan prisons, as did the Black Guerilla Family, a prison gang that urged black inmates to take militant ac-tion against racist prison systems. The Detroit-based Republic of New Af-rika movement—a group that espoused the formation of a new Afrika in the southern United States—claimed disciples as well.[6]

Mr. Karim became a Black Muslim. He heard the voices in the night and read the scraps of paper. He grew interested and asked questions. One night, three months into his incarceration, typed contraband appeared in his cell. "READ," read the note affixed to the worn pages bound by twine. "MUHAM-MAD SPEAKS: The Words of Elijah Muhammad." In his first reading, Mr. Karim was convinced. In his tenth, he was deeply moved. He wept uncon-trollably in his twentieth passage, and by his twenty-fifth, he was ready to serve. Seven days later came the prison yard tap on the shoulder. Otis James was born anew.

On June 19, 1968, after eleven months on the maximum security block at the Marquette facility, Abdul-Rasheed Karim was sent for psychological evalu-ation. By all accounts, the interactions between Mr. Karim and the prison social worker, psychologist, and physician did not go well. "Allah Akbar," Mr. Karim is reported to have said. "This inmate refuses to cooperate," read the social work note. "He repeatedly states that Allah is the only true judge." "Argumentative," added the psychologist. "Tough guy attitude towards white authority figures, paranoid delusions of police plotting against him. Fights continually with officers." "Lacking insight, he tends to project his failure and frustration onto others," added the physician. "Clearly a case of para-noid schizophrenia. Recommend transfer and further evaluation at a foren-sic facility."

Marquette transferred Mr. Karim to the Center for Forensic Psychiatry at Ypsilanti State Hospital on February 1, 1969. Located several miles outside of Ann Arbor, Ypsilanti Hospital was on the verge of becoming a national cen-ter for forensic expertise. To be sure, the hospital employed many dedicated clinicians. But the center's brief evaluation of Abdul-Rasheed Karim was not among its shining moments.

"Otis James appears to have religious delusions," claimed the Bromberg-ian/Simonian note documenting Mr. Karim's three-week stay at Ypsilanti. "He calls himself A. R. Karim, and he states that he will submit to treatment only with a black Muslim therapist. While in jail he was noted to be a problem inmate, considered to be dangerous. This apparently was on the basis of his presenting a threat to guards." The note suggested in no uncertain terms that the defective person reflected the decayed moral environment from which he emerged.

> Otis James' primary education took place in the streets. He appears to have been socialized toward ghetto survival by his brothers telling him he would have to fight his own battles and never run from a fight. . . . He was raised in a slum ghetto where there was a great deal of criminal behavior. . . . Grew up in a broken, deprived, inadequate environment. His neighborhood was one where early use of drugs and alcohol, rough living, and difficulties with the law were the norm . . . cultural retardation is thus a significant factor in his schizophrenic disease . . . his identification with the Black Muslim group is a projection of his feelings of inadequacy.

In other words, the Ypsilanti evaluation committed what the anti-psychiatrist David Cooper rightly described as a "technique of invalidation" by conflating social issues with psychiatric illnesses. By so doing, the report did not stop to consider that racism, police brutality, economic injustice, and even army training may have shaped Mr. Karim's "socialization" as well. Instead, the report read Mr. Karim at face value, and it read him as unsuitable for the Ypsilanti Hospital:[7] "Throughout the processing procedure the patient appeared to be paranoid and potentially explosive. Therefore, it is recommended that because of his potential for acting out behavior, he should be examined at the Ionia State Hospital."

Thus did Abdul-Rasheed Karim arrive at Ionia in March of 1969. He arrived with a rap sheet as long as the Detroit River. Argumentative. Assaultive. Demanding. Hostile. AWOL. Belligerent. Monster. Militant. Terrorist. Schizophrenic. He arrived full of anger and despair. Two years prior, he planned to defend his country. But a punch to the wrong eye of the wrong officer sent him through the levels of hell, from suffering city to eternal pain. He abandoned hope somewhere between incarceration, evaluation, and isolation. His belief in Allah was his only worldly possession, and even that was deemed by his oppressors to be a symptom of mental illness. In other words, Mr. Karim probably appeared very much as his Ionia intake note described:

"possibly one of the most hostile inmates in the institution and his hostility is directed primarily toward authority figures."

Citing his mental condition, a state court found Mr. Karim "incompetent to stand trial," and he became a ward of the Department of Mental Health on January 6, 1970. The department changed Mr. Karim's status at Ionia from observation/evaluation to formal involuntary commitment. His tenure at Ionia was to last until the time in which he was restored to sanity or until he was determined to no longer be a "threat to society." The formal admit note stated that Mr. Karim showed "no evidence of delusions or hallucinations," but that he nonetheless presented "very disturbed behavior, requiring isolation and medication."

Ionia placed Mr. Karim in confinement on its maximum supervision ward. There he lived in and out of seclusion and restraint for the next six years. The medication log described doses of antipsychotic medication that seem beyond comprehension by today's standards: "Thorazine 250mg. QID [four times/daily]." "Unable to control his destructive impulses. Dose upped to Thorazine, 500mg., QID, along with Haldol, 5mg., QID." Or, "Attacked an attendant. Dose changed to Mellaril 500mg. and Haldol 10mg., both QID."

Even half of such doses would put you or me into a long, anti-cholinergic slumber. Thorazine, Mellaril, and Haldol may or may not have been enough to control Mr. Karim's occasional outbursts. But they were clearly strong enough to keep Abdul-Rasheed Karim at Ionia after the buildings closed, and the hospital emptied, and most of the other patients went free.

CHAPTER 18

Power, Knowledge, and Diagnostic Revision

RETURN, ONE LAST TIME, TO the moment of diagnostic tension. A doctor worked in the Ionia receiving hospital in 1969 when the black Muslim soldier arrived. Mr. Karim appeared combative and defiant. He called the doctor a "white devil," even though this particular doctor was born in the Philippines. Mr. Karim then refused to participate in the evaluation. He stared at the ceiling and rolled his eyes. In the absence of the desired cooperation, the doctor rendered observations that were at once reflective of those made by past evaluations and portentive of the rationale for Mr. Karim's future incarceration. *"Hostile and belligerent. Blames others for his problems. Fights with attendants."* The doctor was in no mood for diagnostic revision, even though by his own admission the patient did not manifest hallucinations or delusions. *"Diagnosis: Schizophrenia."*

What led to this diagnosis? More specifically, what was the relationship between the cultural politics of the 1960s and the diagnosis of schizophrenia in Mr. Karim's chart?

Again, it makes a certain sense to answer such questions at the level of the individual clinical interaction. The doctor was biased, we might say, and he failed to consider how social factors influenced Mr. Karim's presentation. Perhaps the doctor was unduly swayed by a Haldol advertisement, or the writings of Bromberg and Simon, or the film *Shock Corridor,* or by a host of other cultural artifacts of the 1960s that conveyed the message that participation in civil rights–era protests *caused* schizophrenia. Perhaps such cultural messages also made it difficult for the doctor to consider depression, bipolar disorder, or other diagnostic options. Or, perhaps the Black Muslims supplied language for Mr. Karim to express what was, in fact, underlying schizophrenic illness.

The poignancy of these individual encounters haunted me as I read through the Ionia charts, and again as I began to collate and describe them. They helped me understand how schizophrenia functioned both as a diagnosis that required treatment, and as a life sentence that promised ongoing incarceration. The painful impacts were individual, material, and above all else, tragic. Ultimately, each individual chart forced me to consider intentions, influences, and alternatives. What could have been done differently in each case, I wondered?

Over time, though, I came to realize the limitations of understanding these moments of diagnostic encounter based solely on the intentions, volitions, experiences, or concerns of individuals—a doctor's racism, for instance, or a patient's membership in the Black Muslims. If these were the central factors, then the problems that arose when race, prejudice, misunderstanding, politics, and power collapsed into decisions about diagnosis could have been fixed by "cultural competency" retraining of "white" doctors and "black" patients, or by some other attempt to teach people of different identities and subject positions to better get along. Such was not the case.

As much as I reflexively understood these encounters as illustrative of the impact of specific events on individual cases, I was increasingly faced with the reality that many different doctors—indeed, many doctors of many different cultural backgrounds—diagnosed or misdiagnosed many African American men with schizophrenia at Ionia. When read as a group, these cases suggested that the interactions between doctors such as Barry Leroy or Sylvan Cabrioto and patients such as Caeser Williams or Abdul-Rasheed Karim were small subsets of much larger wholes.

"I'm not a psychologist or a psychiatrist, I'm a political activist," Stokely Carmichael once said, "and I don't deal with the individual. I think it's a cop-out when people talk about the individual." Carmichael meant that race problems were too often conceptualized based on case by case perceptions and biases. "I don't talk about the individual," he said, "because I feel that whenever you raise questions about racial problems to white western society, each white man says 'Well don't blame me, I'm only one person and I really don't feel that way. Actually I have nothing against you, I see you as an equal. You're just as good as I am—almost.'"

As I've previously described, Carmichael defined such utterances as illustrative of individual racism, the type of racism based on overt acts by individuals that could be communally observed, understood, and condemned. Carmichael argued that, though important, the focus on the individual effaced recognition of racism's more pervasive and pernicious form, which he termed *institutionalized racism*. This was the silent racism of "established and respected forces in the society" that functioned above the level of individual perceptions or intentions, and that worked to maintain the status quo in capitalist societies through such structures as zoning laws, economics, schools, and courts. Institutionalized racism, he argued, "is less overt, far more subtle, less identifiable in terms of specific individuals committing the acts, but is no less destructive of human life."[1]

Had Carmichael been a psychologist or psychiatrist, he might have included the clinic to his list of sites shaped by institutionalized racism—or at least the diagnostic facility at the Ionia Hospital for the Criminally Insane. Here, in a radical turn, schizophrenia became the diagnosis of choice for the hospital's expanding population of African American men, including men with explicit ties to Black Power protests or Detroit riots, and other men found guilty by association. Ionia diagnosed fully 88 percent of post-1960 "U.S. Negro" admissions—96 percent of whom were men—with schizophrenia, compared with only 44.6 percent of "U.S. White" admissions. Ionia doctors, nurses, and attendants also disproportionately described African American men with schizophrenia as being hostile or violent. Over the same time period, health-care professionals decreasingly associated violent intent to patients identified as belonging to other racial and diagnostic groups.[2]

It must have seemed to Ionia staff at the time that an epidemic of angry black male schizophrenia spread through the patient population as if by highly contagious infection. But it would have been much harder for staff to recognize how, in the aggregate, the spread of black schizophrenia at Ionia resulted from a host of decisions that were made at institutionalized levels, long before individual doctors or patients ever entered examination rooms.

Evidence for the impact of institutionalized forces on diagnostic decisions comes from the second part of the chart study. To recall chapter seven, in the time period between 1935 and 1950, Ionia doctors did not consider patients categorized as "Negro" and "Schizophrenia" as disproportionately "Hostile" or "Violent." "Negro male, delusional, incoherent, babbling," read one such chart. Or, "simple, childish, stereotyped behavior . . . neat and clean." Meanwhile, "White" patients with "Other" diagnoses comprised the most volatile group.

How drastically these associations changed between 1960 and 1975. Figures 15 and 16 detail how, during this fifteen-year period, Ionia charts increasingly located hostility and aggression in African American men diagnosed with schizophrenia. Data reveals that Ionia doctors used adjectives connoting hostile intent or aggression toward others far more frequently in charts of persons diagnosed with "Schizophrenia" and categorized as "Negro/Black" (n=20) than they did in charts of persons diagnosed with "Schizophrenia" and categorized as "White" (n=20).

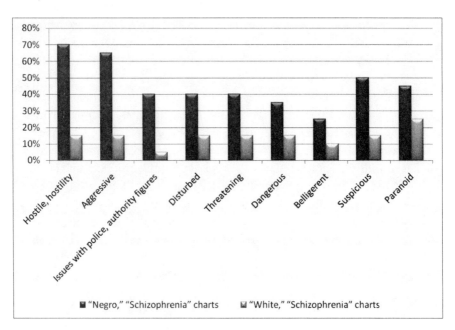

FIG. 15 *Schizophrenia patient descriptions from 1960 to 1975: A comparison of key terms connoting action/aggression/distrust/violence toward others. Results from the second part of the chart study suggest that the definition of schizophrenia shifted on local as well as national levels during the 1960s and 1970s.*

Exact words and phrases used in "Negro" "Schizophrenia" charts (which were, not surprisingly, almost entirely classified as "Paranoid Schizophrenia") included the following.

> 1966: dangerous, volatile, persecutory delusions, antisocial, disposed to-wards violence with minimal provocation, hostile, assaultive, drug dependent, paranoid, suspicious, hostile, very disturbed individual, feels outside of society, aggressive impulses under tenuous control "that could break down suddenly at anytime"
> 1966: bizarre behavior, hostile, sudden outbursts of aggression, guarded, evasive, no insight, disrupting behavior, paranoid, hostile, assaultive, threatening a police officer, persecutory thinking, agitated, appre-hensive, loud, talkative
> 1969: disturbed manner, autistic, hostile, violent for no apparent reason, aggression projected onto others, confused, irrelevant statements,

suspicious, easily distracted, severely threatened by people, poor impulse control, guarded, inappropriate affect, "WHITE MEN ARE AGAINST ME, including police officers"

1970: belligerent, upset, agitated, withdrawn, hostile attitude, uncooperative, over talkative, evasive, lacks insight, defective judgment, "developed a pattern of assaultiveness and an inability to respond to accepted social behavior"

1970: expressed destructiveness and dangerousness, rambling speech, threatened to kill, hostile, destructive feelings, hypomanic, paranoid delusions about state hospital, emotional disturbance is due to aggressive impulses

1970: attacked cell mate and attendants, suspicious, aggressive, disturbed, confused, destructive, restless, unpredictable, hostile, no insight, disturbed, negativistic

1970: "supports Black Power," agitated, threatening, ill tempered at home, fearful, aggressive, highly suspicious, poor impulse control, blunted affect, cooperative, alcoholic, unstable, low frustration tolerance,

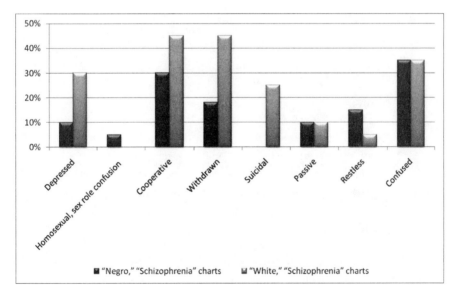

FIG. 16 *Schizophrenia patient descriptions from 1960 to 1975: A comparison of key terms connoting social withdrawal/isolation/violence against the self. Data suggest that the Ionia staff saw white patients with schizophrenia differently—theirs was an illness of isolation and confusion.*

well groomed, fearful, bewildered, unkempt, withdrawn and seclusive on ward, "severe conflict arising from close association of sexual
and aggressive needs"

1971: outbursts, belligerent, history of fighting in jail, unkempt, hostile, defensive, authority figures challenged including "ALL WHITE
PEOPLE," egocentric, fighting stems from doubts about masculinity, "patient's system of values could only be treated by a BLACK
THERAPIST who could provide a strong masculine figure for identification . . . born and raised in deprived and disadvantaged social
situation . . . adopted the Detroit ghetto life by proving himself in an
aggressive way . . . seeks Black identification through interest in Islam," tough guy attitude towards white authority figures, paranoid
delusions of police plotting against him, blames the judge's whiteness
as his reason for being in jail, inadequately integrated

1972: problem inmate, dangerous, threatened guards, paranoid, potentially explosive, disturbed behavior, required confinement

1973: fought with prison personnel, belligerent, "possibly one of the most
hostile inmates in the institution and his hostility is directed primarily toward any authority figures," agitated, low impulse control,
basically an angry person, argumentative, chronically complained,
demanding, believed others had it in for him, long term muteness,
suspicious, guarded, paranoid thinking, "using passive aggressive behavior as a defensive way of defying the prison and showing his hostility"

1975: claimed he was God, confused, bizarre thought associations, suspicious, preoccupied with religion, directed by the Lord, presented
mgmt problems, acted irrationally, overactive, destructive, talked
about killing people, agitated, bizarre behavior, disturbed, uncooperative, unable to adjust in community, rambling speech, required
seclusion due to aggressiveness, threatened police by saying "I'll kill
you"

"White" patients with schizophrenia evenly divided between paranoid,
undifferentiated/chronic, catatonic, simple, schizophrenic, hebephrenic, and
mixed types of schizophrenia. The language in their charts sounded quite
different.

1965: limited ability to relate, friendly, cooperative, passive, unenergetic,
manneristic, withdrawn, flat affect, childish thinking, inappropriate

use of words, quiet, well adjusted, does not create any problems, low intelligence, slow speech, fears sexual contact, feels inadequate, paranoid, persecutory ideation: "I think the police dept and judge are against me"

1967: flat emotions, disturbed, panic reaction, bewildered, confused, inappropriate emotional responses, entertained morbid thoughts, dangerous, narcissistic, no insight, low mental capacity, poor masculine identification, raised in female household, conflicts in regards to his masculine image, over controlled conventional facade, impulsive, explosive acting out, hostile, feelings of inadequacy and impotence, quiet, moody, withdrawn, delinquent set of values

1969: drug usage, basically an aggressive person, suspicious, guarded, grandiose, paranoid, belligerent, aggressive towards parents, cooperative, flat affect, threatening attitudes, angry, "orientation toward drugs and hippie way of life" caused with his deterioration

1970: cooperative, crying at times, comments make no sense, anxious, agitated, suspicious, preoccupied with religious thoughts, bizarre comments, rambling speech, repressed hostility, grandiosity, depression, "mixed up young man," suicidal, belligerent, threatening, moody, paranoid

1973: confused, agitated, uncommunicative, passive, withdrawn, very guarded, flat affect, evasive, disorganized thinking

1973: withdrawn, regressed, apathetic, under-productive, does not show interest in anything, just existing, functioning has deteriorated, smiled inappropriately, no insight, soft spoken, very cooperative

1973: withdrawn, almost mute, unable to function at home, confused, apprehensive, flat affect, sleepy looking, depressed, cooperative, giggles, tangential, tense, restless, "has not been acting right since coming back from Vietnam"

Finally, violence or hostility did not appear in charts of patients diagnosed with Other disorders (for example, depressive neurosis, personality disorders, manic depression, involutional melancholia). Nonschizophrenia control charts for patients categorized as white and as Negro/black contained language suggesting that these patients were quiet and agreeable. White patients were overwhelmingly more likely to be described as depressed.

Results from the second part of the chart study suggest that the definition of schizophrenia shifted on local as well as national levels during the 1960s and 1970s. Doctors, nurses, and attendants disproportionately used

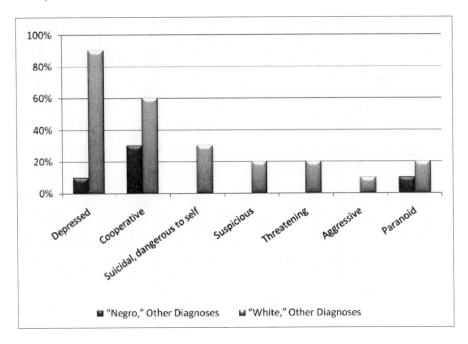

FIG. 17   *Key nonschizophrenia patient descriptions from 1960 to 1975.*

terms such as *hostile, violent, belligerent,* or threatening to describe Ionia's expanding category of "Negro" men with paranoid schizophrenia. Clinicians frequently assumed that black schizophrenic aggression was directed at—or more appropriately, projected onto—authority figures. *"Paranoid delusions of police plotting against him," "fought with prison personnel," "blames the judge's whiteness as his reason for being in jail."* By contrast, the Ionia staff saw patients with "White" schizophrenia differently. Theirs was an illness of isolation and confusion. *"Withdrawn, regressed, apathetic, under-productive, does not show interest in anything, just existing, functioning has deteriorated."* When hostility appeared, it was just as likely to be directed toward the self, in the form of suicidality or self-destructive behavior, as toward others. Meanwhile, unlike earlier time periods, charts of nonschizophrenia patients demonstrated no race-based trends, save a connection between "depressed" and whiteness that becomes important in the next chapter of this book.

One potential explanation for these trends is that African Americans and white Americans actually *did* express mental illness in different ways.

By this logic, black schizophrenia looked different from white schizophrenia because, in essence, it was. Black forms produced hostility while white forms produced confusion. Black forms produced Caesar Williams and Abdul-Rasheed Karim, while white forms produced hippies, wanderers, and apathetic souls.

Ethnically or racially distinct forms of schizophrenia would have been the most likely explanation for the chart findings if we conducted our study epidemiologically in 1970 rather than historically in the present day. As previously discussed, scientific articles from leading journals from the 1960s and 1970s described "racial differences" between black and white patients strikingly similar to those described in the Ionia charts. For instance, in "Hallucinations and Delusions in White and Negro Schizophrenics," Vitols, Waters, and Keeler wrote that schizophrenic symptoms were "phenomenologically" dissimilar between the two races, and that "Negro groups" displayed more hostility, bizarre behavior, and mistrust of medical authority than did "white groups." The authors attributed the higher incidence of hostile psychotic symptoms to a series of "premorbid cultural patterns": "It is often considered that the Negro places particular emphasis on impressions and experiences," they wrote, "causing him to react out of proportion to the stimulus and show a lowered emotional threshold and heightened tension." The article further explained that,

> The Negro . . . has few opportunities to express hostile feelings directly toward white individuals or toward the dominant white society and has many reasons to be hostile. The situation is further complicated by the fact that the Negro may admire the positions and opportunities of the white. It might be expected that a conflict involving unexpressed hostility and envy would manifest itself in psychotic productions.[3]

Before dismissing such arguments for their clear and obvious racism— recall that white psychiatrists were not the only group who might have argued that Ionia charts demonstrated separate black and white forms of schizophrenia. Black Power, Black Rage, and the Rev. Wyatt Tee Walker were but a few of the voices who contended that black schizophrenia was a condition forged from the distinctiveness of black experience. "It was heartening for me to hear of your paranoia," said the Rev. Walker in 1969, "because it allows me to admit to the black community of our schizophrenia." In this formulation, the expression of what the charts described as "hostile feelings" toward white individuals, or toward authority figures "*including ALL WHITE PEOPLE*" enacted the anger, rage, and frustration not just of the psychotic mentally ill, but of the "Negro culture" from which they allegedly emerged.[4]

However, historical analysis is not epidemiological analysis. The latter practice tests for the incidence of prevalence within set categories, while the former questions the formation of the categories themselves. The epidemiologist rightly claims that "Jews are genetically predisposed to Tay-sachs disease [*sic*]," or that "osteoporosis primarily afflicts women." But for the post-Foucault historian, the epidemiologist's seemingly transparent groupings exist in a continuous process of flux. These statements may be true, the historian replies, but their truth claims rest on anything-but-self-evident assumptions about race, gender, biology, sickness, health, power, circumstance, and other context-dependent variables that are historically produced rather than culturally essential.

From a historical perspective, data from the second part of the chart study suggests that the key shift taking place at Ionia in the late 1960s was one of perception. Two decades prior, violent, black schizophrenia was not a category of analysis, let alone a biological fact. Yet by 1975, Caeser Williams, Abdul-Rasheed Karim, and other men became schizophrenic in part because their doctors saw them as black—and because the perception of blackness functioned as the sine qua non of a particularly hostile form of paranoid schizophrenia. Schizophrenia in this context was both a mental illness with tragic material effects and a pernicious cascade of self-perpetuating stereotypes in which observations about "race" and "diagnosis" stood in for a host of other charged assumptions and anxieties.

Locating the diagnosis of schizophrenia in shifting perceptions is not to say that the illness was not real for patients and doctors at what Carmichael called the individual level. Rather, the perceptual systems surrounding the reality of schizophrenia were shaped by institutionalized variables other than the doctors' racism or the patients' skin color. Diagnosing the problem in individual black bodies, or even in monolithic black cultures, then effaced awareness of the structural factors that surrounded and shaped clinical interactions.

In other words, it might well have appeared to Ionia psychiatrists that black schizophrenia was a violent disorder, given the types of patients they saw at the hospital in the post-1968 period. But it would have been much more difficult for these doctors to recognize how policy decisions, changes in the legal system, urban decay, political crisis, and other factors effectively preselected African American patients with histories of violent crime in the first place, while eliminating patients without violent histories well before they arrived at the psychiatrist's door.

As one example, Ionia became a receiving hospital for so-called forensic psychiatric cases in the mid-1960s. Forensic psychiatry was an emerging discipline that combined psychiatry and the law in order to address matters of criminal insanity, competency to stand trial, mental state at the time of offense, and sentencing recommendations for mentally ill defendants. In the aftermath arrived increasing numbers of "hard-core criminal patients" who had histories that included armed robbery, homicide, and attacks on authority figures such as police. Ionia received forensic cases from prisons, lower security hospitals, other forensic centers such as Ypsilanti, and urban Detroit. (Of note, my sample did not produce a single instance of black-on-black crime. Such cases likely remained in jail.) These patients were overwhelmingly, though not entirely, categorized as "Negro"; and being "Negro" was overwhelmingly, though not entirely, associated with paranoid schizophrenia.[5]

Policy decisions in the 1960s and 1970s, such as the Community Mental Health Act and Michigan House Resolution 225, also removed other groups of patients from Ionia's diagnostic purview. Michigan House Resolution 225 of 1967 raised the bar considerably for the determination of criminal insanity. Only the "most disturbed or violent offenders" met the new criteria, while the state sent those deemed as lesser risks to prison or to community parole. Again, Michigan also repealed the infamous Criminal Sexual Psychopath Act in 1968, and, by dictum, "persons who commit sex offenses and are found competent to stand trial" were sentenced to prison instead. Such policies effectively eliminated two categories comprised mainly of persons identified as white. The population of women patients fell from several hundred in the 1960s to below 30 by 1972. And the hospital admitted no perverts, homosexuals, or pedophiles after 1970. Ranks of these patients dropped to 12 by 1975. As a result of these and other changes in the late 1960s and early 1970s, the percentage of Ionia patients classified as "Male," "Violent/Homicidal," and "Schizophrenia" and "Negro" rose in relation to other patient groups.[6]

The economist Glen Loury describes such sample bias as a "self-confirming racial stereotype," a social distortion that ascribes disadvantage "among a group of people to qualities thought to be intrinsic to that group, when in fact that disadvantage is a product of a system of social interactions." Loury uses as his example the refusal of certain taxi drivers to pick up African American men at night in urban settings based on the fear of being robbed. Such fears, Loury argues, result from a myriad of social factors, from the ways that taxi drivers treat African Americans differently to the possibility that robbers are less easily deterred than law-abiding citizens by long waits for cab rides. Loury argues that such concerns often result in assumptions about the intrinsic connections between criminality and race, when they in fact result from "a process that economists call 'adverse selection,'" in which "the set of black men actually hailing taxis after dark may well come to contain a noticeably larger than average fraction of robbers, precisely the circumstance presumed by the drivers in the first place."[7]

If the analogy holds, then adverse selection offers one potential explanation for hostile black schizophrenia at Ionia, where findings that appeared as changes in the numerator resulted from changes in the denominator instead. Policies changed, laws changed, and the patients sent to Ionia had a priori histories of particular crimes. Yet, psychiatric literature, societal bias, and indeed daily clinical experience conveyed the message that "violence" and "schizophrenia" were subsets of "black." This conceptual flaw justified the belief that black schizophrenia became increasingly violent. Violent schizophrenia then became the justification for continued incarceration.

As we have already seen, the charged language of the DSM-II provides another institutionalized explanation for the new category of black, violent schizophrenia at Ionia. Chart data suggests that, in spite of its claims of universality, the 1968 diagnostic text promoted dissimilarities between "Negro" and "white" groups of patients at on the ground clinical levels as well as societal ones. To recall, the DSM-II described paranoid schizophrenia as an illness in which "the patient's attitude is frequently hostile and aggressive, and his behavior tends to be consistent with his delusions," and employed a different set of descriptors for cognitive and mood disturbances. Post-1968 charts in particular show that the former language was preferentially applied to black male patients at Ionia, much as it had been in the mainstream media and in psychiatric journals. "Hostile, violent for no apparent reason, aggression projected onto others." In this anything-but-trickle-down-economy, the DSM created racial differences in psychopathology rather than reflecting them; and race-based differences in symptoms represented not the premorbid cultural patterns of African American patients, but the premorbid professional assumptions of their doctors.

In sum, Ionia charts suggest that institutional factors coded schizophrenia as a black disease in ways that influenced the perceptions, actions, and experiences of doctors and patients. By so doing, the charts function as object lessons for better understanding how seemingly hermetic diagnostic interactions, even those taking place behind layers of barbed wire and bureaucracy at a remote Michigan asylum, connect to larger political tensions and debates.

The sociologist Michel Foucault provides one important way to think about such tensions between the local and the political and the neurobiological. His schema contends that the ever-shifting divide between normal and abnormal exposes relationships between knowledge and power. Defining something as abnormal establishes power relations, and allows those in power to discard, diagnose, or incarcerate threats to prevailing ideologies as transgressive crimes or illnesses. Utterances or actions that signify valid resistance in one context—"Black identification through interest in Islam," or "Supports Black Power"—become symptoms of mental illness in another. Foucault held that the human sciences serve as key actors in creating and maintaining this divide. Far from being value-neutral, timeless, or objective, the human sciences discipline particular subjects in order to reify particular power structures at particular moments in time.[8]

Foucault's arguments apply in obvious instances where totalitarian regimes define political dissent as insanity, and treat it as such. It has been widely reported that the government of the former Soviet Union diagnosed dissidents with schizophrenia before sending them to gulags. And the incidence of schizophrenia rose in China in the period following protests at Tiananmen Square—after all, who but a crazy person would stand in the way of an oncoming tank?[9]

Ionia charts raise the possibility that a similar, though more subtle dynamic occurred in the northern United States during the civil rights era. By this reading, it is far from happenstance that the category of the angry black male schizophrenic appeared in the charts at precisely the historical moment when angry black men and women protested in the streets, Martin Luther King preached patience while Stokely Carmichael preached revolt, Detroit burned, and the country seemed torn by the racial schizophrenia described by the *New York Times*. Only in this context did the DSM-II, mainstream American media, and Ionia doctors conspire to define and produce the category of black schizophrenia under the guise of describing it. In other words, defining black protest as insane was far more advantageous than taking seriously the content of that protest, or allowing it to disrupt the functioning of white bourgeois society. Connections between national-political and local-diagnostic discourse thereby reflected the ways in which, according to Foucault, regulatory power is "produced from one moment to the next, at every point, or rather in every relation from one point to another."[10]

The psychiatrist Frantz Fanon, similarly structuralist, adds the important notion that race-inflected individual pathologies reflect racist societies. "Freud insisted that the individual factor be taken into account through psychoanalysis," he wrote in a quote frequently cited by Stokely Carmichael. "[It will be seen that] the black man's alienation is not an individual question. It is a question of socio-diagnostics." Fanon believed that the social climate of colonial subjugation was so absolute that it forced "the black man" to view himself through the eyes of his "white" oppressors. "The black man has no ontological resistance in the eyes of the white man," Fanon wrote, meaning that the protesting black man discovers himself through the diagnostic lens of the *other*. Fanon thus developed the concept of "sociogeny" ("beside phylogeny and ontogeny stands sociogeny") to describe the ways in which social forces and power relations structured language, pathology, and even claims of identity.[11]

Fanon's work has rightly been critiqued for enforcing rigid categories of black men and white men. Yet, in part because of his insistence on distinct black and white bodies, Fanon vitally provides an alternate reading of race-insanity trends in the Ionia charts. By relocating the "problem" of black schizophrenia from black mind to white society, Fanon's work suggests ways in which adaptation to white society in turn shaped black psyches. By this reading, the Ionia charts demonstrate the profound, psychological impact of racist subjugation, a process in which African American men internalized and then reproduced white notions of black pathology. "I am what you made me," the charts say. "My violence is a response to, and psychical reflection of, yours." Schizophrenia in this context functioned as a survival mechanism and a means of adaptive autobiography.[12]

Take nothing away from the power of the individual clinical encounter, for the power was immense. Patients likely seemed to their doctors to be every bit as ill, and every bit as volatile, as their charts described. "Agitated, threatening, ill tempered, aggressive, highly suspicious, poor impulse control." To be sure, the men came after committing acts of aggression. They also came after years of abuse by the system. They came in chains, in straightjackets, in seclusion, and generally not in peace. Put yourself in the position of the Ionia doctor, or of the Ionia patient for that matter. An angry man gets out of the police car. Or, a physician walks toward you holding a syringe in raised-pistol position. You are not a social constructionist, a postpositive realist, a poet, or a detached narrator at that moment. You reflexively identify a threat and process it through the categories available. Black or white. Psychotic or normal. Friend or foe. The implications are not trivial. Schizophrenia meant neuroleptic medication, prolonged incarceration, even death. You diagnose in the moment. You diagnose the *other,* as Fanon would have it, even as you diagnose yourself.

Yet, the chart data connects the tensions of these moments to the larger social and historical contexts in which they were situated. By so doing, Ionia charts archive connections between racialization-as-local-narrative and racialization-writ-large. The numbers quantify how emerging anxiety about social change embedded into emerging diagnostic language, and emerging diagnostic language embedded into science, law, policy, and common sense. Blacks demonstrated hostile forms of schizophrenia, the new logic implied, because of their social backgrounds or cultural predilections or because of the biology of their black brains. Whatever the cause, the new logic located illness, protest, and revolt within decontextualized black bodies, while conveniently overlooking the economic and social injustices that created the need for protest in the first place. Diagnosis, misdiagnosis, and any number of other symptomatic sequelae, were then the result.

Return of the Repressed

IDEM THE SAME, GERTRUDE STEIN once wrote atop a poem. *Idem* is Latin for "the same," and the phrase translates into a repetition, "the same the same." Stein's invocation foreshadows her poem, "A Valentine for Sherwood Anderson," that is structured through linguistic repetition of seemingly familiar words. "Very fine is my valentine," it begins. "Very fine and very mine. Very mine is my valentine very mine and very fine." Idem the Same signified Stein's belief in the transformative effect of repetition, a process in which words such as *fine, mine,* and *valentine* accrued new associations and new meanings when seen over and over and over again. As the Stein scholar Liesl Olson describes it, Stein believed that repetition ruptured the "delusion" that life ever exactly replicates itself.[1]

Idem-the-Same process describes Alice Wilson's progressive encounters with the mental-health system in the years following her first discharge from Ionia in March 1942. Alice enjoyed prolonged periods of feeling fine. But symptom escalation always ensued. Hospitalization then followed escalation. Alice initially appeared to her doctors to be very much the same. The same issues, the same reactions, the same promises made and broken. But over time, her same came to mean something different.

Alice's first major relapse occurred in spring 1964. Stability seemed the norm in the months prior. George left for work at the paper each morning. Alice cleaned, mothered, and played cards with women from the neighborhood on Tuesday nights. The family attended church each Sunday and ate lunch afterwards at a local diner. Was this how life would be from then on? the family must have wondered. Perhaps the hospitalization never happened. But it was not, and it did.

Darkness was the first sign of trouble—not darkness outside, but inside a house whose every blind and shutter closed in rejection of afternoon sun and its portents. "The light hurts my eyes" was Alice's explanation, which was perhaps believable until she used five rolls of toilet tissue to fill in cracks in the blinds where light seeped through. George came home early one day in March and found Alice curled in the bedroom closet. "They are watching me," she muttered over and again. George made the inevitable call, though it pained him deeply. And the officers came.

Alice was known to Ionia, and to Ionia she returned. "This patient refused to go outside, even to do her shopping," read the court petition for hospitalization. "She refused to do any housework. She continually complained that she didn't have anything to wear, although her husband brought her many dresses. . . . It became necessary for her husband to do all of the housework. . . . The patient complained that the house was extremely dirty. She threatened the neighbors."

The admit note sounded a similar refrain. "Alice Wilson was placed on convalescent status from Ionia Hospital in 1942," wrote the women's ward physician, Walter R. Willis. "She made an adequate adjustment for a number of years, spending most of her time doing housework. As she relapsed, she became greatly confused in attempting any household tasks." The doctor observed Alice to be "a clean, white woman of short stature, 54 years old, who wears upper dentures. Ash-blonde hair, light blue eyes . . . she appears polite, overly talkative, cooperative, depressed, guarded."

"Were you here previously?" Willis asked. "Yes," Alice replied. "I was taken sick while we were visiting in the South with a nervous condition or something."

"How have you been getting along at home?" the doctor followed. "Well," the patient answered, "now I got to where things were awfully hard for me. I couldn't keep my housework up decently. I want to try again."

"Why couldn't you?" posed Willis. "I don't know. Just a weakened condition and nerves, but I'm sure it will get better."

"Have you had any difficulty with your husband?" "I nagged him too much. I guess I just wanted him to do things for me with his own work."

"Have you heard voices when no one was around?" "No."

"Have you been depressed?" "Not nearly as much as I have been before. I'm terribly blue about being here. I didn't want to come, of course."

"Do you feel you can do housework now?"

To read Alice Wilson's extensive hospital chart is to be struck, once again, by the tragic ways that mental illness ruptures everyday life. Yes, the clinical conversation aligned white, middle-class housewifery too closely with sanity. But page after page, quote after quote, suggests that being a white, middle-class housewife was not just an imposed norm; it was a desired one as well. In intake and ward interviews, Alice and her family long repeatedly for the kind of quotidian life that others took for granted. A meal and conversation at the end of the day. Parent-teacher night at school. A summer picnic with the neighbors. Church bingo. These became events of anticipatory trepidation. Alice's spells shattered the delusion of calm and reinforced the notion that she was incapable of maintaining her social network over time. Would Alice attend? Would she create a scene? In time George and the girls reproduced Alice's avoidance of public situations. And moments of normalcy became moments untrusted.

Recall, however, that this is a book about the intersections of race and mental illness. In this context we must also note that a white woman presenting in 1964 with bouts of paranoia still pointed to schizophrenia, albeit in DSM-I-modified form. "This examination shows a well developed, well nourished white female," Dr. Willis dictated at the end of Alice's intake note. "Under questioning it is quite apparent that she displays little insight into her illness . . . she has no hallucinations and she denies any dreams of any sort and she has not been violent." With history as his guide and the DSM-I as his template, Willis concluded that, "it is the writer's opinion that this is a Schizophrenic Reaction, undifferentiated type . . . this apparently is a recurrence of her previous illness."

Thorazine, Stelazine, psychotherapy, group therapy, and arts-and-crafts followed. Five months later came Ward Walk:

> DR. OSLER: She is much improved. The main thing was she just got anxietous [*sic*] and restless and made her husband nervous so she came to the hospital to give him a rest.
>
> DR. AGRAS: Ok, we will give her another trial at home if nobody objects.

Alice's final relapse of record occurred in early March of 1972. By then, Alice was a grandmother several times over. She was far too old to be running through the neighborhood late at night, tapping on unsuspecting windows while announcing herself as Mary, Queen of Scots. And she was certainly past the point of embarrassing her husband in public. But that is precisely what happened.

According to the admit report, "this 62-year-old white woman's problems began when she and her husband were driving to Ohio to visit their daughter and grandchildren." Ten miles into the road trip, Alice became "increasingly anxious, confused, and vocal." George pulled into a rest stop. Alice worsened. "He is out to get me," she yelled, pointing at her husband. "He is taking me against my will!" George coerced Alice back into the car. He drove back home as quickly as his driving skills allowed. "What shall I do? What shall I do? What shall I do?" Alice muttered again and again. She "took three sleeping pills and a [T]horazine tablet, which were ineffective." Over the next several days, she became convinced that "women in her church group" conspired against her. Then she wandered and tapped and shouted and ultimately the police were called. Alice cried all the way back to Ionia. "I've lost control of myself again," she said.

In other words, Alice appeared largely the same. The same as when the trip to Biloxi stressed her to the point of decompensation. The same as when George and the neighbors became the focus of her ideations. Psychiatrists apparently felt the same way. In their intake note, Drs. George Clark and Sylvan Cabrioto described Alice's previous admissions in detail, even referencing quotes from earlier doctors. "Alice continues to feel guilty about the problems that she has caused her family," they added, "and the periods of time when she was away from her children while she was hospitalized."

The doctors noted more of the same in their mental status examination.

Pre-admission information indicates that the patient was unable to care for her basic needs and that her husband had to do them for her. During the admission interview the patient cried and said she was unable to do things at home. . . . She states, "There were so many times when I've broken down—failed." . . . She is neat and clean . . . occasionally would emote inappropriate affect and emotions . . . there was an attitude of chronic anxiety and insecurity . . . physical and neurological examinations were essentially within normal limits.

But something was different: the diagnosis. Alice Wilson was thought schizophrenic for much of the preceding forty years. But this time, Doctors Clark and Cabrioto formulated her case by foregrounding altered mood and cognitions instead of actions. "This patient feels helpless and hopeless," they wrote, "and is often confused." In their view, the most relevant aspect of Alice's presentation was "depression," which, they argued (incorrectly, given past notes), gradually emerged during the so-called involutional years of her middle and late life in conjunction with a worsening sense of paranoia.

Doctors Clark and Cabrioto removed schizophrenic reaction from Alice's diagnostic list and replaced it with a Kraepelinian term that functioned as a tentative diagnosis at first and a definitive diagnosis several days later. Alice's 1972 face sheet appeared as follows.

The doctors prescribed 25 milligrams of Valium thrice daily and 20 milligrams of Serentil at night for their newly, involutionally depressed patient. They advocated the following treatment plan.

> Treatment goals are to increase self-confidence, decrease dependency, teach assertiveness, develop work habits and skills, increase productivity and achievement, increase interactions with others. Treatment approach is active friendliness.

Ionia placed Alice in its new Riverside Center, an open ward for non-criminally insane patients. The center housed Ionia's dwindling population of women—the census was 29 at the time of Alice's admission (26 of these women were classified as white). To understate greatly, these women were not seen as risks to the community. The goal of their treatment was reintegration.[2]

At Riverside, Alice met other diagnostically recast women like herself,

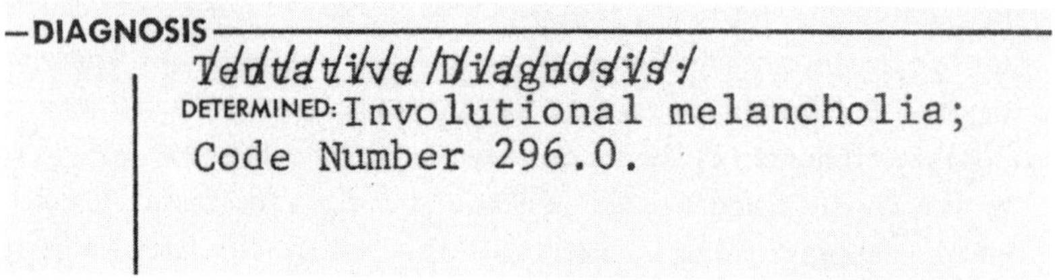

—DIAGNOSIS
Tentative Diagnosis
DETERMINED: Involutional melancholia;
Code Number 296.0.

18A

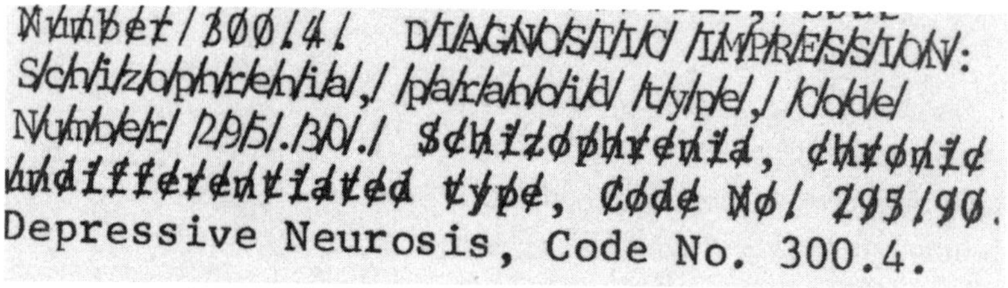

Number 300.4 DIAGNOSTIC IMPRESSION:
Schizophrenia, paranoid type, code
Number 295.30. Schizophrenia, chronic
undifferentiated type, Code No. 295.90.
Depressive Neurosis, Code No. 300.4.

18B

FIGS. 18A AND 18B *In the 1970s, the official diagnosis in Alice Wilson's chart shifted from schizophrenia to involutional melancholia (18a). The face sheets of other women patients showed similar transformations (18b).*

women whose exodus from schizophrenia into depression helped transform the meaning of both illnesses in American society. Treatment regimens for these women included individual and group psychotherapies, art and vocational therapies, "Bingo parties," and a series of "community outings" such as shopping trips into town and visits to the Ionia Free Fair.

Alice's chart described an increasingly "happy, calm woman" whose "emotional distress resolved within the therapeutic milieu." Alice left the hospital two months after her admission. She was not hospitalized in the Michigan psychiatric system again.[3]

Alice Wilson's case is an individual tragedy on par with any in this book. Mental symptoms defined and ruined Alice's life, and she enjoyed few moments of respite. At the same time, the discussion in the preceding chapters complicates the notion that doctors incorrectly diagnosed these symptoms for much of her life before discovering the correct approach. We might be equally skeptical that Alice recovered from schizophrenia over time, or survived the illness, or was cured.

Rather, from a historical perspective, Alice and the other women served as protagonists and victims in what might be called a counter-revisionist mystery in which the same symptoms in the same people in the same settings came to mean different things at different points in time. Only here the repetition identified similarity rather than difference. Rose is a rose, as Stein put it, is a rose is a rose.[4]

Alice Wilson's case history provides another layer in the story of how definitions of race, gender, violence, and schizophrenia changed in relation to one another at Ionia during the 1960s and 1970s. That lesson is: the civil rights era of the 1960s and 1970s altered assumptions not only about what schizophrenia looked like, but also about what it did not. The bar lowered for certain patients, but forced others higher to climb. Doctors saw schizophrenia increasingly in Abdul-Rasheed Karim. But Alice Wilson, whose symptoms had not changed, looked newly, neurotically depressed.[5]

Whiteness is often experienced as invisibility in Western society, the social scientist Ruth Frankenberg once claimed. Whiteness is the control group, the assumed norm. The sociologist Paul Gilroy provocatively argues that whiteness is that which resists observation. Whiteness normalizes power through the differentiation and classification of the other, Gilroy suggests, while—in a counter-Fanonian process—promoting obliviousness to the self.[6]

Professors Frankenberg and Gilroy may just as well have been talking about depression at Ionia. Alice no longer appeared schizophrenic to her doctors in part because of her "symptoms," but also because she was not overly hostile, or threatening, or black. These were the very markers powerfully present in Caeser Williams, Octavius Greene, and other cases defined by their difference even before being defined by their psychic distress. By rhetorical contrast, Alice's was a diagnosis of similarity. Hers became an illness of the white liberated, an illness whose integration into society was eased over time by its invisibility.

In other words, it was a telling diagnostic moment when a doctor decided that Alice Wilson no longer suffered from schizophrenia, both because of the clinical symptoms he observed when proposing the diagnostic switch and, more important, because of the cultural symptoms he subliminally registered but decidedly did not recognize, even though they appeared right in front of him in the examination room.

We might think of the tensions of such a moment through the words of another master of repetition, poet Wallace Stevens. "For the listener, who listens in the snow," Stevens wrote from a white snowy place that was a world away from Ionia or schizophrenia but nonetheless profoundly apt regarding the poetics of same-race-based diagnosis. "And, nothing himself, beholds," he continued in brilliant analysis of the apperceptions, stimuli, and cognitive omissions that shape our encounters with others at times when everything around us appears comfortably the same, *"Nothing that is not there and the nothing that is."*[7]

CHAPTER 20

Rashomon

To the Honorable Doctors at Ionia Hospital,

My brother Otis was attacked by three persons in the street and managed to struggle and defend himself and fight back. While defending himself and being a large man in size and an Army soldier, he was able to win the battle. Police officers were called or happened to the scene. As it was told to me, it appeared as if Otis was attacking the people. Well quite naturally he argued and resisted the Police officers, fighting and struggling with them he was knocked unconscious. Near death, he was thrown in jail—miraculously he survived, totally unable to understand any part of this INSANE experience, he now begs for his life from the state mental institution.

This entire experience leaves my family deeply hurt and weakened. We beg you to either release my brother or to transfer him to a hospital closer to our family home. Please help.

Thank you,

Brother of Otis James (AR Karim), Gerald James

■   ■   ■

JULY 20, 1972

Dear Mr. James,

This is in response to your recent letter regarding your brother, Otis James. He is residing at our hospital because he requires treatment for a mental condition. We can not recommend his release from our hospital at the present time because he is not well enough to function in the open community. Because of his confused and unrealistic thinking he would not be able to care for himself adequately, and he may be a potential danger to others.

We are aware that your brother has expressed dissatisfaction about his hospitalization. However, we feel that his condition has shown some improvement since his admission. We are hopeful that his condition will continue to improve, and that it may be possible to recommend his transfer to another state hospital nearer to his relatives at some point.

We assure you that we will continue to give your brother the best possible care and treatment while he is in our hospital. There is no desire that he remain hospitalized any longer than necessary for his own welfare. We hope you will correspond with your brother to express your support and encouragement during his period of hospitalization.

Sincerely yours,

A. A. Fairman, MD

Medical Superintendent

■   ■   ■

FEBRUARY 2, 1973

To the Doctors in Authority,

I'm writing concerning getting my brother released in my custody or to an Army or VA hospital closer to our family. During my visit I talked to one of the social workers on duty. Learning that he is well enough to leave the hospital providing that he has someone to keep watch that he takes his medicine properly and get proper meals. I can provide those needs.

Gerald James

■   ■   ■

JUNE 14, 1973

Dear Mr. James,

I am sorry for the delay in answering your letter. Your brother remains unstable. Please rest assured that we are doing everything possible for him. We plan to seek transfer to a closer facility as soon as possible once his condition improves, and after necessary court hearings.

Sincerely yours,

A. A. Fairman, MD

Medical Superintendent

■   ■   ■

SEPTEMBER 20, 1973

Leading Doctors in Authority at Ionia State Hospital,

This communication is in regards to a patient named AR Karim (Otis James). It is requested that he be immediately released from confinement.

All indications are that he is healthy and should be free.

I am writing the President, the Governor, the Senator, Mayor, Bar association, Congress man of Michigan and the United Nations as soon as I finish this letter.

You have as usual been very unjust in your dealings with my brother. And you will be dealt with accordingly.

Gerald James

■ ■ ■

NOVEMBER 11, 1973

Dear Sir,

I have been retained by the family of this patient for the purposes of securing the earliest possible date for his release from Ionia. I spoke with a representative from your department of Social Services regarding the case. At that time I confirmed the fact that Mr. James no longer has any criminal matters pending and that the only basis for his enforced hospitalization must flow from a civil commitment.

I am writing to request a full and complete report.

With sincerest thanks for your speedy cooperation in this matter, I am,

Sincerely yours,

Robert Leonard, Attorney at Law

■ ■ ■

DECEMBER 12, 1973

Dear Mr. Leonard,

This is in response to your recent inquiry regarding our patient, Otis James. Since being transferred to our hospital from Ypsilanti, he has been unpredictable, threatening, and has required seclusion and close supervision. His thinking is confused and unrealistic, and he appears to be hallucinating. He is receiving tranquillizing medication for his condition at the present time. Although our diagnostic evaluation has not yet been completed, his condition is tentatively diagnosed as that of schizophrenia. We cannot estimate the duration of this condition.

In view of the fact that Mr. James was transferred to our hospital because of disturbed behavior which indicated a need for treatment in a maximum security setting, we cannot presently recommend transfer or release. If his relatives should care to contact us within six months, we will then be willing to consider a transfer provided his adjustment here has been satisfactory.

We are enclosing a copy of the permanent commitment order entered by the Wayne Country Probate Court. It is hoped this information is helpful to you and Mr. James's relatives.

Sincerely yours,

A. A. Fairman, MD

Medical Superintendent

■   ■   ■

DECEMBER 20, 1973

PROGRESS NOTE: This patient has no insight into his illness. On the ward he is uncooperative and refuses to take his medication. He is combative and threatening to the staff. He appears dangerous. Feelings are released primarily in the form of aggression which he projects primarily onto other individuals . . . speaks constantly of the Black Muslim group . . . sexually he is weak and inadequate. . . . The diagnosis is schizophrenia, paranoid type. Prognosis is poor.

Sylvan Cabrioto, MD

■   ■   ■

FEBRUARY 9, 1974

Dear Staff at Ionia State Hospital,

This communication is in regard to a patient named AR Karim/Otis James. I can feel his agony, you people are not helping him and probably never will.

I am writing the Mayor, Governor, Congress of the United States, Detroit Medical Association, the Michigan Senator, the Congressman for that District, Detroit Bar Association, also to President Nixon. I wrote him first. Also last but not least the United Nations. And I write to you, for my brother's freedom.

If he is healthy and has served his time then why don't you release him? You are playing with the life of a young man who has done you no harm, only prepared to risk his life for this country. It could be your life or your brother one day that may be on the receiving end of the line. I ask you honestly, to free him.

Please settle this matter before it gets out of hand.

Gerald James

CHAPTER 21

Something Else Instead

END OF AN ERA: State Hospital Now an Official Prison
Ionia Sentinel-Standard, January 11, 1977

IONIA—MONDAY afternoon marked the final day of life for Ionia Riverside Center as a mental health institution.

As of 4 pm, the latest mental health patients were transferred to the New Riverside center in Dimondale, according to William Abshire, director of the Riverside Correctional Facility.

Callers to the Riverside Center are now greeted with "Good Morning, Riverside Correctional Facility—may I help you?" something which just began Tuesday, according to Abshire. While Tuesday will still be devoted to moving records and supplies, Riverside will officially become a prison on Wednesday, when the first bus will arrive from the trustee division at Jackson.

"I'm glad we're able to start functioning as a full-time correctional facility," said Abshire on Tuesday morning. "Of course, there's still some staff moving stuff—materials, medical records, and mental health records."

He noted the new prison will still be running two more corrections officer schools for 51 employees not yet oriented to their new jobs. "Ten buildings we'll occupy immediately, then nine, then eleven," he explained. "That leaves seven with extensive work still to be done on the locking system."

Meanwhile, Ionia State Hospital Director Robert Kilpatrick said Tuesday morning all mental health personnel will be out of the Ionia grounds by 6 pm Tuesday.[1]

PART VI

Remnants

FIG. 19 *The Riverside Correctional Facility, in Ionia, Michigan, occupies the site previously inhabited by the Ionia State Hospital for the Criminally Insane. (Photograph by Jonathan Metzl)*

CHAPTER 22

Locked Away

IONIA, MICHIGAN, IS A TOWN of 10,569 residents whose claim to fame these days, besides the Chili-Dawg Challenge and the Ionia Free Fair, is a sprawling set of prisons that occupy the high ground overlooking the Grand River Valley. The expansive campus includes such notorious institutions as the Ionia Maximum Security Facility, aka Ionia Max, the Michigan Reformatory, the Richard A. Handlon Michigan Training Unit for Youthful Offenders, and the Riverside Correctional Facility.

In 2002, Ionia tied Huntsville, Texas, as the U.S. city with the most prison facilities. As the *Detroit News* reporter Francis Donnelly observed at the time, "when this world of servitude collides with that of freedom, Ionia takes on the look of a Norman Rockwell painting defaced by Quentin Tarantino."[1]

You might drive through on a sunny day and never have a clue about Ionia's *other* past. The past immured even from a town whose main currency is incarceration. The past about which townsfolk, when you bring it up in polite conversation, seem surprised, or curious, or unaware.

One set of clues lives on the grounds of the Riverside facility, a 966-bed, closed-custody prison for violent male offenders. From afar, Riverside appears not unlike any other level-2 prison in Michigan. Double fences, electronic detection systems, and spirals of razor-ribbon wire surround the perimeter. Patrol vehicles circle on constant lookout for infrequent escapees. Gun towers with armed guards provide additional layers of security. A booming male voice on a megaphone implores prisoners to move quickly through the yard.[2]

Step closer and several of the buildings in the compound stand out. They appear older, more solid and wise. These brick buildings only begrudgingly wear the silver barbed wire that covers their facades. Shiny bravado, the older buildings say, that undermines rather than enhances the art of containment.

Meanwhile, several flights of cobblestone stairs emerge from slopes in the ground, and lead, randomly, to nowhere. Fragments of old stone fences stand sentry over nothing. An elaborate creek bed winds elegantly beside the driveway, complete with a waterwheel and small waterfall. What type of prison architect constructs steps to nowhere, one wonders, or places a pastoral waterfall within a landscape otherwise dominated by intimidation?

Such structures seem out of place in a modern-day high-security prison because, of course, they are. They are artifacts left by the previous tenants of this land. They are stone and mortar crumbs of institutional memory, devoid, as stones often are, of the ability to resist rearticulation. Or reverse gentrification. Or time. They are shards of the asylum.

CHAPTER 23

Diversity

IONIA IS ALSO A TOWN marked by a particular form of Midwestern multi-culturalism.

Walk down Main Street, and the people you encounter at the café, the restaurants, the courthouse, the library, the hotel, the gas station and seem-ingly everyplace else seem exceedingly white. White like you, if you are me. White like Ionia used to be. "There were no black people that lived in Ionia in the 1970s," a former hospital employee and lifelong resident claimed at the end of an oral history interview. "Wait, there was that one family that lived outside of town, north of town. What was their name?"[1]

The whiteness is not surprising. Like most of rural Michigan, Ionia is dominated by people who self-identify as such. A 2004 study described the noninstitutionalized population of Ionia as 97 percent white, 0 percent black, and 2 percent Latino.[2]

But the whiteness is also a mirage. According to Ionia's 2000 U.S. Census information Web site, "approximately 29% of Ionia is non-white." The Web site actually boasts that "a diverse population is one of the features of the city . . . Ionia rates in the top 3% of Michigan cities for racial diversity." The page lists many other census statistics that seem entirely at odds with the Io-nia you have just seen. Ionia is 21.9 percent African American. Only 25 per-cent of adults are married. The site also explains that "the town is noted for its large share of males," a share that according to the census comprises fully 61.8 percent of the population.[3]

We often think of racial diversity, and indeed of race itself, as an observ-able characteristic. We walk into a room, or a school, or a nightclub, or a town, and see its diversity before almost anything else. This notion of diver-sity tells us about others and about ourselves, about if we fit in or if we do not. About if we should stay or if we should go. But the census reveals how diversity is also defined by indiscernibility; or, by those Ionians you see on a drive through town, as well as those you specifically do not see because, of course, they are locked away.

CHAPTER 24

Inside

RIVERSIDE CORRECTIONAL FACILITY OWES its existence to many factors
unrelated to the DSM, Alice Wilson, or Abdul-Rasheed Karim. The facility
opened during the height of an unprecedented expansion in the American
prison system that occurred, not ironically, in the aftermath of deinstitutionalization. In 1974, state and federal prisons held 218,000 people. By the year
2000, this number had exploded to over 1.3 million. Such growth went hand
in hand with a strategy of so-called economic salvation through incarceration, in which rural towns throughout the United States revived stalled economies by building new facilities or, as with Riverside, by converting existing
structures to meet the country's expanding penal needs.[1]

Riverside also stands as tragic end point to the narrative arcs I have traced
in this book. The first narrative is that of schizophrenia, and of the evolving
belief over the latter half of the twentieth century that symptoms of the illness include hostility, aggression, and rage. The second narrative concerns
increasing levels of security—or, perhaps more aptly, anxiety—that surround
institutions that house afflicted individuals, as represented by changes at the
Ionia State Hospital for the Criminally Insane. I have argued that these two
histories grew together through particular historical relationships to "race,"
here defined in tension between the pathologized races of patients and protesters cast within the system and the normalized races of those outside.

Both narratives were much on my mind when I visited Riverside prison
in the late summer of 2007. My trip capped a year-long negotiation that made
access to the hospital files seem straightforward by comparison. Prisoners
spend much of their time scheming to leave Riverside, legally or otherwise.
Guards recounted several plots, including a spoon-dug tunnel, visits from a
bogus pastor, and a bait-and-switch from a well-meaning friend. Some part
of me felt, melodramatically, as if I had worked nearly as hard to get in. Calls,
letters, and smoke signals to the warden's office. Interactions with the State
Board of Corrections. Communiqués to my senator. "I wish only to study
the hospital, not the prison" was my nearly honest stump speech. "We allow
no academics" would have been one possible answer. "Homeland security"

would have been another. Instead, the constant reply was: "Please wait for a reply. Someone will get right back to you. It's looking good." Followed by silence. Not the silence of night, or a library, or a country road. But the silence of an institution familiar with wasted time.

In the fourteenth month came a surprisingly cordial rejoinder: "Sir, you are clear to tour the facility. We will need the following information to complete a LEIN background check prior to the tour: Your full name. Your driver's license number. Your height. Your weight. Eye color. Race. Date of birth. Next, please select a proposed date and time for your tour. Look forward to hearing from you."[2]

On October 19, I drove north from Ann Arbor for the first of several well-chaperoned tours. As I drove, I reminded myself that the Ionia I knew from archived records, pictures, and articles was not the same structure as Riverside, circa 2007. When the hospital closed in 1977, the state supposedly razed most of the structures inside the compound. And the staff underwent a nearly complete turnover, as did the administration.[3]

Riverside's transition was thus often described with a rhetoric of complete fissure from the past. For instance, throughout the late 1970s, front-page articles in the *Ionia Sentinel Standard* touted ways in which the prison complex completely replaced the psychiatric one. "Riverside Closing Approved," read a headline on September 4, 1976, above an article that explained how "Riverside Center, a part of the Ionia state hospital complex, is to be closed . . . the transfer of the patients is expected to be made as soon as possible." Several weeks later, an article titled "Ionia Residents Give Views About Institutional Changes," described local anxieties about the loss of jobs. "It was a mistake," one Ionia employee is quoted as saying, "to have gone ahead and changed the whole program of the mental health department like this." "Building Demolition Is Scheduled," the paper announced on September 18, beneath a lead picture of demolition machinery at the hospital site. "Doomed for Destruction," read the caption. "Everything will be gone." One week later, front-page photos of wrecking balls and rubble appeared above captions that explained how "hydraulic 'clambuckets' bit greedily into wreckage . . . removing great chunks of debris at a time." "Three-ton wrecking balls ripped into building five at Riverside center," an accompanying article detailed, "giving emphatic reality to the center's changeover to a prison facility . . . the air was filled with the smoke and dust of decades, rudely disturbed by wrecking crews."[4]

I heard much the same message in my correspondence with prison officials in the months leading up to my visit. "Mental health was completely replaced by corrections," the administrator in the warden's office told me. "There's really nothing left from those days."[5]

As I soon learned, such claims spoke to an on-the-ground reality beyond the fact that the hospital closed and the prison opened. From a functional perspective, hospitals and prisons are not the same things, and one would be ill advised to think otherwise. A hospital, even a hospital for insane criminals, operates on the assumption that its inhabitants suffer from illnesses. Palliation, recovery, and reintegration are viable, if elusive goals. But a prison runs on the logic of containment—containment of prisoners from the outside world, and containment of bodies and emotions there within. As a psychiatrist, I felt comfortable with the pressures of the former institution. Resistance to treatment. Concern about other patients. Anger about involuntary commitment. But the tension of a prison was something altogether different. Razor wire. Patrol cars. Mistrust that shaped even friendly interactions. Volatility constantly an option, even in moments of calm.

However, I was struck repeatedly over the course of my visit not by Riverside's disjuncture from the past, but by its continuity with it. Administrators, prisoners, and guards seemed surrounded by shards of the very past that the *Sentinel Standard* claimed had been bulldozed and carted away. Far from functioning as wreckage or debris, these leftovers shaped important aspects of the prison's function and its identity.

Buildings and landscapes were the most immediate points of overlap between past and present. For instance, from records dating back to the 1920s, I knew that Ionia superintendents long considered driveway beautification as vital to the hospital's public image. Countless state funds and untold patient hours helped maintain the winding drive from the county road to the treatment complex, even as conditions within the institution decayed. The state archive contained troves of pictures of patients whose paths to sanity were paved through supervised construction of the driveway's stone creek bed, landscaped hills, groves of pine and oak trees, elaborate flower beds, and Ionia Hospital's signature waterwheel.

I turned off Riverside Drive onto the winding driveway, and there it all was. Water flowed through the perfectly maintained creek bed. The wheel churned. The fall lawn lay green and leafless. And legions of orange-clad prisoners worked, under the close supervision of guards, with mowers, rakes, shovels, and other plowshares.

The scene struck me as beyond surreal. Perhaps idyllic landscapes outside asylums once assuaged public guilt or anxiety. How bad can it be in *there*, the logic implied, if the part we see is so manicured and lovely? We should not feel accountable for locking people away in such a place. Or, we should not feel threatened by this structure in the midst of our town. Today, however, in the aftermath of Attica and Guantánamo, we seem long past self-reproach. I felt certain that if built today, the road to Riverside prison would be marked by barricades and concrete. But history provided flower beds, water, and an endless supply of free labor, and the prison administration clearly went with the flow.

The end of the driveway yielded an even bigger déjá vu: the Ionia Hospital administration building remained fully intact. The massive brick structure opened to great fanfare in June 1967. At the time, local publications hailed the building as a symbol of the hospital's future. "Ionia State Hospital's new administration building is now in full use following recent dedication ceremonies," an article in the *County Bulletin* bragged. "The two-story structure, built and furnished at a cost of $750,000, houses 45 offices and a number of other facilities." When the hospital closed, area newspapers printed letters from citizens enraged by the wasted cost. I assumed that wrecking balls determined the building's ultimate fate. But it now stood before me, fully operational and intact. Even the signage at front, reading ADMINISTRATION BUILDING remained. As far as I could tell, the only evidence of change over time—besides corrections guards mulling near the door—were the spools upon spools of razor wire that covered the building and connected it laterally to armed sentry towers.[6]

I walked inside. A guard marked my hand with a fluorescent pen. Another checked my identification, patted me down, and then worked a metal-detecting wand. I met the administrators who were to be my guides. Neither reticent nor wary, the two men were entirely accommodating (I later learned that the warden had an interest in history and had encouraged their participation). We passed through a series of locked chambers, entered into the prison complex, and toured the facility for the next five hours. We traversed wards, dining halls, and the prison yard. We went on rounds with guards. We spoke to prisoners. We toured the security perimeter, the workshop, and the prison hospital.

I was acutely aware of being interpolated into the very power structure I had spent the past years critiquing. I was a psychiatrist walking through the Ionia compound flanked by guards. "Who is that white man in a tie?" a prisoner asked. That white man in a tie, I could not deny, was me.

I also realized that the continuities between past and present that were so evident outside the prison extended inside as well. While much was new, practically every turn revealed some structure or sign that the prison for male offenders was once a hospital for insane criminals. Erstwhile hospital wards seamlessly functioned as prison wards. Centrally placed nursing stations became central guard posts, ideally situated to allow panoptic surveillance of daily life. Dining halls built so that doctors could observe their patients remained fully operational at meal times. A recreational yard that encouraged sanity through exercise worked well as a field that, as one guard told me, hosted occasional fights between prisoners or gangs. "The old buildings have some dangerous blind spots," a guard told me while explaining the intricacies of modern-day surveillance. "But they are very well made—we don't build like this anymore."[7]

Bodies, and particularly racialized bodies, seemed another point on the historical line from patients to prisoners. To recall, during the first half of the twentieth century, the Ionia census reflected the composition of the county in which it was situated. The hospital identified the majority of its inhabitants as "U.S.-White" and from rural environs, and housed a fair number of women. Over the 1960s and 1970s, however, Ionia Hospital's population became increasingly dissimilar from Ionia per se, and the tensions of the asylum increasingly mirrored Samuel Fuller's urban "street" from *Shock Corridor* more than the gendered, Freudian *Snake Pit* described by Mary Jane Ward. By the time of the transition, the face sheets of the majority of Ionia patients described volatile African American men from Detroit; and the increasingly black hospital in the midst of steadfastly white surroundings signaled the maintenance of sanity as well as of a particular racial order.

Riverside's racial demographics clearly perpetuated those from the Ionia hospital. Like most Michigan prisons, roughly 65 percent of Riverside prisoners were African American men, even though African Americans comprise no more than 14 percent of Michigan's overall population. These men were exceedingly likely to be convicted of so-called assaultive crimes. According to the nonprofit group Injustice Line, such imbalances reflected a prison system in which, "if you are a black person in Michigan, your chances of being a prison inmate during any given year are $8\frac{2}{3}$ times higher than the chances of a white person in Michigan being a prison inmate during that same period."[8]

Riverside's racial configuration impacted prison life in expected and surprising ways. The administration clearly made concerted efforts to employ a diverse corpus of guards, and every ward I visited had at least one African American corrections officer. At the same time, prisoners imposed their own systems of segregation as a means of survival. Black gangs and white gangs protected their own and fought each other. Everyone knew that the dining halls were divided into black and white sections—a longtime employee recalled only one instance in which the color line was crossed, leading to a fight. African American prisoners seemed acutely aware of the implications of their geographical displacement in ways that reflected and inverted the racial anxieties of Ionia itself. "It is safer for me as a black man to be an inmate in this dangerous prison," a man told me, "than for me to drive as a free black man through this scary white town . . . the police stop you just for being black."

Attitudes about mental illness were the most salient holdovers from Ionia. Guards considered persons with schizophrenia the most volatile and unpredictable inmates in the prison. Practically every guard I spoke with told a story about the volatility of "RTPs." The acronym officially stood for the Residential Treatment Program for Mentally Ill Prisoners that had long resided at Riverview. Over time, RTP became a shorthand way for the guards to refer to the prisoners themselves. "A schizophrenic RTP came at me with a knife one time. I have no idea where he got it," said one guard. "We had one RTP guy who cut his stomach open—that's psychotic," said another. Concern about RTPs was so prevalent that, according to the prison legal officer, removal of the treatment program several years prior was the key factor leading to Riverside's transition from a level-4 to a level-2 facility.

From an academic perspective, continuances between Ionia and Riverview were far from surprising. Historians, sociologists, and other social critics have long studied similarities between asylums and prisons. Erving Goffman, Gerald Grob, David Rothman, Nancy Tomes, and Thomas Szasz are but of few of the scholars who have demonstrated the totalizing functions of both institutions. Goffman, for instance, discusses the similar ways in which mental hospitals and prisons regulate and subordinate the lives of individuals there within, while Szasz uses the term *asylum-prisons* to describe singularity of purpose. Meanwhile, Foucault argues that prisons and psychiatric hospitals work within the same disciplinary system to produce particular subjects. His notion of *delinquency,* a category of persons produced at the nexus of medicine, psychology, and criminology, seems particularly useful for explaining the logic whereby institutions use psychiatry and the human sciences to justify the containment of criminals, schizophrenics, protesters, and others whose abnormality is deemed threatening to the state.[9]

More recently, the law professor Bernard Harcourt describes a *continuity of confinement* in which persons once placed in mental institutions for exhibiting certain behaviors now end up in penal facilities instead. "It should be clear," he writes, "why there is such a large proportion of mentally ill persons in our prisons: individuals who used to be tracked for mental health treatment are now getting a one-way ticket to jail."[10]

What was surprising, however, was the forgetting. Prison guards entered work each day through a building constructed as a mental hospital. Convicts traversed a yard still fresh with the footprints of patients. A walled institution within a rural white town contained violent black men and RTP schizophrenics. In this sense, Riverside did not merely look like Ionia; Riverside functioned like Ionia.

Yet an institution built on memories claimed to have no institutional memory. And the rhetoric of replacement blocked access to precisely those vestiges that suggested that which came before. Is there anyone at Riverside who might remember the transition? I asked. Or, do people talk about this prison as having once been a psychiatric hospital? Or, how did things get to be this way?

There is nothing left from that time, I was told in a thousand different ways. Corrections replaced mental health. The records are all in Lansing. We are something else now. It was as if a sign hung over the institution: NOT A MENTAL HOSPITAL.

On my way out, I recalled that I had brought reprints from the Ionia State Hospital photo archive with me for the tour. I took a stack of images from my bag. Some showed the Administration Building, in front of which I now stood. Others revealed smiling orderlies on the wards. Still others had patients working the land. The people in the black-and-white images looked of a different era. Crew cuts, horn-rimmed glasses, too-tight checkered shirts. But the structures appeared markedly, timelessly the same.

A crowd of guards walked by, in full uniforms complete with Tasers and batons. They stopped to look. Their intentions were not corrective. They were curious.

"Are these of the hospital?" "I want to see!" "The old buildings haven't changed at all!" "I work on that same floor." "Look at the Admin building!" "That guy looks so familiar!" The pictures eagerly passed.

"These are amazing," said a guard looking over my shoulder. "Can I get copies? I want to show my wife."

AUTHOR'S ADDENDUM

Several months after my visit, in a cost-cutting move, the Michigan legislature closed the Riverside prison and transferred the prisoners, staff, and administration to another facility. The move was a homecoming of sorts: the state moved Riverside to the campus of the nearby Michigan Reformatory, which had been refurbished and security updated to accommodate violent offenders. To recall, the reformatory was the original home of the Ionia State Hospital from 1885 1890. Idem, the same.

CHAPTER 25

Remnants

A REMNANT IS A FRAGMENT, a shard, a vestige. A left-over piece.

Certain definitions of the term emphasize tactile, observable, or demonstrable matter. A remnant is "that which remains or is left of a thing or things after the removal of a portion; the remainder, rest, residue; now applied only to a small remaining quantity," says the *Oxford English Dictionary*.[1]

Other definitions focus on the archeological function of remnants, and the ways they illuminate seemingly extinct monoliths, masses, or tectonic plates. Astronomers envisage prior stellar constellations by studying supernova remnants. Consumers learn about long-lost ancestors by purchasing tests that analyze genetic remnants.[2]

A third usage implies, conversely, that remnants offer clues to histories that resist articulation, or retain valences because of their connections to specifically forgotten pasts. For Freud, our personalities are remnants of the very childhood crises that we spend the rest of our lives trying to disavow. Similarly, when the French psychoanalyst Jacques Lacan defined *objet petit a* as "the remnant left behind by the introduction of the Symbolic in the Real," he meant that our deepest desire is shaped by charged particles of a traumatic past that *needs* to be forgotten, and forever idealized, in order to enter into the adult world of language and communication.[3]

This third meaning seems the most useful for understanding the amnestic actions of people and institutions when race and schizophrenia are the topics of conversation. Present-day configurations are built on the stone and mortar of earlier moments of crisis. But usage depends, symptomatically, on forgetting; and forgetting is enabled by narratives that demand attention to the present even when the past returns in racialized dreams, hallucinations, and slips of the tongue. As is often the case with stigma, we are then left only with opinions, and with opinions that masquerade as facts.

Put another way, the rhetoric surrounding schizophrenia seems the last place in the world where one would find remnants of the American civil rights movement, and particularly of those aspects of the movement once deemed most threatening to the unity of the American nation. But it is precisely so.

Prisons are obvious sites of residence for such remnants. Not just Riverside prison, where ruins visibly structure daily life, but many other American prisons where ruins reside in the vapor trails of language, thought, and attitude. In the era of Alice Wilson, the notion that prisons were primary institutions for persons with schizophrenia would have seemed counterintuitive, if not crazy. This is not to say that incarceration did not occur, for it did—particularly to African Americans in the South. But asylums were the institutions of choice. To recall 1940s articles in the *American Journal of Psychiatry,* treatments assumed that persons with schizophrenia acted like unruly children who required stern guidance or reprimand. Regimens combined hydrotherapy and, all too often, abuse, with gardening chores, baseball, sewing class, and even shopping trips.

Today, however, shopping trips are decidedly not on the agenda. People diagnosed with schizophrenia in the United States are far more likely to reside in prisons than in psychiatric care facilities. Credible research also demonstrates that rates of schizophrenia in prisons are up to five times higher than in the population at large. The discrepancy is so great that Human Rights Watch, in a 2003 report titled "Ill-equipped: U.S. Prisons and Offenders with Mental Illness," describes prisons as underfunded, understaffed, "pseudo mental hospitals."[4]

According to the Human Rights Watch report, prison workers view their de facto mental-health provider status as inevitable and frustratingly resistant to change. But statistics clearly demonstrate that the present situation emerged at a precise moment in time. Bernard Harcourt usefully compiles data from the Federal Census Bureau, the Department of Health and Human Services, and the Bureau of Justice Statistics to contextualize the incarceration of people with schizophrenia within larger shifts from asylums to prisons that took place in the 1960s and 1970s.[5]

Psychiatrists' offices are another site of remnants. In the free world, far beyond solitary confinements or locked wards, psychiatrists and other health professionals diagnose schizophrenia in African American men far more frequently than in other groups of patients. For instance, to recall the preface of this book, the health-policy researcher John Zeber examined the nation's largest database of mentally ill military veterans, the VA National Psychosis Registry in 2004, looking for "ethnic differences in diagnosis." Zeber and his colleagues took as their starting point the assumption that schizophrenia is a genetic illness that occurs in 1 percent of any given population regardless of race, social class, or geographic location. And yet, once again, the research group found "striking racial differences" among the 134,523 veterans diag-

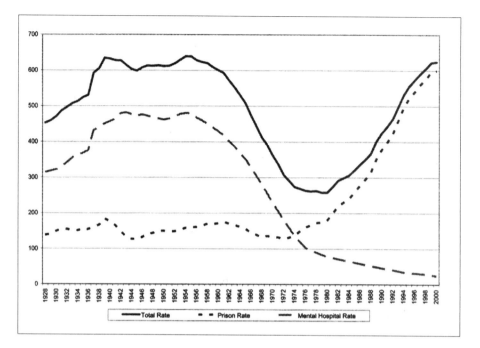

FIG. 20 *Institutionalization in the United States per 100,000. Rates of incarceration of mentally ill offenders rose dramatically in the early 1970s. (Source: Bernard E. Harcourt, "Asylum to Prison: Rethinking the Incarceration Revolution," Texas Law Review 84 (2006): 1752–86. Reproduced with permission of the author.)*

nosed with schizophrenia at the VA: those identified as African American were four times as likely to be diagnosed with schizophrenia as those identified as white.[6]

On June 28, 2005, the *Washington Post* reported Zeber's findings in a prominent cover story titled "Racial Disparities Found in Pinpointing Mental Illness." The article explained how Zeber's analysis uncovered no evidence "that black patients were any sicker than whites." Quoting Zeber, the article detailed how researchers found no significant difference between the two groups regarding severity of illness, financial status, combat exposure, substance use, or a host of "other variables." According to Zeber, "the only factor that was truly important was race."[7]

Racists might argue that such disparities suggest inevitable mental differences between distinct ethnic groups, as if a modern-day drapetomania. But such arguments have a hard time accounting for the fact that racial differences in diagnosis emerged at a predictable historical moment—in fact, the very moment that patients became prisoners in the 1960s and 1970s. Much of the current body of misdiagnosis literature emerged in the aftermath of a 1969 National Institute of Mental Health study that used DSM-II criteria to discover that "blacks have a 65% higher rate of schizophrenia than whites." Several years later came a host of published research reports describing racial disparities in schizophrenia diagnoses. A series of articles published in the *Archives of General Psychiatry* in 1973 uncovered that African American patients were "significantly more likely" than white patients to receive schizophrenia diagnoses, and "significantly less likely" than white patients to receive depression diagnoses. As a result of these and other findings, the research psychiatrists Carl Bell and F. M. Baker rightly note that "since the 1970s studies have reported overdiagnosis of schizophrenia and underdiagnosis of affective disorders among African Americans, compared with the overall prevalence of these disorders in the psychiatric population."[8]

People's minds are another site of remnants, or at least the parts of people's minds that stigmatize schizophrenia as a violent disorder even though compelling evidence suggests that the stigmatization is false. While schizophrenic violence is certainly not unheard of, a convincing body of research demonstrates that the actual number of violent acts committed by persons diagnosed with the illness are equal to, and in some cases lower than, rates of violence committed by everyone else. Psychologist Paul Nestor argues that certain symptoms of schizophrenia actually *reduce* a person's risk of violence over time. And social workers John Brekke and Cathy Prindle have shown that, far from posing a risk to others, "people diagnosed with schizophrenia have a *victimization* rate 65 to 130 percent higher than that of the general public." In their large-scale studies, the risk is exponentially greater that individuals diagnosed with schizophrenia will be assaulted by others rather than the other way around.[9]

And yet, stigmatizations of schizophrenia continue to rise in American culture. Such attitudes may seem the inevitable result of beliefs about the volatility of insanity that date back to burr holes or ships of fools. But the sociologists Bruce Link and Jo Phelan convincingly show that, in the United States, stigmatizations of schizophrenic and psychotic violence are decidedly phenomena of the second half of the twentieth century. In an extensive analysis of surveys of public conceptions about mental illness, Link, Phelan, and colleagues found that

> comparison of 1950 and 1996 results shows that conceptions of mental illness have broadened somewhat over this time period . . . but that

perceptions that mentally ill people are violent or frightening substantially increased, rather than decreased . . . the proportion who described a mentally ill person as being violent increased by nearly 2½ times between 1950 and 1996 . . . there has been a real move toward acceptance of many forms of mental illness as something that can happen to one of "us," but that people with psychosis remain a "them" who are more feared than they were half a century ago.[10]

It is of course the case that prisons, doctors' offices, and people's minds represent different *kinds,* to use the philosopher Ian Hacking's term, and are comprised of different social atoms, molecules, and networks. Each site is subject to dissimilar forces and economies. Comparison must be made with care.[11]

But incarceration, misinterpretation, and stigmatization are connected by the variable of *history.* All three of these dynamics emerged in the context of an intensely charged moment in time; a moment that, thinking of Lacan, might rightly be described as one of crisis in the United States. Marches. Riots. Fires. Threats to the status quo. As I have shown, the 1960s and 1970s represented an era when psychiatry's symbolic order shifted in immutable ways. *Protest* and *psychosis* merged in response to national events, and schizophrenia developed associations with aggression, hostility, rage, Black Power, and Malcolm X as a result.

Present-day configurations reflect this past. Incarcerating persons with schizophrenia only makes sense if schizophrenia is believed to be a disorder that requires containment rather than reintegration. And diagnosing schizophrenia as disproportionately violent or black only makes sense when using the definition of illness that came of age in the 1960s. Before that era, to recall, American psychiatry and the American mainstream often considered schizophrenia to be a broad, psychoneurotic personality reaction that was often suffered in silence.

Like the Ionia buildings at Riverside, these sites of inhabited remembrance are also connected by narratives that encourage collective forgetting. Biological psychiatry. The DSM-IV. Three strikes and you're out. Corrections replacing mental health. Cultural competency training. These and other rhetorics interrogate the present at the expense of the past. *Why do we have racially imbalanced rates of schizophrenia,* the psychiatrist asks, *when schizophrenia is a disorder of dopamine, and dopamine knows nothing of history? Why not execute schizophrenic killers,* the U.S. Supreme Court asks, *when they are clearly culpable of crimes? Why does the census say that a diverse population is one of the features of the city,* a visitor asks, *when Ionia feels so comfortable and safe?* Such questions depend on Lacanian acts of repression and foreclosure in their constructions of the real. For, as Lacan knew, and Heidegger before him, forgetting is neither random nor innocent. Instead, forgetting is an intensely political act, an act that is requisite for the construction of particular forms of truth.[12]

In other words, when read through remnants, incarceration, misidentification, and stigmatization are connected by a logic whereby focusing on the most observable characteristics—the patient, the prisoner, the diagnosis, the molecule, the crime—requires overlooking the historical constructedness of the frames that govern observation in the first place.

For instance, from the perspective of contemporary psychiatry, it makes no sense that schizophrenia is overdiagnosed in African Americans, or considered a violent disease. For one thing, psychiatry considers schizophrenia a biological illness that occurs in all people equally. For another, current versions of the DSM make no mention of aggression in the diagnostic criteria. Indeed, the third edition of the DSM, published in 1980, removed terms such as *anger, hostility,* or *projection* from the diagnostic criteria for schizophrenia, and quietly changed the text from the universal male pronouns of the DSM-II to a gender-neutral, passive, third-person voice. The DSM-III said of paranoid schizophrenia that "the essential features are persecutory or grandiose delusions, or hallucinations with a persecutory or grandiose content. In addition, delusional jealousy may also be present." The current, revised version of the DSM-IV, published in 2000, continues the trend by defining schizophrenia as a disorder marked by peculiarity, altered perceptions, social isolation, or withdrawal.

Characteristic symptoms: Two (or more) of the following, each present for a significant portion of time during a 1-month period (or less if successfully treated):

    (1) delusions

    (2) hallucinations

    (3) disorganized speech (e.g., frequent derailment or incoherence)

    (4) grossly disorganized or catatonic behavior

    (5) negative symptoms, i.e., affective flattening, alogia, or avolition.[13]

A person reading the DSM-IV might rightly surmise that there should be no imbalance, no stigma, no room for racialized misinterpretation if the criteria are correctly applied.

The problem with such logic, though, is that presentist frames control for remnants by ignoring them, or by treating their most visible, immediate manifestations. *Race-based misdiagnosis distorts the objective deployment of diagnostic criteria, so we must teach doctors to speak to patients of different races objectively.* Or, *aggression and hostility were problematic diagnostic terms, so we expunged them from the DSM.*

Again, though, remnants derive their charge from the unseen, the unspoken, the forgotten or overlooked. The black prison that hides behind the water wheel in the William Carlos Williams all-white town. The diagnosis imbued with racial valence long before doctor or patient enters the examination room. Or the structure that, in its structural violence, locks the most needy patients outside the clinic gates so that they cannot even obtain treatment in the first place. In these instances, clinical tensions mask social and political ones. And forgetting not only obfuscates history. It also affords doctors, Ionians, guards, historians, protesters, and others the delusion that they are not themselves prisoners of a rhetorical order, or practitioners of a process of anything but random change over time.

CHAPTER 26

Controllin' the Planet

ACCORDING TO FOUCAULT, ARBITER of things delusional, the setup is far from surprising. His schema suggests that prisons, clinics, and attitudes treat schizophrenia in similar ways because psychiatric discourse is central to decentralized power. In this formulation, incarcerating, misdiagnosing, or fearing persons with schizophrenia all serve the larger purpose of subjugating bodies and controlling populations. Framing the discussion as one concerned with the universal good of mental health simply renders the ideologies and mechanisms of what he calls biopower all the more impervious to critique.[1]

However, a key point of this book is that the white power structure is not the only site of remnants, and subjugation is not the only present-day discourse built on the valences of the past. Remnants also suffuse sites of resistance, and in this context they signify alternate relationships between insanity and the status quo.

Consider music, for example. Or, at least consider forms of popular music indexed by such comprehensive lyrics Web sites as Leo's Lyrics, HipHopDX, UrbanLyrics, and SongLyrics. Leo's Lyrics claims an archive of lyrics to "over 200,000 songs," while SongLyrics more hyperbolically boasts access to "over 4,000,000 tracks." These sites, and quite a few others, invite searches for specific words or phrases within songs. SongLyrics goes so far as to provide tips for the research-challenged.

- Choose a line or a phrase from the song that is unique and characteristic for this song.
- When searching in lyric text think of specific words in the song. Type words from the song that are rarely used in other songs. This will lead to faster and more exact search results. For example, use "placebo crawling dawning" (2.5 seconds to search, 1 result returned) instead of "a friend in need" (6.8 seconds to search, 126 results returned).[2]

It turns out that *depression* and *depressed* appear frequently in songs—far more frequently than *a friend in need*, or, for that matter, than *schizophrenia* or *schizophrenic*. According to Leo's, *depression* and *depressed* appear in 1,034 lyrics. As one might imagine, the uses are as disparate as metal is to folk. Yet trends emerge.

When *depression* or *depressed* reference mental illness, the recording artists are disproportionately white. Songs often allude to affect or emotions, particularly surrounding love relationships. In a surprising gender twist from the historical representation of depression as a white woman's illness, the singers of this intergenre subset are as likely to be men as women, and a good number of songs come from 1970s-era classic rock. For instance, in "Baby Get Your Head Screwed On," the artist formerly known as Cat Stevens empathizes with a woman whose lover has left her—"I know he's left, but don't be depressed"—by telling her that "if you're feelin' low, take it slow." In their megahit "Sister Golden Hair," America croons about the tensions between being friends with a woman and being potentially married to her with the line "Well I tried to make it Sunday, but I got so damn depressed." Art Garfunkel's "Grateful" sounds a similar refrain. When the singer feels his "spirits sink," he tells himself that "I can't stay depressed" when "I remember how I'm blessed."[3]

Current artists often associate depression with white middle-class ennui. For instance, the metalcore group Psychostick takes a parodic approach in its song "Prozak Milkshake." The singer self-critically intones that, after his mother would not allow him to attend a "rated R cool movie" with his friends, he became "depressed" and wrote the song, "to express everything that's wrong." Meanwhile, in corporeal rejection of historical stereotypes of depression as a disease of passive maternal femininity, folk sensation Ani DiFranco intones in "Pick Yer Nose," "i think shy is boring, i think depressed is too."[4]

According to Leo's, *schizophrenia* and *schizophrenic* appear in 135 songs. Here, as well, voices are overwhelmingly male. Yet one cannot help but notice the altered terrain. Artists are frequently identified as African American, often rappers or hip-hop artists, and actions and ideas replace affects. Competition between rappers is a familiar refrain. In "Rampage," the longtime Brentwood hip-hop artists EPMD, rapping with LL Cool J, boast that they smoke M.C.s because their rhyme style is "deadly psychopath or schizophrenic." In "Speak Ya Clout," another East Coast group, the duo Gang Starr, rhymes that they are "Schizophrenic with rhyme plus we're well organized" as a way of warning that they are "stepping rugged and tough." Similarly, in "Standing Ovation," Young Jeezy boasts of "Psychopathic wordplay, schizophrenic flow." And, in the intro track to his brilliant *Beautiful Rhyme,* Buffalo artist Eddie Haskill plays off of the schizophrenia-genius narrative of Sylvia Nasar's biography of John Nash, discussed in the next chapter of this book, to boast that his music is similar to *A Beautiful Mind* "in the sense that I'm a schizophrenic with rhymes."[5]

More frequent are references to physical altercation. In "16 on Death Row," 2Pac contemplates taking action against a witness and the police by warning that "I'm kind of schizophrenic, I'm in this shit to win it." In "Symptoms of Insanity," onetime Psychopathic Records artist Esham warns that, because of symptoms of insanity, "I'm quick to pull the trigger, hoe, schizophrenic, somebody panic." Rapping with Esham, Dayton Family rapper Bootleg menacingly raps that his schizophrenia causes him to "sleep wit' a glock."[6]

Other lyrics urge action in the face of perceived injustice. In "Hidden Crate," A.G. raps about the split of having made money through rap, while holding onto a "poor man's" anger, a condition he describes as a "schizophrenic state." Bizzy Bone's call to arms, "Thugz Cry," is another example. "Nigga, we represent the planet," he raps, "get schizophrenic and panic." And, in the multiartist hit "Everything," Busta Rhymes voices a similar call for action by rapping "Panic and schizophrenic, sylvy-atlantic, Wrap up your face in ceramic, goddammit we controllin' the planet."[7]

Any generalizations about lyrics should be made with high degrees of disclaimer. Lyrics are adjectives and abstractions, even when they are nouns. Lyrics depict bravado or mimesis or fantasy as often as they do actual events. As such, and like all poems, lyrics play to the multiplicities rather than the essences of meaning.

Caveats acknowledged, lyrics databases suggest that the racialization of diagnostic language in popular music mirrors the racialization of diagnoses in the real world. Depression appears a privileged position for those who have time. But schizophrenia is a threat, a crime in progress, an impulse of survival.

How does a diagnostic term coined by a Swiss psychiatrist in 1911 make its way into American rap lyrics nearly a century on? The most obvious answer is that schizophrenia retains its complex historical charge. Overtones of Sufic inspiration recall the alignment of schizophrenia with genius common in the 1920s, 1930s, and 1940s. To recall, popular media described writers and poets touched by schizophrenic grandiloquence, a form of madness that inspired brilliant, otherworldly prose. Similar connotations appear explicitly in Haskill's reference to *A Beautiful Mind,* and implicitly in EPMD's portrayal of a schizophrenic style so potent that it cuts like a knife, Jeezy's boast of schizophrenic flow, or Gang Starr's description of being schizophrenic with rhyme. Meanwhile, in "Thugz Cry" Bizzy Bone depicts the euphoria and the dysphoria of being obsessively trapped in language as a state of living "loco with vocals."

Of course, rap and hip-hop also rearticulate associations between schizophrenia and violence that emerged in the 1960s and 1970s. References to schizophrenic violence keep alive the notion that schizophrenia is a condition marked by uncontrollable aggression and hostility, only here these traits are glorified and sexualized rather than condemned. Get out of the way, the logic implies, because I am capable of anything.

One can rightly critique hip-hop artists for perpetuating stigma in these instances. Rap's mistaken gender politics have been well documented, but it might also be said that rap artists perpetuate the prevalent notion that schizophrenia is an illness marked by uncontrollable, and distinctly male, hostility and rage. The voices of African American women are tellingly missing from the sample, much as they are in many of the sources cited in chapters above. Schizophrenia is a man's anger, society says, and rap lyrics reinforce the message even as they decry the system.

Yet, such critiques also risk simplifying the multiple meanings of *schizophrenia,* and more importantly, of *schizophrenic,* in rap. As I've shown, popular American usage of these terms emerged from several rhetorical traditions. Psychiatry was one locale, but so was African American philosophical thought. The former discourse took its cues from Bleuler, Kraepelin, and the DSM, and subsequently defined schizophrenia as an illness that resided in patients. But the latter took from Du Bois, Frederick Douglass, Robert Williams, Fanon, and other theorists whose work helped code schizophrenia as a healthy adaptation to an insane, racist society. Martin Luther King used schizophrenia to urge nonviolent resistance. Amiri Baraka used the same term to encourage revolt. In both cases—and belying a historical reality often forgotten in our multicultural age—the goal was deeper than simply getting along. The goal was actual change.[8]

Remnants of this latter trajectory reverberate through rap, a musical form whose early innovators drew inspiration from the race politics of the 1960s and 1970s. Grandmaster Flash's classic 1982 song "The Message" and 1980s Public Enemy albums such as *By Any Means Necessary* or *It Takes a Nation of Millions to Hold Us Back* are but a few examples of rap's initial political engagement, a mantle brilliantly picked up by, for instance, the searing critique in Ice Cube's 2008, "Gangsta Rap Made Me Do It." Intended or not, use of the terms *schizophrenia* and *schizophrenic* connect 2Pac's fight against the legal system and Bizzy Bone's call for revolution to King, Du Bois, and also per-haps to Blues traditions in which going crazy was a way of resisting white authority during slavery. Meanwhile, Rhymes, Bone Thugs, and others turn Bromberg and Simon's 1968 notion of a protest psychosis on its head. Yes, we are black, male, and violent, rappers concur. But this violence is not our pathology—it is a response to yours. And, *Goddamnit we controllin' the planet.*[9]

If lyrics are in any way reflective of larger wholes, and if generalizable claims can be made from an admittedly unscientific sampling, then rap's rhymes suggest that *schizophrenia* and *schizophrenic* remain contested terms within an ongoing clinical-cultural dialectic. On one hand, schizophrenia articulates the expert opinion of the doctor, whose trained knowledge is req-uisite for a correct diagnosis. On the other hand, schizophrenia signifies a rejection of medical authority by a power vested in the people.

In no way do I mean to conflate black rappers with black patients. Rather, I wish to point out that rap's use of the terms *schizophrenia* and *schizophrenic* connotes not only a disease, but also an identity claimed in response to a sys-tem that misperceives survival strategies as insanity. "It was heartening for me to hear of your paranoia," the Reverend Wyatt Tee Walker said in 1969, "because it allows me to admit to the black community of our schizophrenia. We are desperately trying to survive in a racist society." *Idem the same* (aka, word), say African American rappers today, with a Steinian poetic repetition that uses the same words to highlight the ways in which current race strug-gles are also so very, very different.

Rap lyrics remind us that diagnosis is an inherently political interaction because diagnostic terminology is inherently politicized. Psychiatric defini-tions provide levels of clarity for patients and families struggling to under-stand painful life events. Psychiatric diagnoses also serve as the first steps toward treatment and palliation, if not complete cure. But wholesale accep-tance of psychiatric terms and frameworks involves entry into a potentially racially subjugating symbolic order in which biomedical definitions of illness supplant cultural ones.[10] Here, the doctor's diagnosis serves as the entry point into a cascade of reinforcement. Biomedical diagnoses become requisite for insurance company reimbursement. The longer patients stay in the system, the more diagnoses they accrue. Over time, persons with schizophrenia be-come *doubly* stigmatized, both by a diagnosis that carries poor prognosis, and by a medical system that forces acceptance of hegemonic descriptors of well-being at the expense of autobiographies of protest or survival. To enter the doctor's rhetorical system, rhetorically speaking, is to give up the fight.

All the while, it becomes ever-more difficult to contest the logic of diagnosis itself; or, as Fanon did, to use diagnosis to better understand not the patient, but the society in which he is forced to endure and get ahead.

In this sense, even a correct diagnosis is always already a misdiagnosis. And true cultural competence means more than understanding the ways in which difference shapes the expression of symptoms in other people. It also involves recognition of the ways in which we are ourselves symptomatic, doctors and patients both, of a set of enduring negotiations about the meanings of health, illness, and civil rights.

CHAPTER 27

Conclusion

A PATIENT WALKS INTO a doctor's office, the old joke goes. More aptly, a patient negotiates the bureaucracy and the paperwork and the waiting room delays before being led into the examination room. Then it is the doctor who enters.

What follows is a rhetorical narrowing. Open-ended questions give way to specific queries. Descriptions of generalized symptoms lead to close inspection of particular body parts. Hypotheses bring about lab tests. Only at the end of the process, it is assumed, does a generalized, differential diagnosis produce a specific diagnosis, followed by a planned intervention.

In an ideal world, such narrowing should winnow out stereotypes based on a patient's race, culture, class, gender, or other categories that are largely extraneous to the diagnostic process. We do not have separate categories for black or white schizophrenia, any more than we do for women's depression or poor person's narcolepsy. The fact that we make no such associations represents marked progress from earlier epochs, when, to recall, doctors believed that pauperism, spinsterism, negritude, onanism, and a host of other identities, lifestyles, economic conditions, or object choices caused particular forms of mental illness.

To be sure, cultural generalizations remain central to many doctor-patient interactions, and rightly so. Recognition of a patient's socioeconomic status helps a doctor consider possible risk factors for illnesses ranging from stroke to heart disease to anorexia nervosa. As scholars such as the academic psychiatrist Arthur Whaley point out, a patient's racial background can also affect the ways in which he or she experiences or expresses particular symptoms. Patients also frequently make group generalizations when selecting practitioners. Women who seek treatment with female obstetricians, or immigrants who visit family doctors from their home countries, do so out of the valid belief that health-care providers of similar backgrounds to their own might better understand their bodies and their concerns.[1]

Schizophrenia is far from the only case in which a patient's membership in a particular racial, cultural, gendered, or socioeconomic group correlates with worse care. Women notoriously are given more antidepressant and antianxiety medications than are men. Hispanic patients with chronic pain receive insufficient narcotic doses from their doctors. Black patients with diabetes or asthma fare worse than white patients with diabetes or asthma, even after controlling for socioeconomic differences and disease severity. And Hispanic, Native American, Asian and Pacific Islander, and South Asian patients all rate far lower than comparable white patients on a host of measures including physician-patient communication, access to care, and health-care coordination.[2]

One would think that these disparities should be relatively easy to fix. Issues such as race-based misdiagnosis evolve from cultural misperceptions on the part of doctors, the logic goes. If doctors and other health-care professionals misperceive cultural difference, or worse, think racist thoughts, then we should simply train them to think and act otherwise.

Such sentiments undergird the so-called cultural competency approach, which represents medicine's most sustained recent attempt to impart clinical understandings of the cultural and cross-cultural aspects of health care. In 2000, the Association of American Medical Colleges (AAMC) instructed American medical schools to teach students the skills of "understanding the manner in which people of diverse cultures and belief systems perceive health and illness and respond to various symptoms, diseases, and treatments." Around that same time, virtually every professional health-care provider organization added cultural competency to its list of requisite clinical skills. The American Psychiatric Association outlined sets of core "Cultural Competencies for the Clinical Interaction" for its members, while hospitals and clinics required cultural sensitivity training modules for all employed personnel. The hospital where I work tested clinicians on their mastery of sets of beliefs and behaviors that were allegedly specific to particular groups of patients such as "Asians," "Latinos," or "African Americans." Meanwhile, leading physicians such as Abraham Verghese argued that "bias in health care must be corrected not by medical ombudsmen, or by legislation, but by a focus on the individual—individual patients and individual doctors."[3]

The allure of such an approach seems obvious. We live in an increasingly multicultural world, and medical interactions have become increasingly multicultural as a result. Talking across cultural difference is exceedingly difficult under any circumstance, and all the more so when one of the participants in the conversation is under duress.

At the same time, the arguments traced in this book suggest that cultural competency misses the proverbial boat, and might even exacerbate cross-cultural disconnect, by reinforcing the very hierarchies it attempts to work against. For one thing, the discourse of cultural competency often assumes fixed definitions of culture, or conflates culture and race in problematic ways. Medicalized race categories are exceedingly complex, as the Ionia charts powerfully demonstrate: a person's racial identity may or may not be the same as the race category ascribed to that person by a doctor or a medical chart. Moreover, the tensions inherent in an interaction between a doctor from Cleveland and a patient from Thailand are not the same as those that arise between a white American doctor and an African American patient, and the two scenarios require different sensibilities. Such distinction is often lost not just in cultural competency criteria that collapse divergent forms of difference based on alterity from the norm, but also in emerging scientific approaches to cross-cultural medicine. Research in cross-cultural psycho-pharmacology, for instance, often uses social categories of difference, such as those derived from the U.S. census, to make biological claims about variances in drug metabolism among racial groups. This type of research often overlooks how census categories are comprised thorough self-identification rather than on (ever elusive) genetics, while at the same time positing that knowing what is happening to a racial group biologically tells us something about what is happening to them culturally. As researchers Jamie Brooks and Meredith King Ledford aptly put it, race-based genetic research thus constructs "biological reality" out of "social reality."[4]

Another problem is that, for understandable reasons, cultural competency presupposes biomedical interactions as the framework for interpersonal ones. Patients describe, while doctors listen, analyze, diagnose, and treat. Cultural competency shores up this framework by in effect empowering doctors to make another diagnosis when they enter the room: that of the patient's race, ethnicity, or culture. If not well-handled, a cultural competency approach risks conveying the altogether false notion that professional sensitivity training enables one person to achieve competent mastery over the beliefs, family structures, practices, or attitudes of another person. By so doing, cultural competency interactions oversimplify the complex ways in which people negotiate difference, a process that is based on the intersubjective responses of two participants rather than the diagnostic observations of just one.

Critics note that cultural competency's unidirectional flow reinforces racialized power grids while leaving the culture of the doctor free from diagnostic scrutiny. Medical educators Melanie Tervalon and Jann Murray-Garcia argue that cultural competency should be replaced by "cultural humility," a phrase that emphasizes respect across cultural boundaries along with the humbling premise, first developed by the philosopher Emmanuel Levinas, that the Other always lies beyond the comprehension of the self. The anthropologist Linda Hunt writes that in the cultural humility approach, "the most serious barrier to culturally appropriate care is not a lack of knowledge of the details of any given cultural orientation, but the providers' failure to develop self-awareness and a respectful attitude toward diverse points of view." Picking up this theme, pediatrician Sayantani DasGupta asserts that doctors who assume that their reading of a patient's narrative is the "definitive interpretation" risk closing themselves off to awareness of the patient's "valuable nuances and particularities."[5]

The most important limitation of the cultural competency approach is the idea that cultural differences can be resolved through individual interactions at all. Verghese, to recall, argues that clinical bias should be confronted through the actions of "individual patients and individual doctors," and even cultural humility proponents assume that moments of cultural discord need be addressed in the medical examination room, after physicians have received the requisite training.

My central argument in this book, however, has been that racialized assumptions and biases are historically embedded into the very DNA of healthcare delivery systems, and shape interactions and outcomes long before the participants appear on the scene. As such, I believe that focusing on the individual obscures the impact of the structural, while putting undue pressure on even well-intentioned patients or doctors to solve problems in ten-minute office visits that have taken decades or even centuries to evolve.

Structural violence is the term often used to describe how even seemingly benevolent social institutions can dominate, oppress, or exploit minority populations. The concept emerged in the 1960s. In an infamous 1969 article titled "Violence, Peace, and Peace Research," the Norwegian sociologist Johan Galtung described structural violence as the largely invisible process that separated a person's "actual, somatic, and mental realizations" from their "potential realizations." Similar sentiments lay behind Stokely Carmichael's 1968 description of *institutional racism* as the silent process whereby "established and respected forces in the society" worked to maintain the status quo through a set of institutions that were "destructive of human life."

Structural violence's present-day champion is the medical anthropologist Paul Farmer, who powerfully describes how even institutions ostensibly set up to help marginalized populations end up harming them, particularly by reinforcing rather than eliminating economic and health disparities. For Farmer, structural violence produces illness by creating "political economies of risk" in which particular populations are rendered vulnerable to disease because of economic, political, or cultural forces in addition to infectious or biological ones.[6]

Economies, attitudes, health-care systems, food distribution networks, legislations, policies, dictums, and zoning laws are but a few of the entities shown to perpetuate structural violence and institutional racism. My book has added another entry to this list: psychiatric diagnoses, and their oft-invisible racial hierarchies and histories. Undeniably, diagnoses aid afflicted persons by legitimizing their suffering and providing the first step toward treatment. Even the most stigmatized or debilitating psychiatric diagnosis thus represents categorical relief for the majority of patients. You are not alone, the diagnosis implies, and the experiences of others like you help us better understand the course of your illness and the interventions necessary to try to arrest its downward trajectory.

As we have seen, psychiatric diagnoses can also define, circumscribe, and contain abject populations in ways that harm people in these populations under the guise of helping them. Not coincidentally, these people are, in a Farmerian sense, already vulnerable; or, they reside in categories that elicit public antipathy or fear during particular moments of historical stress. Unruly housewives, for instance, or addicted war veterans, or inattentive children. Or angry black men. At the level of the structural unconscious, concerns about the actions or proclivities of such people impacts the ways in which we aggregate symptoms into diagnoses, and the ways in which certain populations come under our diagnostic purview as a result.

When viewed as such, the limitations of a cultural competency approach to clinical moments of cultural inquietude come into greater focus. Cultural competency concentrates entirely on the races, cultures, and backgrounds of the two participants in the room, and works to ease the diagnostic process through enhanced cross-cultural communication. But it practically trains doctors to remain blind to the ways in which the diagnoses themselves convey profoundly racial and cultural meanings. For instance, during the 1960s, the shifting frame surrounding paranoid schizophrenia led to the formation of the category of angry black male schizophrenic subjects. Cultural sensitivity training would have made the matter worse by helping doctors to overcome their cultural misperceptions, thereby easing the diagnostic encounter, leading eventually to ever more diagnosis. But those doctors would have had no way of recognizing that the diagnosis itself was part of the problem. Treating the individual only perpetuated the structural disease.[7]

Let me repeat that mental illness is real. I regularly encounter patients with symptoms such as auditory hallucinations, paranoia, delusions, mania, or social withdrawal. Some of these patients embody the very categories I have discussed in this book. Paramedics bring African American men from Detroit to the University of Michigan Psychiatric Emergency Room where I work. Some of these men hallucinate, others remain mute, while others feel, rightly or wrongly, that the state is out to get them. Other sets of patients force me to confront how my own preconceived stereotypes and expectations limit my clinical observations. Seemingly placid white secretaries who plot to bomb their neighbors or accomplished university professors from India who lock themselves in their bedrooms for weeks on end.

It would be nothing short of malpractice for me to assert that the symptoms suffered by these and other persons are inauthentic. "I've just written a book about the history of schizophrenia," malpractice me would unethically contend, "and I've learned that mental illness is socially and politically constructed. Thus we need to change the culture rather than treating the individual." Such an answer is as irresponsible as it is incorrect. Psychosis, mania, and a host of other symptoms result from biological or chemical anomalies in addition to social, environmental, or even iatrogenic ones. Psychiatry has an absolute responsibility, a social contract, to ease such suffering no matter the cause, whether through social support, talk therapy, medications, safe housing, ongoing research, or all of the above.

Yet researching and writing this book has taught me how, for better and sometimes for worse, the frames aggregating certain symptoms into particular psychiatric diagnoses exist in an ongoing state of flux. Recognizing such a process does not mean that psychiatrists should vote about whether a particular diagnosis is either socially constructed or real. Indeed, the polarizing dichotomy serves no one, and makes it harder to see how mental illness is always already both. Rather, psychiatrists should remain continually aware of how social contexts, historical moments, and violent structures shape perceptions of psychiatric reality. Psychiatry, in other words, must persist in its pursuit of the ontology of mental illness. But it must also develop better methods for recognizing what, or who, its ontologies, categories, and provider networks leave out.

There is no easy answer to the question of how a profession might develop what might be called structural competency, no magic bullet for imparting the humility needed to observe forces that shape interactions but remain elusive to the interactants. Psychiatry, however, has a rich history of uncovering the unseen, and a long tradition of exploring how here-and-now exchanges reflect evanescent expectations and desires. Perhaps libratory promise exists not in rejecting its past through high-resolution brain scans, but in recuperating at least part of the expertise required to understand the biological in the context of the structural or the historical or the political.

Undoubtedly the most important interventions are those that correct structural disparities and socialize political economies of risk. Current efforts at national health reform, parity coverage for mental illness, and expanded social support services promise betterment if not outright change. Vital to this effort, doctors, policy experts, and organizations have shifted focus from racial attitudes to race-based health disparities in order to address underlying barriers to care. Former U.S. surgeon general David Satcher's report *Mental Health: Culture, Race, and Ethnicity* argues for profound reorganization of the structure of health-care delivery systems in order to change the ways in which "racial and ethnic minorities bear a greater burden from unmet mental health needs and thus suffer a greater loss to their overall health and productivity." The Henry J. Kaiser Family Foundation's 2008 report, *Eliminating Racial/Ethnic Disparities in Health Care: What are the Options?* similarly argues that racial and ethnic health-care disparities need be addressed through improvements in insurance coverage, access, and quality of care.[8]

Psychiatry's first steps away from economic interdependence with pharmaceutical companies will also help. While psychopharmaceuticals help millions of people live their lives, the rhetorics surrounding these pharmaceuticals often create two-tier systems that promote particular diseases while rendering other diseases as invisible. Advertisements for brand-name pharmaceutical treatments for depressive and anxiety disorders flood television, magazines, newspapers, and the Internet, for instance, while advertisements for antipsychotic medications rarely appear outside of professional journals. Critics of drug ads note that these strategies emphasize outpatient treatments for insured persons who can afford them. Indeed, the few campaigns that tout antipsychotic medications advertise the medications not as anti-schizophrenia treatments for the poor or indigent, but as off-label adjunct therapies for anxiety or insomnia in white, middle-class women.[9]

Psychiatry would also benefit from more ongoing, engaged, political analysis of the ways in which cultural forces impact diagnostic categories. Even though the profession has moved well beyond the DSM-II, which described paranoid schizophrenia as an illness of anger, hostility, and projection and posited homosexuality as a mental disease, diagnosis-based controversies still arise with regularity. At these times, and indeed in the many other silent instances where the culture of the doctor inadvertently shapes the diagnosis of the patient, psychiatry's understanding is hampered both by presentist science that locates mental illness strictly within the brains of patients, and by a five-axis diagnostic system that asks clinicians to separate real mental illness on Axis I from "psychosocial, environmental, and cultural" factors on Axis IV. As we have seen, culture and diagnosis are not so readily detached.[10]

Such a conversation, were it to take place, would also benefit from productive consideration of the limits of psychiatric expertise. In the 1960s, psychiatry got into trouble for playing along with the notion that its diagnostic tools and therapeutic modalities assuaged social "pathologies" in addition to clinical ones. Research articles deployed psychiatric language to diagnose urban unrest, while pharmaceutical advertisements posited antipsychotic medications as treatments for angry black men in the streets. When the dust settled, it turned out to be a reach: the diagnoses were wrong, Haldol had little impact beyond the asylum walls, and doctors' abilities to help people suffered from their profession's attempts to position itself as an authority on a situation it knew little about. Present-day psychiatry has surely learned from these mistakes. Current versions of the DSM-Instruct clinicians to treat only those symptoms observed in the exam room, and the profession as a whole sounds apolitical about national matters almost to a fault. Yet, in very different ways, the pressures of medicalization push diagnostic boundaries constantly outward. Pharma ads tout antidepressants as cures for troubled marital relationships, while popular desires for these medications frequently outpace actual physiological effects. At these times and others, the question that was not asked in the 1960s needs to be continually addressed: what mechanisms exist for defining what is *not* a psychiatric disease, in addition to defining what is?

Anti-stigma and public information campaigns might also benefit from considering how race-based historical tensions impact attitudes about mental illness. Most published stigma studies assert that people who stigmatize schizophrenia should be taught that the illness is a biomedical condition similar to diabetes or heart disease. In 2004, psychologist Amy Watson and colleagues found in a vignette study that Chicago police officers were much more likely to ascribe violent intent to "minimally violent" perpetrators if those perpetrators were described as having schizophrenia. The researchers argued that police should undergo expanded educational training about how mental illnesses are real, biologically based diseases. Organizations such as the National Alliance on Mental Illness (NAMI) similarly fund public information campaigns that emphasize how schizophrenia is an illness "twice as common as HIV/AIDS. It does not discriminate. It strikes people of all races and both genders, and cuts across all social and economic classes."[11]

History suggests, however, that at least part of the stigma against schizophrenia, and particularly negative beliefs about schizophrenic violence, emerged precisely because of such discrimination. Often invisibly, this history continues to impact attitudes in the present day. The vignettes in Watson's police study made no mention of race, for instance, but the officers read them through a set of clearly racial assumptions. Here, the lesson is not that stigma directly links schizophrenia to black bodies. Rather, stigma itself is racialized in ways that shape perceptions about schizophrenia more broadly. In this sense, teaching police officers, members of the general public, doctors, or other citizens about mental illness would address only half of the reason why people might associate schizophrenia with violence. In the transformation from clinical diagnosis to cultural trope to protest metaphor, schizophrenia developed meanings associated with race as well.

Stigma is of course gendered as well, in as much as stigmatizations of race intersect with those of gender, and of class. This system makes it very easy to see connections between fears of violence, negative beliefs about mental illness, and cultural anxiety about angry black men. We have a historic lexicon that helps us to identify these men and to contain them. As I have suggested at various points throughout this book, and not often enough, such representational strategies make it harder to see those people who fall outside of stereotypes or mass-depictions. African American women, for instance, remain largely invisible in the sources I examine, from hospital charts to media depictions to rap lyrics. Again, such invisibility is the focus of vital work coming out of African American studies, feminist studies, and political science. As but one example, the political scientist Melissa Harris-Lacewell explores the negative psychological consequences of the "myth" of the domineering, never-depressed black woman and its correlation to a cultural paucity of terms to describe black women's emotions, needs, or desires. I am in no way suggesting that stigma should be all-inclusive. Rather, the absence of cultural rhetoric regarding black women's mental illness likely represents the reality that it is harder for these women to have their suffering validated, or to get help.[12]

Recognizing stigma's racial undercurrents would also allow psychiatry and patient activist groups to more thoughtfully critique mainstream depictions of schizophrenic illness. Stigmatizing media accounts of schizophrenic crime have been well documented. But almost no attention has been paid to the racial assumptions of allegedly *destigmatizing* representations, and of decisions regarding which stories American culture holds up as destigmatizing, and which stories it chooses to suppress.[13]

For instance, the most visible schizophrenia narrative of recent memory is Sylvia Nasar's 1998 biography, *A Beautiful Mind: The Life of Mathematical Genius and Nobel Laureate John Nash,* which later became a Ron Howard film. As is now well known, the complex book, and oft-oversimplified film, tell the story of mathematician John Nash, who, at twenty-one, developed a model for noncooperative game theory that later helped explain the actions of businesses, corporations, and international trade organizations. Soon thereafter, delusions, auditory hallucinations, paranoia, ideas of reference, and other psychotic symptoms derailed Nash's meteoric career and his personal relationships. In his seventies, Nash suddenly returned to math, and to his wife, and soon thereafter won the Nobel Prize.[14]

A Beautiful Mind rightly garnered a host of important honors. Nasar's book earned the 1998 National Book Critics Circle Award for Biography, Howard's film received the Academy Award for Best Picture, and the American Psychiatric Association (APA) lauded both for attracting long overdue attention to schizophrenia. Nasar even signed copies of her book and gave out DVDs of the film at a pharmaceutical company booth at the 2002 APA annual convention.[15]

Yet, in addition to raising public consciousness, *A Beautiful Mind* also subtly promoted racial stigma. The book and film conveyed the downward spiral of schizophrenia through the image of the beautiful, white male schizophrenic genius. As I discuss in chapter four, associations between whiteness, maleness, schizophrenia, and genius emerged in the 1930s to 1950s, and worked to shore up, not the frailty of white masculinity, but the dominance of white men. During that era, mainstream media touted great white men whose schizophrenic "grandiloquence" produced immortal works of art, while mainstream American society's fixation with idealized forms of white schizophrenia effaced the recognition of mental illness in minority populations.

Book and film versions of *A Beautiful Mind* played to these conventions. Nasar's text repeatedly described Nash's beautiful, troubled white body as a metaphor for his beautiful, troubled white mind. Howard's *Beautiful Mind,* meanwhile, presented an all-white, segregated landscape in which the first spoken words by a person of color appeared four minutes before the end of the 2 hour, 16-minute film. Both constructed the "reality" of schizophrenia through a nostalgic, one-in-a-million, individualized narrative largely divorced from the true social realities of schizophrenia in the present day.

One might claim, of course, that *A Beautiful Mind*'s narrative conventions humanize schizophrenia in ways that enable its mass appeal. But contemporary American culture is replete with stories that engage the complex race tensions of schizophrenia but do not get made into Ron Howard films. As but one example, in the same year that *A Beautiful Mind* won the academy award, an African American novelist named Victor LaValle published a brilliant novel about schizophrenia titled *The Ecstatic, or, Homunculus*. LaValle's main character, Anthony, is the anti–John Nash: a large, unkempt African American man who drops out of college and returns home, where he undertakes a series of tragic, hilarious, and soulful quests.

LaValle's *Ecstatic* vitally relocates psychopathology from individual to social domains. Anthony's insanity, manifest by a horrific insatiability of appetite, is shared by other characters in various ways. Even seemingly sane characters hoard money, or misrepresent themselves, or seek sex obsessively. These actions represent understandable, if unsettling attempts to build community or to stay alive. Life is lonely. Society is racist. People are hungry. People are poor. In LaValle's landscape, hoarding or sex or overeating represent exaggerated, essential responses to these disparities. Symptoms thus also represent complex survival strategies.

In this sense, *The Ecstatic* works as an extended critique of the fixed, individualized schizophrenia diagnosis on which *A Beautiful Mind* depends. Indeed, the book constantly tricks readers who might apply psychiatric reasoning into various forms of misdiagnosis. Anthony is a large black schizophrenic man who should act violently; yet in moments of conflict he becomes meek and timid—hence the biological joke in the book's title (homunculus literally means little man in the brain). Instances that appear as if psychotic symptoms (a cow starts talking) are later revealed to have wholly rational explanations (there was a midget behind the cow). Men outside of hotel windows seem as if visual hallucinations, but are in fact robbers. At these and other moments, *The Ecstatic* conveys lessons vital to clinicians who wish to probe present-day interactions between race and psychiatry: that to understand illness, one must understand social context. And, that a psychiatric lens promotes particular explanations, while foreclosing others. These are destigmatizing concepts indeed.[16]

Approaching diagnosis structurally, categorically, and historically can also promote recognition of the multiple meanings conveyed by psychiatric terms. Psychiatric diagnoses of course represent the expert opinions of doctors. Patients come to doctors seeking definitive answers in moments of need. At the same time, this book has shown that psychiatric diagnoses retain complex political connotations as well. Rappers and hip-hop artists employ the term *schizophrenic* to describe survival strategies. Poets describe the schizophrenia of being a minority person living in a white dominated world. And present-day pastors cite Martin Luther King Jr.'s claim that "a persistent schizophrenia leaves so many of us tragically divided against ourselves" to describe the distinctiveness of black humanity.[17]

It would be a mistake to write off these instances as mere co-optations of scientific terms. Instead, they provide hints to the ways in which popular *and* medical definitions of schizophrenia continue to evolve from numerous locales, and in relation each to the other. Psychiatry's definition of schizophrenia, as a mental illness embedded in brains, abuts the language of pastors, rappers, Baraka, and Black Power, who claim schizophrenia as an adaptation to, or repudiation of, the society in which black brains live and work. Potential tensions between these uses help us think about why medical outreach efforts struggle to overcome resistance and skepticism from minority populations. Outreach efforts often promote biomedical understandings; but in a historical sense, biomedicine imposes a framework that is ironically at odds with vitality, voice, or survival. Uncritical acceptance of medical terminology means giving in to what the medical establishment represents. One wonders what an outreach effort that took account of this complex dichotomy might look like.[18]

Finally, attention to the shifting structures of mental illness wards off the learned helplessness that often surrounds attempts to protest injustice. Many mental-health professionals feel that something is deeply wrong with a system that incarcerates so many mentally ill persons, or that posits prisons as primary treatment centers. The illnesses themselves too often become life sentences. Symptoms so frequently get worse, and the prison rhetoric of containment precludes improvement, recovery, or reintegration. We are not apologists for crime. Yet, most mental-health providers believe that even nightmare scenarios, in which mental illnesses contribute to criminal acts, demonstrate the importance of treating such illnesses proximally, in the community, rather than distally, after the deed is done.

The monolith often feels inevitable. *This is the way it is,* prison walls say, *and this is the way it will always be.* The great lesson of the Ionia charts, however, is that it was not always so. During the first half of the twentieth century, the idea that even criminally insane persons might improve with treatment and return to their lives functioned as a viable concept. The goal of institutions such as Ionia was not merely to warehouse people, but to recuperate them. Oft-barbaric treatments such as hydrotherapy or insulin shock combined with extensive vocational rehabilitation, skills training, even field trips into local communities. This is in no way to romanticize the past: as this book has made clear, Ionia was far from summer camp. But the hospital stood as testament to the belief that *insane,* a mental disease, helped explain and differentiate a category of *criminal,* and that society had a responsibility to help these people even as it condemned their actions.

The notion of recuperation fell by the wayside as hospitals became prisons. Sentences grew ever longer, moats deeper, and barbed wire sharper. Empathy gave way to fear, fear to anger, and anger ultimately to indifference. "Everything changed when mental health was taken over by Corrections" was a refrain I heard again and again during oral history interviews with staffers who worked at Ionia during the transition to Riverside. "Corrections told us to stop caring for people," an elderly gentleman who worked as an attendant told me, "even though in some cases we had these people in the hospital for years. Corrections made clear that our job was just to keep them quiet. No one gave a damn about their needs."[19]

This book has shown that the racialized process whereby corrections replaced mental health, and whereby notions of paranoid schizophrenia as an illness gave way to anxieties about paranoid schizophrenia as a threat, was not preordained. It did not result from natural forces, natural progressions, or the natural history of a disease. Instead, change occurred because of specific decisions, actions, and events. We as a society deinstitutionalized patients we deemed unthreatening to the "community," while locking the thereby community-threatening others within the system. We cut social support services and community treatment centers. We put too much faith in psychotropic drugs. We changed the frames surrounding disease. We watched too much nightly news. We looked askance. Only at the end of our decisions and life choices did the monster of our volition, the prison qua asylum, come into being. People, on all sides of the issue, suffered as a result.

We, of course, did not always mean badly. Safety and security were essential goals and noble ends. Funds were scarce. The error, though, was in our logic. We took the system at face value and let it shape our perceptions, our observations, and our common sense. Schizophrenia is a violent disease, the logic told us, and we need more prisons as a result. Along the way, though, we forgot to notice that we were in part the creators of the diagnostic categories through which we viewed the world. Misdiagnosis was not just a problem, it was a reflection. We observed culture; the culture was us.

I believe that there is a power in knowing these things about ourselves, because knowing them helps us think about ways to create structures that are more egalitarian and fair. Such construction requires more than funding, legislation, or good will, though these are surely essential components. Architecture that addresses injustice also requires ongoing self-reflection about the ways in which our buildings, our attitudes, our anxieties, and our stigmatizations reflect our values and our ideals. Perhaps Levinas was right that one cannot truly know the Other. But to help others, we—psychiatrists, Americans, criminals, policemen, doctors, patients all— must also strive to realize what the very category of Other reveals about the American cultural self.

In other words, the racial schizophrenia of prisons tells us something about the criminal actions of incarcerated bodies, but it tells us even more about a racialized logic that emerged in the 1960s and 1970s, whereby schizophrenia came to represent a threat to civilized society. This logic remains invisible to us today, precisely because it became embedded into common sense.

Historical reflection helps us develop the competency and the humility to grapple with this, our cultural past. History thus lets us begin to understand why, in the present day, schizophrenia remains at once pathologized and pathologizing, and signifies both the need to maintain order and a political imperative to disrupt it. Contained within vignettes, lyrics, newspaper clippings, drug ads, prison cells, and, most of all, archived hospital charts, are clues to a time when psychiatric definitions of schizophrenia became enmeshed in public discourse, and in an often unarticulated set of attitudes and assumptions, in ways that shaped diagnostic practices. These sources also help us recognize how, at a particular moment in time, schizophrenia became both a racialized disease and a metaphor of race in the United States. By so doing, the history of schizophrenia provides a larger, cautionary object lesson about the ways that ideologies that inform diagnosis have extraordinary consequences for society at large; and, conversely, that stigmatizations of psychiatric disorders need to be contextually understood if they are to be effectively treated in clinical settings.

WRITING A BOOK, AS ANY author knows, involves much more than putting words to a page. Book writing reflects many stages of thinking and rethinking, of revising and working through. Each part of the process represents a stratum of development. Passages that make euphoric sense in the middle of the night appear as gibberish the morning after. Long-held attitudes fall away. Certain efforts lead to vast new expanses, others to impenetrable façades. Writing begets more writing, and only then does one truly begin to write. Near the end of each chapter, an author begins to understand how seemingly random shards of information fit into larger scripts, stories, or narratives, and how once-vital pieces of evidence need be left on the cutting-room floor. Then you revise. And then, when each part seems nearly finished, you begin again. A book emerges over time.

We often code writing as a highly individual practice, and understandably so. The process frequently rewards the *sol* component of solipsism. Authors cancel dinner plans or stay home from vacations. Obsessions, compulsions, ruminations, and other seeming symptoms of mental illness emerge as requisite free-time activities. To be sure, euphoria can result from discovering something unique or idiosyncratic from within archives of the mundane. But there is always a cost to the discovery. And in any case, speaking metrically, life can be isolating when reading against the cultural grain.

At the same time, the fantasy of individual authorship effaces the ways in which literary work results also, and at times primarily, from the personal and institutional support systems in which each author is embedded. Here as well, the writing process is as fluid as it is complex, and represents many varied forms of love, care, welfare, or assistance that an author receives over the life of a project. A book chronicles stages of an author's relationships to others. And the name that ultimately appears on the front cover, as if by fait accompli, in fact signifies a series of social networks and networked relations.

I have benefitted from many such networks and support systems while researching and writing *The Protest Psychosis*. At the most elemental level, the project would not have been possible without the foresight of administrators, archivists, interview subjects, and volunteers in Lansing and Ionia.

Harry McGee and Cynthia Kelley of the Michigan Department of Community Health's Policy, Regulations and Professions Administration enabled my access to the hospital files. Dave Johnson and Mark Harvey of the Michigan Historical Center provided expert archival support and advice. Joan and Joe McCord of the Ionia County Historical Society opened the beautiful John C. Blanchard House to me and my research assistants, and invaluably contacted the surviving staff workers from the Ionia Hospital with whom we met. Those workers then shared freely of their memories and their time. The warden, guards, and legal representatives of the now closed Riverside Correctional Facility patiently answered my many questions, and chaperoned guided tours. I can only hope that I have done justice to the efforts of these and other remarkable persons. And, of course, I hope that I have rightly honored the life stories that their efforts have helped me reveal, while at the same time remaining vigilant about protecting all aspects of anonymity.

I am deeply grateful to the various funding agencies that supported my research. Grants from the National Alliance for Research on Schizophrenia and Depression (NARSAD), the American Council of Learned Societies (ACLS), the Robert Wood Johnson Health and Society Program, the National Science Foundation (NSF), and the John S. Guggenheim Foundation endowed significant components of my data gathering and analysis. Faculty fellowships from the University of Michigan Institute for the Humanities and the University of Sydney School of Philosophical and Historical Inquiry provided time, space, and energized communities of interlocutors.

Amy Caldwell at Beacon Press continually provided vision and vital feedback, while Alex Kapitan and P. J. Tierney provided sage advice. I simply cannot express my full gratitude to the excellent student collaborators with whom I have had the privilege to work. Sacha Feirstein wowed the Ionia community with thoughtful aplomb. Joni Angel and Angela Wuest became methods experts. And Sara McLelland proved once again that she sees numbers and charts like Keanu Reeves saw the matrix at the end of *Matrix I*. Sara's excellent quantitative sensibilities appear in many of the book's data sections.

My colleagues at the University of Michigan-Ann Arbor are remarkable, brilliant, generous, and kind. Valerie Traub, Carol Boyd, John Greden, and Gregory Dalack have provided the type of visionary leadership that makes a split medicine-humanities appointment possible. John Carson, Anna Kirkland, and Sherie Randolph are once-in-a-lifetime friends. And Joel Howell, Kevin Gaines, Tim Johnson, Abby Stewart, Frieda Ekotto, Paul Anderson, Holly Peters-Golden, Maria Cotera, Lisa Disch, Debby Keller-Cohen, Elizabeth Wingrove, Dina Goodman, and Adrienne Carson have all given unwavering support.

Collaborators from beyond Michigan have also shaped the contents of this book. I am so very lucky to be a member of the world's most supportive, thoughtful, and downright splendid writing group. Members of the group, called Oxidate, are Lochlann Jain, Jake Kosek, Joe Masco, Miriam Ticktin, Elizabeth Roberts, Jackie Orr, Diane Nelson, Cori Hayden, and Michelle Murphy. The project has also been deeply enriched by the wisdom and sustenance of scholars and friends, including Melissa Harris-Lacewell, Emily Martin, Keith Wailoo, Elizabeth Lunbeck, Elizabeth Wilson, Jamie Saris, Martin Summers, Victoria de Menil, Furaha Norton, G6, Stefan Ecks, Andrea Tone, Annette Leibing, Rebecca Herzig, Susan Craddock, Sue Antonick, Elise Frasier, Ali Fidler-Metzl, and Walter Ricci. Domna Stanton will always remain my mentor. Thoughts of Parna Sengupta suffuse the words of each page, and the empty spaces between them.

My family, as always, has seen me though. My parents, Marilyn and Kurt Metzl, taught me the meaning of social responsibility. My father and my late grandparents came to the United States in the aftermath of the Second World War. Having lost everything they owned and everyone except one another, they started again. My mother's father worked in a box factory, went to law school at night, and then became a New York City lawyer. From these origins, my parents came to embody the ways in which standing up for others comes to define the self. The lesson is not lost on me or my brothers. Two of my siblings, Jordan and Joshua, work as physicians, while a third, Jamie, is a policy expert. Individually, we support one another other. Collectively, we form a net that ensures that no one will fall too far before bouncing back.

Thank you, all.

PREFACE

1. Samuel A. Cartwright, "Report on the Diseases and Physical Peculiarities of the Negro race," *New Orleans Medical and Surgical Journal* (1851): 691–715; A. B. Evarts, "Dementia Praecox in the Colored Race," *Psychoanalytic Review*, no. 1 (1914): 388–403; J. E. Lind, "The Color Complex in the Negro," *Psychoanalytic Review*, no. 1 (1914): 404–14.

2. Shankar Vedantam, "Racial Disparities Found in Pinpointing Mental Illness," *Washington Post*, 28 June 2005, A1 (italics mine); Frederic C. Blow, John E. Zeber, John F. McCarthy, Marcia Valenstein, Leah Gillon, and C. Raymond Bingham, "Ethnicity and Diagnostic Patterns in Veterans with Psychoses," *Social Psychiatry and Psychiatric Epidemiology* 39, no. 10 (2004): 841–51.

3. *Diagnostic and Statistical Manual of Mental Disorders DSM-IV-TR* (text revision) (Washington, DC: American Psychiatric Association Press, 2000); Takanori Hashimoto, H. Holly Bazmi, Karoly Mirnics, Qiang Wu, Allan R. Sampson, and David A. Lewis, "Conserved Regional Patterns of GABA-Related Transcript Expression in the Neocortex of Subjects with Schizophrenia," *American Journal of Psychiatry* 165 (2008): 479–89; Paul J. Moberg, David R. Roalf, Raquel E. Gur, and Bruce I. Turetsky, "Smaller Nasal Volumes as Stigmata of Aberrant Neurodevelopment in Schizophrenia," *American Journal of Psychiatry* 161 (2004): 2314–16; D. A. Regier, W. E. Narrow, D. S. Rae, et al., "The De Facto US Mental and Addictive Disorders Service System. Epidemiologic Catchment Area Prospective 1-Year Prevalence Rates of Disorders and Services," *Archives of General Psychiatry* 2, no. 50 (1993): 85–94.

4. For a few examples, see C. Taube, *Admission Rates to State and County Mental Hospitals by Age, Sex, and Color, United States, 1969* (Washington, DC: Department of Health, Education, and Welfare, National Institute of Mental Health, Biometry Branch, 1971), statistical note 41, 1–7; R. J. Simon, J. L. Fleiss, B. J. Gurland, et al., "Depression and Schizophrenia in Black and White Mental Patients," *Archives of General Psychiatry*, no. 28 (1973): 509–12; J. L. Liss, A. Welner, E. Robins E, et al., "Psychiatric Symptoms in White and Black Inpatients," *Comprehensive Psychiatry* 14 (1973): 475–81; H. Chung, J. C. Mahler, T. Kakuma, "Racial Differences in Treatment of Psychiatric Inpatients," *Psychiatric Services* 46 (1995): 586–91; S. P. Segal, J. R. Bola, and M. A. Watson, "Race, Quality of Care, and Antipsychotic Prescribing Practices in Psychiatric Emergency Services," *Psychiatric Services* 47 (1996): 282–86; S. Mukherjee, S. Shukla, J. Woodle, A. M. Rosen, and S. Olarte, "Misdiagnosis of Schizophrenia in Bipolar Patients: A Multiethnic Comparison," *American Journal of Psychiatry* 140 (1983): 1571–74; J. Delahanty, "Differences in Rates of Depression in Schizophrenia by Race," *Schizophrenia Bulletin* 152, no. 1 (2001): 29–38. For an excellent overview, see F. M. Baker, Carl C. Bell, "Issues in the Psychiatric Treatment of African Americans," *Psychiatric Services* 50, no. 3 (1999): 362–68. As discussed below, the first round of such arguments appeared, in perni-

cious fashion, in the late 1930s. See, for example, the notorious study, R.E.L. Faris, "Demography of Urban Psychotics with Special Reference to Schizophrenia," *American Sociological Review* 3 (1938): 203–9.

5. Vedantam, "Racial Disparities Found," A1. For an important medical perspective, also see Thomas D. Sequist, Garrett M. Fitzmaurice, Richard Marshall, et al., "Physician Performance and Racial Disparities in Diabetes Mellitus Care," *Archives of Internal Medicine* 168, no.11 (2008): 1145–51; Kevin Sack, "Doctors Miss Cultural Needs, Study Says," *New York Times,* June 10, 2008, D1.

6. Stokely Carmichael, "Black Power, A Critique of the System of International White Supremacy & International Capitalism," in *The Dialectics of Liberation,* ed. David Cooper (New York: Penguin, 1968), 151. Also see, E. Bonilla-Silva, "Rethinking Racism: Toward a Structural Interpretation," *American Sociological Review* 62 (2003): 465–80.

7. Arthur P. Noyes, *A Textbook of Psychiatry* (New York: Macmillan, 1927), 127–28.

8. See chapter four for a full discussion. "Shyness Is Blamed in Mental Illness," *New York Times,* December 29, 1929; "Writes in Defense of Lincoln's Wife," *New York Times,* March 2, 1935; "Insanity Ascribed to Some Authors: Psychiatrists Are Told of 'Literary Artists' Who Evidence Schizophrenia: Grandiloquence Is Sign," *New York Times,* May 15, 1935; Donald Cooley, "Don't Tell Them We're All Going Crazy," *Better Homes and Gardens* (July 1947): 122–25; Alicia Marsden, James Adams, "Are You Likely to Be a Happily Married Woman," *Ladies' Home Journal* (March 1949): 31.

9. B. Klopfer, "Is Inclination to Mental Disease within a Population Group a 'Racial' Factor?" *Psychiatric Quarterly* 18 (1944): 240–72; "Insanity: Mental Illness Among Negroes Exceeds Whites, Overcrowds Already-Jammed 'Snake Pits,'" *Ebony* (April 1949): 19–23.

10. Walter Bromberg, Frank Simon, "The 'Protest' Psychosis: A Special Type of Reactive Psychosis," *Archives of General Psychiatry* 19 (1968): 155–60.

11. "FBI Adds Negro Mental Patient to '10 Most Wanted' List," *Chicago Tribune,* July 6, 1966, A4; Bosley Crowther, "The Screen," *New York Times,* September 12, 1963.

12. *Mental Disorders: Diagnostic and Statistical Manual (*Washington, DC: American Psychiatric Association Press, 1952), 26–27; *Diagnostic and Statistical Manual of Mental Disorders,* 2nd ed. (Washington, DC: American Psychiatric Association Press, 1968), 33–35.

13. Clayborne Carson and Peter Holloran, eds., *A Knock at Midnight: Inspiration from the Great Sermons of Reverend Martin Luther King, Jr.* (New York: Warner Books, 1998), 187–200; Martin Luther King Jr., *Where Do We Go from Here: Chaos or Community?* (Boston: Beacon Press, 1968); J. Leo, "Negro 'Paranoia' Assayed in Book," *New York Times,* July 25, 1968.

14. E. Fuller Torrey, *Surviving Schizophrenia: A Manual for Families, Consumers, and Providers,* 4th ed. (New York: Quill, 2001), xxi–xxii.

15. Ideology and politics are absolutely vital to the practice of medicine, of course. Otherwise doctors would be no different from anyone else.

16. See Roy Porter, *Madness: A Brief History* (Oxford, England: Oxford University Press, 2002), 10–33.

17. But, as we will see, the two processes developed in relation to each other over time. Concerns about threats posed by angry black men impacted American perceptions of, and definitions of, schizophrenia. Meanwhile, stigmatizations of schizophrenia as a violent disorder provided language for certain avenues of society to pathologize the larger category of black men. Segal, "Race, Quality of Care, and Antipsychotic Prescribing Practices," 282–86;

Chung, "Racial Differences in Treatment of Psychiatric Inpatients," 586–91; http://mental health.samhsa.gov/publications/allpubs/SMA00-3457/intro.asp, accessed July 1, 2007; Vedantam, "Racial Disparities Found," A1.

18. *Ill-Equipped: U.S. Prisons and Offenders with Mental Illness* (New York: Human Rights Watch, 2003).

19. Angela Davis, *Women, Race, and Class* (New York: Random House, 1981), 174–201; Ruth Frankenberg, "Growing Up White: Feminism, Racism, and the Social Geography of Childhood," *Feminist Review* 45 (1993): 51–84. Also see Vanessa Northington Gamble, *Making a Place for Ourselves: The Black Hospital Movement, 1920–1945*. So too, Daniel Robinson's *Wild Beasts and Idle Humors* is just one of many important books that trace how psychiatric definitions of insanity developed in connection to, and at times in disjuncture with, juridical ones. For a vital anthropological perspective, see Byron Good, Mary-Jo DelVecchio Good, Sandra Hyde, and Sarah Pinto, "Postcolonial Disorders: Reflections on Subjectivity in the Modern World," in *Postcolonial Disorders* (Ethnographic Studies in Subjectivity), eds. DelVecchio Good, Hyde, Pinto, and Good (Berkeley: University of California Press, 2008).

CHAPTER 2

1. http://www.infomi.com/city/ionia/, accessed July 1, 2007; according to event organizer Bill Lynch, the record for eating the most chili dogs was set in 1999, the first year the event was held, "by a fifteen-year-old boy who ate fifteen chili dogs in fifteen minutes." Since then, the winner has typically eaten approximately thirteen chili dogs. "Last year's winner, Dylan Prescott, ate thirteen and one-half chili dogs." Lynch said he thinks Ionia may hold the only contest of this kind in the world. Laura Rico, "Chili-dawg Chow-down," *Ionia Sentinel-Standard,* October 25, 2005. In 2005, vendors sold thirty-eight hundred chili dogs in three hours. Laura Rico, "Chili-dawg Meets the Challenge," *Ionia Sentinel-Standard,* October 29, 2005; http://www.michigan.gov/cgi. For projected data about Ionia Country, including population comparisons by race, see http://quickfacts.census.gov/qfd/states/26/26067.html (both sites accessed July 1, 2007).

2. The asylum at Auburn State Prison in New York opened in 1855.

3. Annual Reports of the Ionia State Hospital 1937–1956, group 70–47, box 1, Michigan State Archives, Executive/Mental Health Collection.

4. See Annual Reports of the Ionia State Hospital for the Fiscal Year 1937–38, 2–3; in Annual Reports of the Ionia State Hospital 1937–1956, group 70–47, box 1, Michigan State Archives, Executive/Mental Health Collection; Audit Reports for the Ionia Hospital for the Criminally Insane, RG79–9 B3F2, State Archives of Michigan, Lansing.

5. Annual Reports of the Ionia State Hospital 1937–1956, group 70–47, box 1, Michigan State Archives, Executive/Mental Health Collection.

6. "Bedlamites Run Wild: Razor Madmen Elude Posses," *Los Angeles Times,* June 4, 1930; "Operation Reformed Him: Holshay, Bandit, Went Under Knife After His Capture 15 Years Ago," *New York Times,* August 11, 1906; " 'Witch' Slayers Due in Court: Man and Wife May be Judged Insane," *Los Angeles Times,* July 22, 1929; "Dr. Small Freed from Asylum," *New York Times,* September 9, 1954; "Legal Briefs," *Time,* July 23, 1973; "Cow Sets All-Time Record, Gives 230,723 Lbs. of Milk," *New York Times,* July 21, 1940.

7. A. A. Birzgalis, "Statement of the Medical Superintendent for Employee Information

Program" (January 5, 1972): 5; "Changes and Corrections as of March 10, 1965, on the Report of the Ionia State Hospital Made By the Central Inspection Board of the American Psychiatric Association in 1957," 2a.

8. Department of Mental Health Records, Ionia State Hospital for the Criminally Insane, 1875–1976, accession numbers RG 89–373, boxes 322–624, State Archives of Michigan, Lansing.

9. See Erving Goffman, *Asylums: Essays on the Social Situation of Mental Patients and Other Inmates* (New York: Anchor Press, 1961); Gerald N. Grob, *The State and the Mentally Ill: A History of Worcester State Hospital in Massachusetts, 1830–1920* (Chapel Hill: University of North Carolina Press, 1966); David J. Rothman, *The Discovery of the Asylum: Social Order and Disorder in the New Republic* (Boston: Little Brown, 1971); Michel Foucault, *Discipline and Punish: The Birth of the Prison* (New York: Random House, 1975); Thomas Szasz, *Schizophrenia: The Sacred Symbol of Psychiatry* (Syracuse, NY: Syracuse University Press, 1988); Nancy Tomes, *The Art of Asylum-Keeping: Thomas Story Kirkbride and the Origins of American Psychiatry* (Philadelphia: University of Pennsylvania Press, 1994). For an excellent analysis of race at St. Vincent's, see Matthew Gambino, " 'These Strangers Within Our Gates': Race, Psychiatry, and Mental Illness Among Black Americans at St. Elizabeths Hospital in Washington DC, 1900–40," *History of Psychiatry* 19, no. 4 (2008): 387–408.

10. As I detail below, there were many ways to end up at Ionia in the first half of the twentieth century because the number of possible admission diagnoses was superseded only by the many potential types of insane crime. Schizophrenia became the most common admitting diagnosis in the mid-1930s, but it was just one in a long list of options.

11. Annual Reports of the Ionia State Hospital, 1937–1972, group 70–47, box 1–4. Michigan State Archives, Executive/Mental Health Collection, accessed June 1, 2004–December 31, 2007.

12. The archive inhabits a large set of rooms on the second floor of the Michigan Library and Historical Center, a huge granite building that also hosts the Michigan Historical Gift Store, the Library of Michigan, the Michigan Historical Museum, and a seemingly endless stream of schoolchildren on field trips. To get to the archive, one must first pass through the First Settlers of Michigan exhibition, in which mannequins dressed in "Indian pelts" stand at the ready while listening to the sounds of computer-generated geese. Although the schoolchildren likely felt otherwise, the bizarre scene appeared as far away as humanly possible from Ionia's locked wards and life sentences.

13. Michigan Dept of Community Health Institutional Review Board Project #98-MH-SAHCFMH. Approval granted June 2, 2004.

14. George Dowdall, "Mental Hospitals and Deinstitutionalization," in *Handbook of the Sociology of Mental Health*, eds. C. Aneshensel and J. Phelan (New York: Kluwer Academic, 1999); Mark Schlesinger, Bradford Gray, "Institutional Change and Its Consequences for the Delivery of Mental Health Services" in *Handbook of the Sociology of Mental Health*, eds. C. Aneshensel and J. Phelan (New York: Kluwer Academic, 1999); H. Richard Lamb, "Deinstitutionalization at the Beginning of the New Millennium," *Harvard Review of Psychiatry* 6 (1998): 1–9; D. A. Rochefort, "Origins of the 'Third Psychiatric Revolution': The Community Mental Health Centers Act of 1963," *Journal of Health Politics, Policy and Law* 9, no. 1 (1984): 1–30.

15. Interviews with former employees of Ionia State Hospital, conducted October 24,

2005, at the Ionia Historical Society, Ionia, Michigan. Interviewer Jonathan Metzl, accompanied by Sacha Firestein.

16. Though beyond the scope of my analysis here, white perpetrators have also historically claimed insanity as a way of avoiding punishment for racist crimes. As but one high-profile example, policeman Charles Guerand famously employed the insanity defense to escape full punishment for the murder of Hattie McCray. See "Policeman Seeking Lunacy Board Aid," *Times-Picayune* (New Orleans), April 22, 1930, AI; also see, Adam Fairclough, *Race & Democracy: The Civil Rights Struggle in Louisiana, 1915–1972* (Athens: University of Georgia Press, 1999), 19.

17. See, for example, "AAAS Honors Scientist for Uncovering Abuse of Psychiatry," http://www.aaas.org/news/releases/2003/1212reich.shtml, accessed March 10, 2009; Michel Foucault, *The History of Sexuality: An Introduction* (New York: Random House, 1978), 93; Michel Foucault, *Society Must Be Defended* (New York: Penguin, 1997/2003), 254–63; Frantz Fanon, *Black Skin, White Masks,* trans. Charles Lam Markmann (New York: Grove Press, 1967), 13, 17–18, 38; Frantz Fanon, "Le syndrôme nord-africain" [1952], in *Pour la révolution africaine: Écrits politiques* (Paris: Maspéro, 1964), 13–25. Also see Richard C. Keller, *Colonial Madness: Psychiatry in French North Africa* (Chicago: University of Chicago Press, 2007).

CHAPTER 3

1. Case files for this section come from Ionia State Hospital case files 3466–3590, accession number RG 80–13, lot number 39, boxes 52–59v, case files 4062–4195. State Archives of Michigan, Lansing.

CHAPTER 4

1. David Hackett Fischer, *Historians' Fallacies: Toward a Logic of Historical Thought* (New York: Harper Torchbooks, 1970), 135–40, 141.

2. John McDermott, "Emily Dickinson Revisited: A Study of Periodicity in Her Work," *American Journal of Psychiatry* 158 (2001): 686–90; Dietrich Blumer, "The Illness of Vincent van Gogh," *American Journal of Psychiatry* 159, no. 4 (2002): 519–26; Thurman Sawyer and George Bundren, "Witchcraft, Religious Fanaticism and Schizophrenia—Salem Revisited," *Early America Review* (Fall 2000), http://www.earlyamerica.com/review/2000_fall/salem_witch.html, accessed June 24, 2006. Also see James W. Thompson, "Trends in the Development of Psychiatric Services, 1844–1994," *Hospital and Community Psychiatry* 45 (1994): 987–92. See also http://www.medterms.com/script/main/art.asp?articlekey=39219, accessed January 10, 2008: "Samson may, it is thought, have had antisocial personality disorder. The Bible tells of his lies to his parents, his cruelty to animals, his torching the Philistine fields, his frequent brawls, and his unremitting bragging after killing a thousand men, actions fitting the diagnosis of antisocial personality disorder."

3. Report of the Metropolitan Commissioners in Lunacy to the Lord Chancellor 1844, http://www.mdx.ac.uk/WWW/STUDY/4_09.htm, accessed June 1, 2006; Sylvanus Stall, *What a Young Boy Ought to Know* (Philadelphia: Vir Publishing, 1897); "Masturbatory Insanity," http://www2.hu-berlin.de/sexology/ECE6/html/masturbatory_insanity.html, accessed

March 10, 2009; E. H. Hare, "Masturbational Insanity: The History of an Idea," *Journal of Mental Science* 108 (1962): 1–25.

4. John Haslam, *Observations on Madness and Melancholy* (New York: Arno Books, 1809/1970), 64–67; Irving Gottesman, *Schizophrenia Genesis: The Origins of Madness* (New York: W. H. Freeman, 1991), 5–6; B. A. Morel, *Traites des Maladies Mentales* (Paris: Masson, 1852).

5. Emil Kraepelin, *Psychiatrie. Ein Lehrbuch für Studirende und Aerzte. Sechste, vollständig umgearbeitete Auflage. I. Band. Allgemeine Psychiatrie. II. Band. Klinische Psychiatrie* (Barth Verlag: Leipzig, 1899).

6. According to Kraepelin, such patients were prone to suicidality and violence. See, for example, Emil Kraepelin, *Lectures on Psychiatry by Dr. Emil Kraepelin: Authorized Translation from the Second German Edition,* ed. Thomas Johnstone (New York: William Wood & Company, 1913), 26–29.

7. Paul Eugen Bleuler, *Dementia praecox or the Group of Schizophrenias,* trans. Joseph Zinkin (New York: International Universities Press, 1950), 7. Originally published as "Dementia praecox oder die Gruppe der Schizofrenien," in *Handbuch der Psychiatrie,* ed. Gustav Aschaffenburg (Leipzig and Vienna, 1911–1928).

8. Bleuler, *Dementia praecox or the Group of Schizophrenias,* 8, 9, 40, 41, 42. For a discussion of the links between Bleuler and Freud, see Thomas G. Dalzell, "Eugen Bleuler 150: Bleuler's reception of Freud," *History of Psychiatry* 18, no. 4 (2007): 471–82.

9. Bleuler, *Dementia praecox or the Group of Schizophrenias,* 8, 9, 40, 41, 42.

10. J. G. Howells, ed., *The Concept of Schizophrenia: Historical Perspectives* (Washington, DC: American Psychiatric Press Association, 1991); Adityanjee Yekeen, A. Aderibigbe, D. Theodoridis, W. V. R. Vieweg, "Dementia Praecox to Schizophrenia: The First 100 Years," *Psychiatry and Clinical Neurosciences* 53, no. 4 (1999): 437–48.

11. For an important historical perspective, see Richard Noll's republication of Harvard neuropathologist Elmer Ernst Southard's classic paper, "Non-dementia non-praecox." Richard Noll/E. E. Southard, "Classic Text No. 72 Non-Dementia Non-Praecox: Note on the Advantages to Mental Hygiene of Extirpating a Term," *History of Psychiatry* 18, no. 4 (2007): 483–502.

12. See, for example, Emil Kraepelin, *Psychiatrisches aus Java. Centralblatt für Nervenheilkunde und Psychiatrie 27* (1904b), 433–37. For a fascinating perspective, also see, Byron Good, Mary-Jo DelVecchio Good, Sandra Hyde, and Sarah Pinto, "Postcolonial Disorders: Reflections on Subjectivity in the Modern World."

13. Cartwright, "Report on the Diseases and Physical Peculiarities of the Negro Race," *New Orleans Medical and Surgical Journal* (1851).

14. Sander Gilman, *Difference and Pathology: Stereotypes of Sexuality, Race and Madness* (Ithaca, NY: Cornell Press, 1985). Also see Harriet A. Washington, *Medical Apartheid: The Dark History of Medical Experimentation on Black Americans from Colonial Times to the Present* (New York: Harlem Moon, 2006), 36.

15. A. B. Evarts, "Dementia Praecox in the Colored Race," *Psychoanalytic Review,* no. 1 (1914): 388–403. See also J. E. Lind, "The Color Complex in the Negro," *Psychoanalytic Review* 1 (1914): 404–14. Also see, E. B. Southard, "On the Topographical Distribution of Cortex Lesions and Anomalies in Dementia Præcox, with Some Account of Their Functional

Significance," *American Journal of Insanity* 71 (1915): 603. For an important discussion of Evart's subsequent career at St. Elizabeths Hospital, see Gambino, " 'These Strangers Within Our Gates.'"

16. "Steamship Agents Clash with Dawes; Defend System of Immigration Inspection That Is Aimed to Detect Insanity. Does Not Suit State Board; Head of Governor's Commission Thinks Examinations by Alienists Necessary—Demand for Law Expected," *New York Times,* December 10, 1912.

17. "Shibley Cries Out at Court's Ruling; Father of Murdered Boy Denounces Refusal to Hold Insane Suspect for the Crime. Committed for Assault Fredericks Identifies Dennison as the Man Who Shot Him—Grand Jury to Consider Murder Charge," *New York Times,* February 4, 1910; "Dennison, Insane, Was Boy's Slayer; Lunacy Commission Finds It Was He Who Shot Lomas and Shibley Lads at Highbridge Park. Has Dementia Praecox Methods Which Permitted Him to Leave Asylums Blamed and a Law Urged to Forbid Them," *New York Times,* March 23, 1910; "Commission Certain to Pass on Charlton; Extradition Proceedings Must Await Determination of Wife Slayer's Sanity. View of Italian Consul: Prisoner Should Be Turned Over to Italy for the Determination of His Responsibility, He Thinks," *New York Times,* June 26, 1910. Also see "Emotional Insanity and Crime," *New York Times,* September 7, 1924.

18. "DECLARES INSANITY CAN BE EXTIRPATED; Chicago Justice Tells How Psychopathic Laboratory Sorts Criminals. 15 Per Cent Demented; Honor System Dangerous in Prison Where Sane and Those with Mental Diseases Are Placed," *New York Times,* November 20, 1915.

19. "Check on Society's Defectives Seen as Urgent Need of Nation; Laboratory Experiments in Chicago Show That Aid for the Unfit Encourages Their Spread—How Municipal Chief Justice Would Curb the Subnormal and Develop Better Stock," *New York Times,* September 2, 1923.

20. Eugen Bleuler, *Textbook of Psychiatry* (New York: Macmillan, 1924/1976), 200–210.

21. In the 1930s insanity was also considered to be a virus that spread among inhabitants of urban "slums." R. E. L. Faris, "Demography of urban psychotics with special reference to schizophrenia," *American Sociological Review* 3 (1938): 203–9.

22. In 1933, Kretschmer resigned as president of the AÄGP (general medical society for psychotherapy) to protest racial hygiene laws.

23. Arthur P. Noyes, *A Textbook of Psychiatry* (New York: Macmillan, 1927): 127–28.

24. Ibid., 130–31.

25. Committee on Statistics of the American Medico–Psychological Association, *Statistical Manual for the Use of Institution for the Insane* (New York: American Medico-Psychological Association, 1918), 24. See Gerald Grob, "The Origins of DSM-I: A Study in Appearance and Reality," *American Journal of Psychiatry* 148 (1991): 421–31.

26. Noyes, *Textbook of Psychiatry* (1927), 148.

27. M. G. Martin, "A Practical Treatment Program for a Mental Hospital 'Back' Ward," *American Journal of Psychiatry* 103 (1947): 758–60; Barbara Betz, "Strategic Conditions in the Psychotherapy of People with Schizophrenia," *American Journal of Psychiatry* 106 (1950): 203–15; Otto Fenichel, *Outline of Clinical Psychoanalysis,* trans. Bertram Lewin (New York: Norton, 1934).

28. Livingston Welch, "The Psychic Ills That Trouble Us," *New York Times Book Review*, August 2, 1936, 8; Leslie C. Barber, "The Age of Schizophrenia," *Harper's Magazine* 176 (December 1937): 70–78.

29. "Insanity Ascribed to Some Authors: Psychiatrists Are Told of 'Literary Artists' Who Evidence Schizophrenia: Grandiloquence Is Sign," *New York Times*, May 15, 1935.

30. Ibid.; "Dual Personality Revealed By Meter," *New York Times*, September 11, 1932; Michela Robbins, "Would You Share Your Home with a Mental Case? The Tuckers Did," *Colliers* (December 1952): 20–22; Ina May Greer, "Occupational Therapy in Mental Hospitals," *Hygeia* (April 1939): 341–44.

31. Donald Cooley, "Don't Tell Them We're All Going Crazy," *Better Homes and Gardens* (July 1947): 122–25; Alicia Marsden, James Adams, "Are You Likely to Be a Happily Married Woman," *Ladies' Home Journal* (March 1949): 31; Joan Younger, "Mental Illness," *Ladies' Home Journal* (March 1949): 44–45, 214. Also see Carol A. B. Warren, *Madwives: Schizophrenic Women in the 1950s* (New Brunswick: Rutgers Press, 1991).

32. W. A. Evans, *Mrs. Abraham Lincoln: A Study of Her Personality and Her Influence on Lincoln* (New York: Alfred A. Knopf, 1934); R. L. Duffus, "Justice Done to Mary Todd, the Wife of Lincoln," *New York Times Book Review*, March 6, 1932, 3; "Writes in Defense of Lincoln's Wife," *New York Times*, March 2, 1932.

33. Mary Jane Ward, *The Snake Pit* (New York: Signet, 1946) 1, 48.

34. Ibid., back cover; Isa Kapp, "A Novelist's Dramatic View of Schizophrenia," *New York Times*, April 7, 1946; Edwin Schallert, " 'Snake Pit' Powerful Film Event," *Los Angeles Times*, December 27, 1948; Orville Prescott, "Books of the Times," *New York Times*, April 5, 1946; Hedda Hopper, "Olivia De Havilland Looks at 'Snake Pit' Role as Most Important in All Career," *Los Angeles Times*, December 12, 1948, D1. The British censorship bureau found the film so disturbing that it banned its showing in Great Britain. See Hedda Hopper, "British 'Snake Pit' Ban Lifting Sought," *Los Angeles Times*, January 6, 1949, A6.

35. Faris, "Demography of Urban Psychotics."

36. "Insanity: Mental Illness Among Negroes Exceeds Whites, Overcrowds Already-Jammed 'Snake Pits,' " *Ebony* (April 1949): 19–23.

37. Laura D. Hirshbein, "Science, Gender, and the Emergence of Depression in American Psychiatry, 1952–1980," *Journal of the History of Medicine and Allied Sciences* 61 (2006): 187–216.

38. For a vivid description, see Ward, *The Snake Pit*, 119–21.

CHAPTER 6

1. Case files for this section: Ionia State Hospital case files 3466–3590, accession number RG 95–190, lot number 245, boxes 200–216. State Archives of Michigan, Lansing.

2. Eric Arnesen, *Black Protest and the Great Migration: A Brief History with Documents* (New York: Bedford/St. Martin's, 2002).

3. As detailed below, the *Statistical Manual for the Use of Institutions for the Insane* (first printing, 1918) was the first formal psychiatric nomenclature adopted for widespread use in America. The manual was first published in 1917 by the National Committee for Mental Hygiene in collaboration with the American Medical Psychological Association. See Gerald

Grob, "The Origins of DSM-I: A Study in Appearance and Reality," *American Journal of Psychiatry* 148 (1991): 421–31. Also see Lucy Ozarin, "Moral Insanity: A Brief History," *Psychiatric News* 36, no. 10 (2001): 21. For a fascinating counterperspective, see Ben Karpman, "The Myth of the Psychopathic Personality," *American Journal of Psychiatry* 104 (1948): 523–34.

CHAPTER 7

1. Talal Asad, "Ethnographic Representation, Statistics and Modern Power," *Social Research* 61, no. 1 (1994): 55–88.

2. Department of Mental Health Records, Ionia State Hospital for the Criminally Insane, 1875–1976, accession numbers RG 89-373, boxes 322–624, State Archives of Michigan, Lansing.

3. See Grob, "The Origins of DSM-I," 421–31.

4. Though it is beyond the scope of this study, pre-1935 charts seem to support associations between dementia praecox and alien others. In 1930, for instance, Negro, Slavonic, Mexican, Norwegian, Finnish, and "mixed" patients made up the majority of praecox cases, English and Germans suffered disproportionately from psychoses with mental deficiency, an Italian was one of two psychoneurotics, and the hospital's single identified Jewish patient appeared under the category of "psychopathic personality without psychosis."

5. George Lipsitz, *The Possessive Investment in Whiteness: How White People Profit from Identity Politics* (Philadelphia: Temple, 1998); Hua Tang, Tom Quertermous, Beatriz Rodriguez, et al., "Genetic Structure, Self-Identified Race/Ethnicity, and Confounding in Case-Control Association Studies," *American Journal of Human Genetics* 76, no. 2 (2005): 268–75; D. J. Witherspoon, S. Wooding, A. R. Rogers, et al., "Genetic Similarities Within and Between Human Populations," *Genetics* 176, no. 1 (2007): 351–59.

6. Farhad Dalal, *Race, Colour and the Process of Racialization: New Perspectives from Group Analysis, Psychoanalysis and Sociology* (London: Brunner-Routledge, 2002), 3, 178; Jamie D. Brooks, Meredith King Ledford, "Geneticizing Disease: Implications for Racial Health Disparities," http://biopoliticaltimes.org/downloads/2008_geneticizing_disease.pdf, accessed March 10, 2009.

7. Again, the remaining charts divided evenly into twenty other nativity categories, none of which comprised more than 3 percent of the new admissions for any given year. These smaller categories have been eliminated from the sample for the sake of clarity and comparison.

8. See Melissa Harris-Lacewell, "No Place to Rest: African American Political Attitudes and the Myth of Black Women's Strength," *Women and Politics* 23, no. 3 (2001): 1–33; Susan Douglas and Meredith Michaels, *The Mommy Myth: The Idealization of Motherhood and How It Has Undermined All Women* (New York: Free Press, 2004).

9. Gloria Hull, Patricia Bell-Scott, and Barbara Smith, eds., *All the Women Are White, All the Blacks Are Men, but Some of Us Are Brave: Black Women's Studies* (Boston: Feminist Press, 1982); Combahee River Collective, "Combahee River Collective Statement," in *Capitalist Patriarchy and the Case for Socialist Feminism,* ed. Zillah Eisenstein (New York: Monthly Review, 1978) ; Gloria Anzaldua, *Borderlands/La Frontera: The New Mestiza* (San Francisco: Aunt Lute Books, 1987); Cherrie Moraga and Gloria Anzaldua, eds., *This Bridge Called My*

Back: Writings by Radical Women of Color (New York: Kitchen Table: Women of Color Press, 1981); Chela Sandoval, *Methodology of the Oppressed* (Minneapolis: University of Minnesota Press, 2000). Also see, Assata Shakur, *Assata* (Chicago: Lawrence Hill Books, 1987).

10. "Preliminary Report of the Special Committee on Mental Health Legislation for Criminal Cases," 1. In accordance with the law, Ionia Hospital remained the receiving hospital for "sexual psychopathic persons." Men convicted of sexual deviance were remanded to Ionia for a sixty-day period of observation and treatment, after which time the hospital made disposition recommendations to the State Hospital Commission. Roughly half of these people were transferred to state prisons, while the other half remained at Ionia. Ionia State Hospital Report for the Fiscal Year 1937–38, 2–3, and Ionia State Hospital for the Fiscal Year 1940–41, 2–5, in Annual Reports of the Ionia State Hospital, 1937–1956, group 70–47, box 1, Michigan State Archives, Executive/Mental Health Collection. Also see Ian Robert Dowbiggin, *Keeping America Sane: Psychiatry and Eugenics in the United States and Canada 1880–1940* (Ithaca: Cornell University Press, 1997).

11. Ionia State Hospital Report for the Fiscal Year 1937–38, pp. 2–3, and Ionia State Hospital Report for the Fiscal Year 1940–41, pp. 2–5, in Annual Reports of the Ionia State Hospital, 1937–1956, group 70–47, box 1, Michigan State Archives, Executive/Mental Health Collection.

CHAPTER 10

1. Ionia State Hospital Report for the Fiscal Year 1950–1951, 2–4, in Annual Reports of the Ionia State Hospital, 1937–1956, group 70–47, box 1, Michigan State Archives, Executive/Mental Health Collection.

2. Ionia State Hospital Report for the Fiscal Year 1954–55, 1–11, in Annual Reports of the Ionia State Hospital, 1937–1956, group 70–47, box 1, Michigan State Archives, Executive/Mental Health Collection.

3. Ionia State Hospital Report for the Fiscal Year 1957–58, 2–7, and Changes and Corrections as of March 10, 1965, on the Report on the Ionia State Hospital Made by the Central Inspection Board of the American Psychiatric Association, 1957, 2, 6–10, 22, in Annual Reports of the Ionia State Hospital, 1957–65, group 70–47, box 2–4, Michigan State Archives, Executive/Mental Health Collection.

4. See, Jonathan M. Metzl, *Prozac on the Couch: Prescribing Gender in the Era of Wonder Drugs* (Durham, NC: Duke University Press, 2003), 71–126.

5. Ionia State Hospital Report for the Fiscal Year 1954–55, 2–4.

6. "Death Increases Fear of Reprisal Against Guards Held as Hostages," *The Washington Post*, April 22, 1952, 1; Edwin Kennedy, "Convicts End 4 Day Revolt to Eat Steak," *Chicago Daily Tribune*, April 25, 1952, 1; "Felon Mutiny Ends; Hostages Set Free," *Los Angeles Times*, April 25, 1952, 1; Ira Henry Freeman, "Prison Revolts Dramatize Need For Various Reforms," *New York Times*, April 27, 1952, E7. For an interesting perspective, also see Edward M. Kennedy, "Prison Overcrowding: The Law's Dilemma," *Annals of the American Academy of Political and Social Science* 478 (March 1985): 113–22.

7. Ira Henry Freeman, "Prison Revolts Dramatize Need for Various Reforms," *New York Times*, April 27, 1952.

8. See "Convicts Bully a Sovereign State," *Life* (May 5, 1952): 27–33; Austin H. MacCormick, "Behind the Prison Riots," *Annals of the American Academy of Political and Social Science* 293 (May 1954): 17–27.

9. Ionia State Hospital Report for the Fiscal Year 1954–55, 1–11, in Annual Reports of the Ionia State Hospital, 1937–1956, group 70–47, box 1, Michigan State Archives, Executive/Mental Health Collection.

10. See Gerald Grob, "The Origins of DSM-I: A Study in Appearance and Reality," *American Journal of Psychiatry* 148 (1991): 421–31.

11. *Mental Disorders: Diagnostic and Statistical Manual* (Washington, DC: American Psychiatric Association Press, 1952), 26–27.

12. Metzl, *Prozac on the Couch*, 1–126.

13. David Healy, *The Creation of Psychopharmacology* (Cambridge, MA: Harvard University Press, 2002), 97–98.

14. Ionia State Hospital Report for the Fiscal Year 1954–55, 1–11, in Annual Reports of the Ionia State Hospital, 1937–1956, group 70–47, box 1, Michigan State Archives, Executive/Mental Health Collection. Also see Gerald N. Grob, *Mental Institutions in America—Social Policy to 1975* (New York: Free Press, 1973); Grob, *The Mad Among Us: A History of the Care of America's Mentally Ill* (New York: Free Press, 1994).

15. Sam Cooke, "A Change Is Gonna Come," *Ain't That Good News,* RCA Records, December 1964.

CHAPTER 11

1. Elie Abel, "Michigan Prisoners Isolated By Troopers in 20–Hour Riot; At the Scene of the Jackson State Prison Mutiny in Michigan Police Stem Prison Riot," *New York Times,* April 22, 1952, 1.

2. *Mental Disorders: Diagnostic and Statistical Manual* (Washington, DC: American Psychiatric Association Press, 1952), 26–27.

3. Ibid., 25.

4. Ibid., 14–16.

5. Ibid., 38, 97.

CHAPTER 12

1. See Gregory Bateson, et al., "Toward a Theory of Schizophrenia," *Behavioral Science* 1 (1956): 251–64; Gregory Bateson, *Steps to an Ecology of Mind: Collected Essays in Anthropology, Psychiatry, Evolution, and Epistemology* (Chicago: University of Chicago Press, 1972).

CHAPTER 13

1. *Diagnostic and Statistical Manual of Mental Disorders,* 2nd ed. (Washington, DC: American Psychiatric Association Press, 1968), vii, viii.

2. Ibid., ix. For a discussion of Margaret Mead's unfinished manuscript, "Learning to Live in One World," see http://www.loc.gov/exhibits/mead/oneworld-learn.html, accessed January 10, 2007.

3. Conversation with Robert Spitzer, Princeton, New Jersey, December 2, 2008. Also see Mitchell Wilson, "*DSM-III* and the Transformation of American Psychiatry: A History," *American Journal of Psychiatry* 150 (1993): 399–410.

4. *Mental Disorders: Diagnostic and Statistical Manual* (Washington, DC: American Psychiatric Association Press, 1952), 26–27. An "attitude of hostility and aggression" was less prominently mentioned in the DSM-I.

5. Conversation with Robert Spitzer, Princeton, New Jersey, December 2, 2008.

6. Stokely Carmichael, *Ready for Revolution: The Life and Struggles of Stokely Carmichael (Kwame Ture)* (New York: Scribner, 2005); Clayborne Carson, *In Struggle, SNCC and the Black Awakening of the 1960's* (Cambridge, MA: Harvard University Press, 1981); John Lewis, *Walking with the Wind: A Memoir of the Movement* (New York: Simon & Schuster, 1998); Imari Abubakari Obadele, *Foundations of the Black Nation* (Detroit: House of Songay, 1975); Kwame Afoh, Chokwe Lumumba, and Ahmed Obafemi, *A Brief History of the Black Struggle in America, with Obadele's Macro-Level Theory of Human Organization* (Baton Rouge: House of Songhay, Commission for Positive Education, 1991); "Malcolm X (1925–1965), U.S. African-American leader," Oxford Union Society Debate, December 3, 1964.

7. R. A. Schermerhorn, "Psychiatric Disorders Among Negroes: A Sociological Note," *American Journal of Psychiatry* 112 (1956): 878–82. Also see C. R. Lafferty, Wilma J. Knox, "Schizophrenia In Relation to Blood Groups Abo and Blood Types Rh. D. and Mn," *American Journal of Psychiatry* 115 (1958): 161–62.

8. Walter Bromberg, Frank Simon, "The 'Protest' Psychosis: A Special Type of Reactive Psychosis," *Archives of General Psychiatry* 19 (1968): 155–60.

9. C. M. Pierce, L. J. West, "Six Years of Sit-Ins: Psychodynamic Causes and Effects," *International Journal of Social Psychiatry* 12, no. 1 (1966): 29–34; A. Raskin, T. H. Crook, and K. D. Herman, "Psychiatric History and Symptom Differences in Black and White Patients," *Journal of Consulting & Clinical Psychology* 43, no. 1: 73–80; E. B. Brody, "Social Conflict and Schizophrenic Behavior in Young Adult Negro Males," *Psychiatry: Journal for the Study of Interpersonal Processes* 24, no.4 (1961): 337–46, 343; M. M. Vitols, H. G. Waters, and M. H. Keeler, "Hallucinations and Delusions in White and Negro Schizophrenics," *American Journal of Psychiatry* 120 (1963): 472–76.

10. See, for example, Gregory Zilboorg, "Suicide Among Civilized and Primitive Races," *American Journal of Psychiatry* 92 (193): 1347–69; Gambino, "'These Strangers Within Our Gates'"; Dalal, *Race, Colour and the Process of Racialization*. Of course, going back to at least the mid-nineteenth century, insanity was thought to be a disease of civilization and primitives were thought to be relatively immune from it. See Charles Rosenberg, "Pathologies of Progress: The Idea of Civilization as Risk," *Bulletin of the History of Medicine* 72 (1998); Peter McCandless, *Moonlight, Magnolias, and Madness: Insanity in South Carolina from the Colonial Period to the Progressive Era* (Chapel Hill: University of North Carolina Press, 1996); Todd Savitt, *Medicine and Slavery: The Diseases and Health Care of Blacks in Antebellum Virginia* (Champaign-Urbana: University of Illinois Press, 1978).

11. R. J. Simon, J. L. Fleiss, B. J. Gurland, et al., "Depression and Schizophrenia in Black and White Mental Patients," *Archives of General Psychiatry*, no. 28 (1973): 509–12; J. L. Liss, A. Welner, E. Robins E, et al., "Psychiatric Symptoms in White and Black Inpatients," *Comprehensive Psychiatry* 14 (1973): 475–81; Arturo De Hoyos and Genevieve De Hoyos, "Symptomatology Differentials Between Negro and White Schizophrenics," *International*

Journal of Social Psychiatry 11 (1965): 245–55. For a fascinating early example of racism described as schizophrenic illness, see the comments of journalist and historian of psychiatry Albert Deutsch in Earl Conrad, "Schizophrenia of Racism," *Chicago Defender,* November 24, 1945.

12. V. R. Adebimpie, "White Norms and Psychiatric Diagnosis: Overview," *American Journal of Psychiatry* 138: 279–85; A. Thomas, S. Sillen, *Racism and Psychiatry* (Secaucus, NJ: Citadel Press, 1979); Charles A. Pinderhughes, "Understanding Black Power: Processes and Proposals," *American Journal of Psychiatry* 125 (1969): 1552–57; J. Spurlock, ed., *Black Psychiatrists and American Psychiatry* (Washington, DC: American Psychiatric Association Press, 1999), 14–15.

13. www.ajp.psychiatryonline.org, accessed May 20, 2006, to August 20, 2006.

14. For full analysis, see Jonathan M. Metzl and Sara McClelland, "Race-Based Trends in Scientific Literature, 1940–1980," in press.

15. Racism, as Fanon rightly details, drives men into madness. For another excellent perspective on this point, see Erica James's description of "traumatic citizenship" in Erica Caple James, "The Political Economy of 'Trauma' in Haiti in the Democratic Era of Insecurity," *Culture, Medicine and Psychiatry* 28, no. 2 (2004): 127–49.

CHAPTER 14

1. Elaine Showalter, *The Female Malady: Women, Madness, and English Culture, 1830–1980* (New York: Pantheon, 1985); Christopher Lane, *Shyness: How Normal Behavior Became a Sickness* (New Haven: Yale University Press, 2007).

2. Proquest Historical Newspapers search engine contains articles from such papers as the *New York Times* from 1851 to 2003, *Los Angeles Times* from 1881 to 1985, and *Chicago Tribune* from 1852 to 1985. The site also provides text searches of one so-called black press newspaper, the *Chicago Defender,* dating back to 1905. (A related site, Ethnic News Watch Historical, begins its coverage of black papers in 1960.) Periodical databases such as the Reader's Guide Electronic or the *Time* Electronic Archive contain full-text articles as far back as the 1920s. Sites accessed through www.lib.umich.edu on January 4–6, 2007. At the time of this writing, these sites contain no comparable databases for performing historical text searches for mainstream newspapers from the southern United States.

3. Sites accessed through www.lib.umich.edu on January 4–6, 2007.

4. The *Defender* archive on Proquest dates to the turn of the twentieth century, but as of this writing, Ethnic News Watch goes back only to 1960. Thus only the *Defender* numbers are listed here.

5. The *Chicago Defender,* founded by Robert S. Abbott on May 5, 1905, once heralded itself as "The World's Greatest Weekly." The newspaper was the nation's most influential black weekly newspaper by the advent of World War I, with more than two-thirds of its readership base located outside of Chicago. Of note, the *Defender* rarely used the words *Negro* or *black* in its pages. Instead, African Americans were referred to as "the Race" and black men and women as "Race men and Race women."

6. "Circumstances of Pressure," *Time,* January 28, 1957.

7. "The End for Eddie," *Time,* December 28, 1962.

8. "Two Boys, 12, Face Slaying Hearing," *New York Times,* October 19, 1964.

9. "U.S. Prison Escapee, 42, on FBI's Top List of 10," *Chicago Defender,* June 8, 1963, 19; "FBI Adds Negro Mental Patient to '10 Most Wanted' List," *Chicago Tribune,* July 6, 1966.

10. One high-profile exception was Marcus Wayne Chenault's 1974 murder of Alberta Williams King, mother of Martin Luther King Jr., as she played the organ during Sunday services at Ebenezer Baptist Church.

11. Layhmond Robinson, "More Is Called For Than Social Protest and Desegregation," *New York Times Book Review,* October 11, 1964.

12. "Books: Leaders in the Field," *New York Times Book Review,* June 6, 1965.

13. Gene Roberts, "Integration in South: Erratic Pattern," *New York Times,* May 29, 1967.

14. "Black Pride," *Time,* October 6, 1967. See also, David Boroff, "The College Intellectual, 1965 Model," *New York Times,* December 6, 1964.

15. "The Negro After Watts," *Time,* August 27, 1965.

16. Kirk Sale, "The Amsterdam News: Black Is Beautiful—Ugly—Comfortable—Sensational—Moderate—Militant," *New York Times,* February 9, 1969.

17. Martin Arnold, "There Is No Rest for Roy Wilkins: Nixon to the Left of Him, Black Militants to the Right," *New York Times,* September 28, 1969.

18. Bosley Crowther, "The Screen," *New York Times,* September 12, 1963.

19. Kenneth B. Clark, *Dark Ghetto: Dilemmas of Social Power* (New York: Harper and Row, 1965). Also see Shelly Eversley, "The Lunatic's Fancy and the Work of Art," *American Literary History* 13, no. 3 (2001): 445–68. Psychological language appeared in the controversial 1965 report *The Negro Family: The Case for National Action,* which later became known as the Moynihan Report.

20. See Allan Bloom, trans., *The Republic of Plato* (New York: Basic Books, 1991). Also see, Daryl Scott, *Contempt and Pity: Social Policy and the Image of the Damaged Black Psyche, 1880–1996* (Chapel Hill: University of North Carolina Press, 1997).

21. Jackie Robinson, "Counter Revolution," *New York Amsterdam News,* April 11, 1964.

22. "The Negro After Watts," *Time,* August 27, 1965.

23. "U.S. Students in 1st Fight for Freedom," *Tri-State Defender,* April 16, 1960.

24. Williams, Nat D., "Dark Shadows," *Tri-State Defender,* March 24, 1961.

25. "U.S. Music Taste Jim Crow, Says Jerry Butler," *Oakland Post,* February 23, 1969.

26. "Chicago's Growing Racial Crisis," *Chicago Defender,* March 4, 1963.

27. See also, Edwin C. Berry, "System to Blame for Segregation," *Chicago Daily Defender,* February 28, 1967.

28. Augustus Hawkins, "What Chance Is There?" *Sacramento Observer,* October 30, 1969.

29. Harold Sims, "The Court and the Poor," *Sacramento Observer,* May 13, 1971.

30. Similar assumptions even appeared in the extensive coverage of the slaying of white civil rights protester William L. Moore. Moore, a postal worker from Binghamton, New York, was shot and killed on an Alabama highway in April 1963 while attempting to deliver a letter decrying segregation to Mississippi governor Ross Barnett. (The letter begged Barnett and citizens of his state to relent in their treatment of Negroes, for "the white man cannot be truly free himself until all men have their rights.") According to the *New Pittsburgh Courier,* the Congress of Racial Equality (CORE), and even Moore himself, mental anguish *caused by*

segregation led to Moore's desperate act of protest. Moore aptly titled his self-published autobiography *The Mind in Chains: Autobiography of a Schizophrenic.* The *Courier* used similar language to describe an admittedly "eccentric," sympathetic white man who sought a "dialogue with America, a case of pointing out that this man's murder, while an isolated act, was symptomatic of the schizophrenia in American life." See, "In Alabama: CORE to Continue Freedom Walk to Honor Slain Postman," *New Pittsburgh Courier,* May 4, 1963; "Discrimination Made Slain Man 'Sick at Heart,'" *New Pittsburgh Courier,* May 6, 1963.

31. "Dr. M. L. King Declares: 'Maladjust Yourselves to Fight for Rights,'" *New Pittsburgh Courier,* October 14, 1961.

32. Martin Luther King Jr., *Where Do We Go from Here: Chaos or Community?* (Boston: Beacon Press, 1968), 191.

33. Clayborne Carson, Peter Holloran, eds., *A Knock at Midnight: Inspiration from the Great Sermons of Reverend Martin Luther King, Jr.* (New York: Warner Books, 1998), 187–200. Hear audio excerpts of the Unfulfilled Dreams speech at: http://www.stanford.edu/group/King/publications/sermons/680303.000_Unfulfulled_Dreams.html; Also see, Dr. Martin Luther King Jr., "Sit In, Stand In, Wade In, Kneel In," *New York Amsterdam News,* May 25, 1963.

34. The fascinating, terrifying FBI file is reproduced at http://foia.fbi.gov/malcolmx/malcolmx1.pdf, accessed January 10, 2007: "In May 1953, the FBI concluded that Malcolm X had an 'asocial personality with paranoid trends (pre-psychotic paranoid schizophrenia),' and had, in fact, sought treatment for his disorder. This was further supported by a letter intercepted by the FBI, dated June 29, 1950. The letter said, in reference to his 4-F classification and rejection by the military, "Everyone has always said . . . Malcolm is crazy, so it isn't hard to convince people that I am."

35. "FBI Hunts NAACP Leader," *New York Amsterdam News,* September 23, 1961. Also see, Timothy B. Tyson, *Radio Free Dixie: Robert F. Williams & the Roots of Black Power* (Chapel Hill: University of North Carolina Press, 1999), 182.

36. Robert F. Williams, *Negroes with Guns* (Detroit: Wayne State Press, 1998 reprint of 1962 text), 54–55, 72–73; Angela Davis, *Angela Davis: An Autobiography* (New York: International Publishers, 1989). Importantly, whites were not the only ones who used the language of schizophrenia to pathologize black militancy. See, for instance, Jackie Robinson, "Counter Revolution," *New York Amsterdam News,* April 11, 1964.

37. Stokely Carmichael, "Black Power," July 28, 1966, speech. Full text reproduced at http://www.answers.com/topic/black-power-speech-28-july-1966-by-stokely-carmichael, accessed February 1, 2008.

38. Hughes wrote that "a Negro's mental and nervous system can be just as gravely injured by Jim Crow shock as it can be injured by the contusion of explosives." Langston Hughes, Christopher Santis, *Langston Hughes and the *Chicago Defender*: Essays on Race, Politics, and Culture, 1942–62* (Champaign-Urbana: University of Illinois Press, 1995), 149–51; Kim Brewster, "Book Corner," *Bay State Banner,* July 18, 1968; See also, John Leo, "Negro 'Paranoia' Assayed in Book: White Racism Said to Push Blacks to the Brink," *New York Times,* April 25, 1968. Also see, W. H. Grier, "When the Therapist Is Negro: Some Effects on the Treatment Process," *American Journal of Psychiatry* 123 (1967): 1587–92.

39. William H. Grier, Price M. Cobbs, *Black Rage* (New York: Basic Books, 1968), 93–95, 133–35; Dianne Thompson, "How to Survive with a Sense of Dignity," *New York Amsterdam*

News, February 15, 1969. Also see "Grier Talks on Book Beat," *Chicago Daily Defender,* September 3, 1968.

40. "Leroi Jones Tells MSU Pupils of 2d U.S. 'Nation,'" *Chicago Daily Defender,* May 12, 1969; Milton Esterow, "New Role of Negroes in Theater Reflects Ferment of Integration," *New York Times,* June 15, 1964.

41. W.E.B Du Bois, *The Souls of Black Folk* (New York: Vintage Books, 1990), 9.

42. See, for instance, D. Bruce Dickson Jr., "W.E.B. Du Bois and the Idea of Double Consciousness," in *W.E.B. Du Bois, The Souls of Black Folk: Authoritative Text, Contexts, Criticism,* eds. Henry Louis Gates Jr. and Terri Hume Oliver (New York: W.W. Norton, 1999), 236–44.

43. W.E.B Du Bois, *The Souls of Black Folk* (New York: Vintage Books, 1990), 142–43.

44. Shelly Eversley, "The Lunatic's Fancy and the Work of Art," *American Literary History* 13, no. 3 (2001): 445–68; Ralph Ellison, *The Invisible Man,* 2nd Vintage International ed. (New York: Vintage, 1947/1995), 575–80. See also Sara Slack, "Baldwin Hits White Liberals," *New York Amsterdam News,* October 26, 1963, 21. In very different form, early debates between Du Bois, *Chicago Defender* publisher Robert Abbott, activist Marcus Garvey, and others revolved around the African American "split personality" that divided African Americans from American white culture, or African Americans from their African homelands. See, for example, Samuel Lubell, *White and Black: Test of a Nation* (New York: Harper & Row, 1964), 30–45.

45. Frantz Fanon, *Black Skin, White Masks,* Charles Lam Markmann, trans. (New York: Grove Press, 1967), 13, 17–18, 38. For a useful discussion of connections between Du Bois and Fanon, see T. Owens Moore, "A Fanonian Perspective on Double Consciousness," *Journal of Black Studies* 35 (2005): 751–62.

46. I. Shenker, "50 Rabbis and Negro Clergymen Searching for Racial Peace," *New York Times,* January 31, 1969. See also Ernest Boynton, "Violence, the Church: Some Reflections," *Chicago Daily Defender,* April 19, 1969.

47. For a brilliant analysis, see Adam Gussow, "'Shoot Myself a Cop' Mamie Smith's 'Crazy Blues' as Social Text," *Callaloo* 25, no. 1 (2002): 8–44. Or, as the comedian Dick Gregory described it in a 1972 performance, "What baffles me is so many white folks in America keep wantin' to know w-w-w-what's wrong with 'em? Niggers must be crazy! I hope they understand one thing. Niggers' got more sense today then ever before in the history of America. And when Niggas was basically crazy, that's when he thought we had good sense." Dick Gregory, "Speech," in *Nationtime,* Gary Williams Greaves Productions Inc., 1972. Also see, Dick Gregory, "Black Politics," *Humanist* 28, no. 5 (1968): 11–12.

CHAPTER 15

1. Case files for this section come from: Ionia State Hospital case files 8425–9764, accession number RG 80–13, box 450–624, location 54/18/5-54/18/3. State Archives of Michigan, Lansing.

CHAPTER 16

1. Thomas S. Szasz, "The Myth of Mental Illness," *American Psychologist* 15 (1960): 113–18.

2. David G. Cooper. *Psychiatry and Anti-Psychiatry* (New York: Paladin, 1967), ix; David G. Cooper, *The Language of Madness* (New York: Penguin, 1978).

3. See David Cooper, ed., *The Dialectics of Liberation* (New York: Penguin, 1968).

4. R. D. Laing, *The Divided Self: An Existential Study in Sanity and Madness* (Harmondsworth: Penguin, 1960); Gilles Deleuze and Félix Guattari, "Anti Oedipus" in *Capitalism and Schizophrenia,* vol. 1, trans. Robert Hurley, Mark Seem, and Helen R. Lane (London and New York: Continuum, 2004); Joseph Heller, *Catch-22* (New York: Simon & Schuster, 1961); Gregory Bateson with Don D. Jackson, Jay Haley, and John Weakland, "Toward a Theory of Schizophrenia," *Behavioral Science* 1, no. 4 (1956), reprinted in Bateson, *Steps to an Ecology of Mind* (San Francisco: Chandler Publishing Co., 1972); Robert Jay Lifton, "The American as Blind Giant Unable to See What It Kills," *New York Times Book Review,* June 14, 1970. For an excellent overview, see Michael Staub, "Madness Is Civilization: Psycho Politics in Postwar America," *Occasional Papers* from the Princeton School of Advanced Study, no. 34 (October 2008).

5. H. Richard Lamb, "Deinstitutionalization at the Beginning of the New Millennium," *Harvard Review of Psychiatry* 6 (1998): 1–9. Also see L. D. Ozarin and S. S. Sharfstein, "The Aftermaths of Deinstitutionalization: Problems and Solutions," *Psychiatric Quarterly* 50 (1978): 128–32; E. Fuller Torrey, *Nowhere to Go: The Tragic Odyssey of the Homeless Mentally Ill* (New York: Harper & Row, 1988).

6. "Final Report of the Citizen's Mental Health Inquiry Board to Gov. G. Mennen Williams, December 1, 1960"; Letter to the editor by Holden Cook, "Ionia Hospital Charged with Haphazard Care," *Detroit Free Press,* March 30, 1964; "Additional Reports on the Gonococcal Infection of Male Patients at the Ionia State Hospital," February 12, 1965; "Michigan Department of Mental Health Memorandum from James A. Peal, MD, to R. A. Kimmich, MD, April 22, 1965"; "Preliminary Report of the Ionia State Hospital Medical Audit Committee, September 20, 1965."

7. "Michigan Mental Health: A Synopsis of Michigan's Program for the Mentally Disordered Criminal Offender," January 23, 1964; "Preliminary Report of the Special Committee on Mental Health Legislation for Criminal Cases," 1–2; "Conversion of Ionia State Hospital to General Regional Mental Hospital for Western Central Michigan," March 10, 1967, 1–4; "Preliminary Report of the Ionia State Hospital Medical Audit Committee," September 20, 1965.

8. "Preliminary Report of the Special Committee on Mental Health Legislation for Criminal Cases," August 1, 1968, 1–2. "Ionia State Hospital Booklet," May 1971, 5; "Conversion of Ionia State Hospital to General Regional Mental Hospital for Western Central Michigan," March 10, 1967, 1–4; Albert Lee, CPA, "Audit Report, Ionia State Hospital, June 1, 1969 through September 30, 1972," Lansing: State of Michigan Office of the Auditor General, August 26, 1969, 14.

Also see: "Michigan Mental Health: A Synopsis of Michigan's Program for the Mentally Disordered Criminal Offender," January 23, 1964; "Michigan Department of Mental Health Memorandum from James A. Peal, MD, to R. A. Kimmich, MD, April 22, 1965"; "Conversion of Ionia State Hospital to General Regional Mental Hospital for Western Central Michigan," March 10, 1967, 1–4; "Ionia Case Proves the Power of Aroused Public Opinion," *Battle Creek Inquirer and News,* December 2, 1965; A. A. Birzgalis, "'Protection of Society' Cited as One of Hospital's Key Goals," news release, July 13, 1967; "Ionia State Hospital Booklet," May 1971; Albert Lee, CPA, "Audit Report, Ionia State Hospital, July 31, 1965 through May 31, 1969,"

Lansing: State of Michigan Office of the Auditor General, August 26, 1969; "Changes and Corrections as of March 10, 1965 on the Report to the Ionia State Hospital Made by the Central Inspection Board of the American Psychiatric Association in 1957"; "Discharging Mental Patients Failed in California, Ionia Employees Say," *Ionia Sentinel-Standard,* May 6, 1973; "Death Is Blamed on Plastic Bag at State Hospital," *Ionia Sentinel-Standard,* January 6, 1973; "Patient at Ionia State Hospital Is a Walkaway," *Ionia Sentinel-Standard,* January 25, 1973; "Dr. Yudashkin Has Said 'He Will Deny It,'" *Ionia Sentinel-Standard,* February 28, 1973; "Hospital Employees Have Explanation," *Ionia Sentinel-Standard,* March 23, 1973; "Employees Cut off at Hospital," *Ionia Sentinel-Standard,* April 28, 1973: "Governor Meets State Employees," *Ionia Sentinel-Standard,* March 13, 1973; "Aiding, Abetting Mental Patient Is the Charge," *Ionia Sentinel-Standard,* September 4, 1973; "Patient at State Hospital Is Missing," *Ionia Sentinel-Standard,* September 4, 1973; "Four Patients Walk Away," *Ionia Sentinel-Standard,* 14 August 1973; "One of 4 Missing Patients Returns," *Ionia Sentinel-Standard,* August 15, 1973.

CHAPTER 17

1. "We Will Serve the Patient Effectively as Long as We Are Here," *Riverside Review* IV, no. 2 (May 1976).

2. See, "When Life in the Projects Was Good," *New York Times,* July 31, 1991; http://info.detnews.com/history/story/index.cfm?id=185&category=events, accessed May 1, 2007.

3. Sidney Fine, *Violence in the Model City* (Ann Arbor, MI: University of Michigan Press, 1989); "Return to 12th Street: A Follow-Up Survey of Attitudes of Detroit Negroes," *Detroit Free Press,* October 7, 1968.

4. Hubert G. Locke, *The Detroit Riot of 1967* (Detroit: Wayne State University Press, 1969); Thomas Sugrue, *The Origins of the Urban Crisis: Race and Inequality in Post-War Detroit* (Princeton, NJ: Princeton University Press, 1996), 260.

5. See C. Eric Lincoln, *The Black Muslims in America* (Boston: Beacon Press, 1961); Henry J. Young, *Major Black Religious Leaders Since 1940* (Nashville: Abingdon, 1979), 66–67; Clifton E. Marsh, *From Black Muslims to Muslims* (Metuchen, NJ: Scarecrow Press, 1984), 52.

6. David M. Oshinsky, *Worse Than Slavery: Parchman Farm and the Ordeal of Jim Crow Justice* (New York: Free Press, 1997); Peter Charles Hoffer, *Seven Fires: The Urban Infernos That Reshaped America* (New York: Public Affairs Press, 2006); Imari Abubakari Obadele, *Foundations of the Black Nation* (Detroit: House of Songay, 1975); Brother Imari (Imari Obadele), *War In America: The Malcolm X Doctrine* (Chicago: Ujamaa Distributors, 1977).

7. Cooper, *Psychiatry and Anti-Psychiatry.*

CHAPTER 18

1. Stokely Carmichael, "Black Power, A Critique of the System of International White Supremacy & International Capitalism," in *The Dialectics of Liberation,* ed. David Cooper (New York: Penguin), 151.

2. Albert Lee, CPA, "Audit Report, Ionia State Hospital, July 31, 1965 through May 31, 1969," Lansing: State of Michigan Office of the Auditor General, August 26, 1969; "Discharging Mental Patients Failed in California, Ionia Employees Say," *Ionia Sentinel-Standard,* May 6, 1973.

3. Vitols, "Hallucinations and Delusions in White and Negro Schizophrenics."

4. More recently, the research psychiatrist Arthur Whaley has done vital research into the "Cultural Relativity" hypothesis, which assumes that "Blacks and Whites have different modes of expressing psychopathology" and that "clinicians are unaware of or insensitive to cultural difference." See Arthur L. Whaley, "Ethnicity/Race, Paranoia, and Psychiatric Diagnosis: Clinician Bias Versus Sociocultural Differences," *Journal of Psychopathology and Behavioral Assessment* 19, no. 1 (1997): 1–20.

5. Lee, "Audit Report, Ionia State Hospital."

6. "Officials Tour State Hospital," *Ionia Sentinel-Standard,* August 2, 1973, 2; Lee, "Audit Report, Ionia State Hospital, July 31, 1965 through May 31, 1969," 14; "Preliminary Report of the Special Committee on Mental Health Legislation for Criminal Cases," 1–2; "Ionia State Hospital Booklet," May 1971, 5.

7. Glen Loury, *The Anatomy of Racial Inequality* (Cambridge, MA: Harvard University Press, 2002), 23, 26, 30–31.

8. Michel Foucault, *Discipline and Punish: The Birth of the Prison* (New York: Random House, 1975); Foucault, *The History of Sexuality: An Introduction* (New York: Random House, 1978), 93; Foucault, *Society Must Be Defended* (New York: Penguin, 1997/2003), 254–63.

9. Erik Eckholm, "A China Dissident's Ordeal: Back to the Mental Hospital," *New York Times,* November 30, 1999.

10. Foucault, *History of Sexuality,* 93. By this interpretation, the definition of schizophrenia at Ionia widened to encompass black protest, black protesters, and many other men who were guilty by association. Men who sought *"Black identification through interest in Islam,"* or *"supports Black Power"* clearly met criteria. Soon, men who protested their incarceration at Ionia or who fought against medication or prolonged restraint fell under schizophrenia's diagnostic gaze. *"Problem inmate, dangerous, threatened guards . . . required confinement."* All the while, psychiatry's increasing emphasis on real-time clinical observations, and then on biological explanations of mental illness, made it more difficult for psychiatrists to recognize the political implications of their clinical actions.

11. Frantz Fanon, *Black Skin, White Masks,* trans. Charles Lam Markmann (New York: Grove Press, 1967), 13, 17–18, 38.

12. After all, supporting Black Power and telling a psychiatrist that one *"supports Black Power"* are not one and the same.

CHAPTER 19

1. Gertrude Stein, *Valentine to Sherwood Anderson* (New York: Peer International Corp, 1951); Liesl M. Olson, "Gertrude Stein, William James, and Habit in the Shadow of War," *Twentieth Century Literature* 49, no. 3 (2003): 328–59. Stein termed this phenomenon "insistence" rather than repetition, as influenced by the psychologist William James, who associated habits with character-building behavior. Also see Thomas Fahy, "Iteration as a Form of Narrative Control in Gertrude Stein's 'The Good Anna,'" *Style* 34, no. 1 (2000): 25–36.

2. "Women do not present much of a problem . . . there is not the prison-like custodial management of the women that there is of the men." Michigan Department of Mental Health Memorandum from James A. Peal, MD, to R. A. Kimmich, MD, April 22, 1965, 3–5; "The

female patient population has been reduced to 40 in 1969, from 114 in 1965," Lee, "Audit Report, Ionia State Hospital."

3. See, "Ionia State Hospital Booklet," May 1971, 8.

4. Gertrude Stein, "Sacred Emily," in *Geography and Plays* (Madison: University of Wisconsin, 1922/1993).

5. Or perhaps depression looked more like Alice Wilson. In either case, Alice stood still, while the frame through which she was viewed changed around her. For a discussion of the gendering of depression in the United States, see Jonathan Metzl, *Prozac on the Couch: Prescribing Gender in the Era of Wonder Drugs* (Durham, NC: Duke University Press, 2003). The discussion of poetics in this chapter is also meant to signify changing associations between genius and mental illness. To recall, schizophrenia was considered closely aligned with artistic temperament, genius, or hyperproductivity in the 1930s, and the late 1950s saw brief fetishization of so-called schizophrenic art. But such associations shifted almost entirely to mood disorders after schizophrenia became a somatic illness in the 1970s. See Emily Martin, *Bipolar Expeditions: Mania and Depression in American Culture* (Princeton, NJ: Princeton University Press, 2007).

6. Ruth Frankenberg, "Whiteness as an 'Unmarked' Cultural Category," in eds. Karen E. Rosenblum and Toni-Michelle C. Travis, *The Meaning of Difference: American Constructions of Race, Sex and Gender, Social Class, and Sexual Orientation,* 3rd ed. (New York: McGraw-Hill, 2003), 92–98; Paul Gilroy, *Against Race: Imagining Political Culture beyond the Color Line* (Cambridge, MA: Belknap Press, 2002), 42; Frantz Fanon, *The Wretched of the Earth* (London: Pelican, 1983), 173.

7. Wallace Stevens, "The Snow Man," *The Collected Poems of Wallace Stevens* (New York: Knopf, 1954/1991), 9–10. See also Sara J. Ford, *Gertrude Stein and Wallace Stevens: The Performance of Modern Consciousness* (New York: Routledge, 2002).

CHAPTER 21

1. Excerpt from "End of an Era: State Hospital Now an Official Prison," *Ionia Sentinel-Standard,* January 11, 1977.

CHAPTER 22

1. Francis X. Donnelly, "Ionia finds stability in prisons," *Detroit News,* July 2001.

2. www.michigan.gov/corrections, accessed May 31, 2005.

CHAPTER 23

1. Interview transcription excerpts, former employees of Ionia State Hospital, October 24, 2005; interviewer: Jonathan Metzl; location: Ionia Historical Society, Ionia, Michigan.

2. See Prisoners of the Census: Ionia County, Michigan, http://www.prisonersofthecensus.org/toobig/countydetail/05000US26067, accessed November 25, 2007.

3. Ionia MI Info, http://www.citytowninfo.com/places/michigan/ionia, accessed November 25, 2007.

CHAPTER 24

1. Lynne Duke, "Building a Boom Behind Bars: Prisons Revive Small Towns, but Costs Are Emerging," *Washington Post,* 8 September 2000. Also see Calvin Beale, "Population Change in Rural and Small Town America: 1970–2000," *Rural Voices* 6, no. 3 (2001): 2–5; Peter Wagner, "Detaining for Dollars: Federal Aid Follows Inner-City Prisoners to Rural Town Coffers," (Springfield, MA: Prison Policy Initiative, 2002); Sarah Lawrence, Jeremy Travis, *The New Landscape of Imprisonment: Mapping America's Prison Expansion* (Washington, DC: Justice Policy Center Publications, 2004).

2. LEIN e-mail exchange August 1–15, 2007. Facility tour September 2007. Names omitted by request of prison staff.

3. Visits occurred on October 19, 22, 23, and 24, 2007. On each visit I was accompanied by the prison legal officer.

4. "Riverside Closing Approved," *Ionia Sentinel-Standard,* September 4, 1976; "Ionia Residents Give Views About Institutional Changes," *Ionia Sentinel-Standard,* September 15, 1976; "Building Demolition at Riverside Is Scheduled," *Ionia Sentinel-Standard,* September 18, 1976; "Jaws," *Ionia Sentinel-Standard,* September 22, 1976.

5. Correspondence with Riverside warden's office, 8/6/2007.

6. "New Administration Building," *C.O. Bulletin* III, no. 19 (June 7, 1967): 1; "From the Mailbag," *Ionia Sentinel-Standard,* March 7, 1973.

7. Foucault's triad, as described in *Discipline and Punish,* of hierarchical observation, normalizing judgment, and constant examination seemed a particularly apt point of connection between nursing stations and guard posts, in as much as both function in the project of supervision and control.

8. See "Commitments by Race for Men," *Michigan Department of Corrections 1998 Statistical Report,* Lansing: Dept. of Corrections, 72–74, or at http://www.michigan.gov/documents/1998stats_2143_7.pdf, accessed December 1, 2007; http://www.injusticeline.com/blacks.html, accessed December 1, 2007; Karen Firestone, "Michigan Prison Population and Capacity: A Report for the Michigan Department of Corrections," December 1997. This report can be found at http://www.senate.michigan.gov/sfa/Publications/Issues/PRISPOP/PRISPOP1.html#INTRO, accessed December 1, 2007.

9. See Erving Goffman, *Asylums: Essays on the Social Situation of Mental Patients and Other Inmates* (New York: Anchor Press, 1961); Gerald N. Grob, *The State and the Mentally Ill: A History of Worcester State Hospital in Massachusetts 1830–1920* (Chapel Hill: University of North Carolina Press, 1966); David J. Rothman, *The Discovery of the Asylum: Social Order and Disorder in the New Republic* (Boston: Little Brown, 1971); Michel Foucault, *Discipline and Punish: The Birth of the Prison* (New York: Random House, 1975); Thomas Szasz, *Schizophrenia: The Sacred Symbol of Psychiatry* (Syracuse, New York: Syracuse University Press, 1988); Nancy Tomes, *The Art of Asylum-Keeping: Thomas Story Kirkbride and the Origins of American Psychiatry* (Philadelphia: University of Pennsylvania Press, 1994).

10. Harcourt also perpetuates assumptions about schizophrenic violence by contending that high rates of psychiatric institutionalization in the 1950s correlated with lower homicide rates. Bernard E. Harcourt, "The Mentally Ill, Behind Bars," *New York Times,* January 15, 2007; Bernard Harcourt, "From the Asylum to the Prison: Rethinking the Incarceration Revolution," *Texas Law Review* 84 (2006): 1751–86.

CHAPTER 25

1. http://dictionary.oed.com, accessed November 25, 2007.

2. Some Seventh Day Adventists claim that they will identify vaporized nonbelievers, after the axe falls, by their exclusion from the church of *eschatological remnants*.

3. See, for example, Jacques Lacan, *The Four Fundamental Concepts of Psycho-Analysis* (London: Tavistock, 1977); Dylan Evans, *An Introductory Dictionary of Lacanian Psychoanalysis* (New Brunswick: Rutgers, 1966): 125.

4. *Ill-equipped: U.S. Prisons and Offenders with Mental Illness* (New York: Human Rights Watch, 2003); Linda Teplin, "The Prevalence of Severe Mental Disorder Among Male Urban Jail Detainees: Comparison with the Epidemiologic Catchment Area Program," *American Journal of Public Health* 80, no. 6 (1990); Jeffrey L. Metzner, et al., "Treatment in Jails and Prisons," in *Treatment of Offenders with Mental Disorders,* ed. Robert M. Wittstein (New York: Guilford Press, 1998), 211; American Psychiatric Association, *Psychiatric Services in Jails and Prisons,* 2nd ed. (Washington DC: American Psychiatric Association Press, 2000), introduction, xix; Paige M. Harrison and Allen J. Beck, *Prisoners in 2002* (Washington, DC: U.S. Department of Justice, Bureau of Justice Statistics, July 2003); National Commission on Correctional Health Care, "The Health Status of Soon-to-be-Released Inmates, A Report to Congress," vol. 1 (March 2002): 22.

5. Harcourt, "The Mentally Ill, Behind Bars," "From the Asylum to the Prison."

6. Frederic C. Blow, John E. Zeber, John F. McCarthy, Marcia Valenstein, Leah Gillon, and C. Raymond Bingham, "Ethnicity and Diagnostic Patterns in Veterans with Psychoses," *Social Psychiatry and Psychiatric Epidemiology* 39, no. 10 (2004): 841–51.

7. Vedantam Shankar, "Racial Disparities Found in Pinpointing Mental Illness," *Washington Post,* June 28, 2005, A1 (italics mine).

8. See, as but a few examples, C. Taube, *Admission Rates to State and County Mental Hospitals by Age, Sex, and Color, United States, 1969* (Washington, DC: Department of Health, Education, and Welfare, National Institute of Mental Health, Biometry Branch, 1971), 1–7, statistical note 41; R. J. Simon, J. L. Fleiss, B. J. Gurland, et al., "Depression and Schizophrenia in Black and White Mental Patients," *Archives of General Psychiatry* no. 28 (1973): 509–12; J. L. Liss, A. Welner, E. Robins, et al., "Psychiatric Symptoms in White and Black Inpatients," *Comprehensive Psychiatry* 14 (1973): 475–81; H. Chung, J. C. Mahler, and T. Kakuma, "Racial Differences in Treatment of Psychiatric Inpatients," *Psychiatric Services* 46 (1995): 586–91; S. P. Segal, J. R. Bola, and M. A. Watson, "Race, Quality of Care, and Antipsychotic Prescribing Practices in Psychiatric Emergency Services," *Psychiatric Services* 47 (1996): 282–86; S. Mukherjee, S. Shukla, J. Woodle, A. M. Rosen, and S. Olarte, "Misdiagnosis of Schizophrenia in Bipolar Patients: A Multiethnic Comparison," *American Journal of Psychiatry* 140 (1983): 1571–74; J. Delahanty, "Differences in Rates of Depression in Schizophrenia by Race," *Schizophrenia Bulletin* 152, no. 1 (2001): 29–38. For an excellent overview, see F. M. Baker, Carl C. Bell, "Issues in the Psychiatric Treatment of African Americans," *Psychiatric Services* 50, no. 3 (1999): 362–68.

9. Benedict Carey, "A Psychiatrist Is Slain, and a Sad Debate Deepens," *New York Times,* September 19, 2006; Paul G. Nestor, "Mental Disorder and Violence: Personality Dimensions and Clinical Features," *American Journal of Psychiatry* 159 (2002): 1973–78; John S. Brekke, Cathy Prindle, S. W. Bae, and J. D. Long, "Risks for Individuals with Schizophrenia Who Are Living in the Community," *Psychiatric Services* 52 (2001): 1358–66. Also see, Amy

Green, "Attacks on the Homeless Rise, with Youths Mostly to Blame," *New York Times,* February 15, 2008.

10. Jo C. Phelan, Bruce G. Link, Ann Stueve, and Bernice A. Pescosolido, "Public Conceptions of Mental Illness in 1950 and 1996: What Is Mental Illness and Is It to be Feared?" *Journal of Health and Social Behavior* 41, no. 2 (2000): 188–207. In recent work, Phelan and Link importantly connect the "social patterning of disease" to such factors as access to resources such as money, knowledge, power, prestige, and the social connections that determine the extent to which people are able to avoid risks. For instance, Bruce G. Link, and Jo C. Phelan, "Understanding Sociodemographic Differences in Health—The Role of Fundamental Social Causes," *American Journal of Public Health* 86, no. 4 (1996): 471–73.

11. Ian Hacking, "The Looping Effect of Human Kinds," in *Causal Cognition: An Interdisciplinary Approach,* ed. D. Sperber (Oxford, England: Oxford University Press, 1995), 351–83.

12. "In every entry of being into its habitation in words, there's a margin of forgetting, a lethe complementary to every *aletheia,*" Jacques Lacan, *The Seminar of Jacques Lacan, Book I,* trans. John Forrester, ed. J. A. Miller (Cambridge: Cambridge University Press, 1988), 192. See also Martin Heidegger, *Being and Time* (Oxford, England: Blackwell, 1967).

13. *Diagnostic and Statistical Manual of Mental Disorders,* 3rd ed. (Washington, DC: American Psychiatric Association Press, 1980), 191; *Diagnostic and Statistical Manual of Mental Disorders,* 4th ed., text revised (Washington, DC: American Psychiatric Association Press, 2000).

CHAPTER 26

1. See Nik Brown, "Hope Against Hype—Accountability in Biopasts, Presents, and Futures," *Science Studies* 16, no. 2 (2003): 3–21; Paolo Palladino, "Life . . . on Biology, Biography, and Bio-Power in the Age of Genetic Engineering," *Configurations* 11 (2003): 81–109; Kaushik Sunder Rajan, *Biocapital: The Constitution of Postgenomic Life* (Durham, NC: Duke University Press, 2006).

2. http://www.songlyrics.com/searchtips.php, accessed December 12, 2007. On my search, "placebo crawling dawning" actually yielded zero results.

3. Cat Stevens, "Baby Get Your Head Screwed On," *Matthew & Son,* Universal UK, 1967; America, "Sister Golden Hair," *Hearts,* March 19, 1975, Warner Brothers, producer George Martin; Art Garfunkel/ John Bucchino, "Blessed," *Across America,* Hybrid Recordings, May 21, 1997.

4. Psychostick "Prozak Milkshake," *We Couldn't Think of a Title,* Rock Ridge Music, producer Joshua Key, May 16, 2003; Ani DiFranco, "Pick Yer Nose," *Puddle Dive,* Righteous Babe Records, 1993.

5. EPMD with LL Cool J, "Rampage," *Business as Usual,* Def Jam Records, 1990; Gang Starr, "Speak Ya Clout," *Hard to Earn,* producer DJ Premier, coproducer Guru, Chrysalis/ EMI Records, March 8, 1994; Young Jeezy, "Standing Ovation," *Let's Get It: Thug Motivation 101,* producer Drumma Boy, CTE/Island Def Jam, July 26, 2005; Eddie Haskill, "Intro," *Beautiful Rhyme,* Has-Skill Productions, 2003.

6. Tupac, "16 On Death Row," *R U Still Down (Remember Me),* producer Afeni Shakur, Amaru/BMG/Jive Records, November 25, 1997; Esham, "Symptoms of Insanity," *KKKill the Fetus,* Reel Life Productions, June 16, 1993; Esham, Shoestring/Bootleg/Ghetto E, "Fuck a

Lover," TVT Records, June 19, 2001. In an interesting act of mimesis, the moniker schizophrenic is also claimed by a small subset of white rappers when boasting about their street credibility. See, for instance, the Beastie Boys, "Looking Down the Barrel of a Gun," or, more recently, Twiztid's "Meat Cleaver."

7. Show and A.G., "Hidden Crate," D.I.T.C. Records, May 24, 1998; Bizzy Bone, "Thugz Cry," *Heaven'z Movie,* Ruthless/Relativity/Mo Thugs, October 6, 1998; Busta Rhymes/Rampage/Spliff Star/Rah Digga/Baby Sham, "Everything," *The Imperial,* Elektra, 1998. Also see, Bone Thugs-n-Harmony with Tupac, "Thug Luv."

8. See Alice Richardson, "Baraka's Fiery Launching of Studio Museum Series," *New York Amsterdam News,* April 13, 1985.

9. Jeff Chang, *Can't Stop Won't Stop: A History of the Hip-Hop Generation* (New York: St. Martin's Press, 2005); Adam Gussow, " 'Shoot Myself a Cop': Mamie Smith's 'Crazy Blues' as Social Text," *Callaloo* 25, no.1 (2002): 8–44.

10. Once through the racial mirror stage, as Lacan might have predicted, attempts to increase clinical vocabulary take doctors and patients ever farther away from the Real source of conflict. Ironically, the more they talk, the more they misperceive.

CHAPTER 27

1. Number of fast-food restaurants in neighborhood associated with stroke risk, http://americanheart.mediaroom.com/index.php?s=43&item=666, accessed February 25, 2009; Arthur L. Whaley, "Ethnicity/Race, Paranoia, and Psychiatric Diagnosis: Clinician Bias Versus Sociocultural Differences," *Journal of Psychopathology and Behavioral Assessment* 19, no. 1 (1997): 1–20.

2. Jonathan Metzl, *Prozac on the Couch: Prescribing Gender in the Era of Wonder Drugs* (Durham, NC: Duke Press, 2003); "Black Patients with Diabetes Fared Worse Than White Patients," http://www.sciencedaily.com/releases/2008/06/080609162108.htm, accessed March 10, 2009; "Black Patients with Asthma May Fare Worse Regardless of Disease Severity," http://www.sciencedaily.com/releases/2007/09/070924163024.htm; "Racial and Ethnic Disparities Detected In Patient Experiences," http://www.sciencedaily.com/releases/2008/10/081028184826.htm, accessed March 10, 2009; K. H. Todd, T. Lee, and J. R. Hoffman, "The Effect of Ethnicity on Physician Estimates of Pain Severity in Patients with Isolated Extremity Trauma," *JAMA* 271, no. 12 (1994): 925–28.

3. See http://www.aamc.org/meded/tacct/culturalcomped.pdf, accessed March 1, 2009; J. R. Betancourt, "Cross-cultural Medical Education: Conceptual Approaches and Frameworks for Evaluation," *Academic Medicine* 78, no. 6 (2003): 560–69; M. L. Kelley, ed., *Understanding Cultural Diversity: Culture, Curriculum, and Community in Nursing* (Sudbury, MA: Jones, 2000); Abraham Verghese, "Showing Doctors Their Biases," *New York Times,* March 1, 1999. Also see Liaison Committee on Medical Education, "Accreditation Standards," June 8, 2004, www.lcme.org/standard.htm (December 27, 2004); and AAMC, "Diversity Initiatives," www.aamc.org/diversity/initiatives.htm (December 20, 2004).

4. Albert Gaw, "Cross-Cultural Psychopharmacology," in *Concise Guide to Cross-Cultural Psychiatry,* ed. Albert Gaw (Washington, DC: American Psychiatric Association Press, 2001); A. J. Wood, "Racial Differences in Response to Drugs—Pointers to Genetic Differences," *New England Journal of Medicine* 34, no. 18 (2001): 1394–96; H. H. Zhou, and Z. Q. Liu, "Eth-

nic Difference in Drug Metabolism," *Clinical Chemistry and Laboratory Medicine* 38 (2000): 899–903. For an important critical perspective, see http://www.americanprogress.org/ issues/2008/01/geneticizing_disease.html, accessed March 10, 2009; Jamie D. Brooks, Meredith King Ledford, *Geneticizing Disease: Implications for Racial Health Disparities,* http:// biopoliticaltimes.org/downloads/2008_geneticizing_disease.pdf, accessed March 10, 2009.

5. Linda M. Hunt, "Beyond Cultural Competence: Applying Humility to Clinical Settings," *Park Ridge Center Bulletin* 24 (2001): 3–4; Sayantani DasGupta, "Narrative Humility," *Lancet* 371, no. 9617 (2008): 980–81; Rita Charon, "Narrative Medicine: A Model for Empathy, Reflection, Profession, and Trust," *JAMA* 286 (2001): 1897–1902.

6. Johan Galtung, "Violence, Peace, and Peace Research," *Journal of Peace Research* 6, no. 3 (1969): 167–91; Stokely Carmichael, "Black Power, A Critique of the System of International White Supremacy & International Capitalism," in *The Dialectics of Liberation,* ed. David Cooper (New York: Penguin, 1968), 151; Paul Farmer, *Infections and Inequalities: The Modern Plagues* (Berkeley: University of California Press, 2001), 79. Writing of the HIV epidemic in third-world countries, Farmer argues that AIDS transmission "is a result of structural violence: neither culture nor pure individual will is at fault; rather, historically given (and often economically driven) processes and forces conspire to constrain individual agency. Structural violence is visited upon all those whose social status denies them access to the fruits of scientific and social progress."

7. A related argument can be seen in *Inclusion: The Politics of Difference in Medical Research* (Chicago: University of Chicago, 2007), where the sociologist Steven Epstein argues that inclusive research practices have drawn attention away from the tremendous inequalities in health that are rooted not in biology but in society.

8. David Satcher, *Mental Health: Culture, Race, and Ethnicity,* http://mentalhealth .samhsa.gov/cre/toc.asp, accessed March 10, 2009; "Eliminating Racial/Ethnic Disparities in Health Care: What are the Options?" http://www.kff.org/minorityhealth/upload/7830.pdf, accessed March 10, 2009; Institute of Medicine, *Unequal Treatment: Confronting Racial and Ethnic Disparities in Health Care,* 2002.

9. Alex Berenson, "Drug Files Show Maker Promoted Unapproved Use," *New York Times,* December 18, 2006.

10. *Diagnostic and Statistical Manual of Mental Disorders DSM-IV-TR* (text revision) (Washington, DC: American Psychiatric Association Press, 2000); "The Art of Diagnosis," NPR, *On the Media,* http://www.onthemedia.org/transcripts/2008/12/26/05, accessed March 10, 2009.

11. Amy C. Watson, Patrick W. Corrigan, and Victor Ottati, "Police Officers' Attitudes Toward and Decisions About Persons with Mental Illness," *Psychiatric Services* 55 (2004): 49–53, http://www.nami.org/Content/NavigationMenu/SchizophreniaSurvey/Summary_ Schizophrenia_Survey_2008_NAMI_Harris_Interactive.htm. Also see http://www.nami .org/Content/Microsites254/NAMI_Tuscarawas-Carroll_Co_/Home239/Resources132/ SchizophreniaAwareness.pdf. Both accessed March 10, 2009.

12. Harris-Lacewell, "No Place to Rest: African American Political Attitudes and the Myth of Black Women's Strength." For a vital perspective on affect, also see Eva Tettenborn, "Melancholia as Resistance in Contemporary African American Literature," *Melus* 31, no. 3 (fall 2006): 101–21.

13. Otto F. Wahl, *Media Madness: Public Images of Mental Illness* (New Brunswick, NJ:

Rutgers University Press, 1997): Patrick W. Corrigan, Amy C. Watson, Gabriela Gracia, Natalie Slopen, Kenneth Rasinski, and Laura L. Hall, "Newspaper Stories as Measures of Structural Stigma," *Psychiatric Services* 56 (2005): 551–56.

14. Sylvia Nasar, *A Beautiful Mind: The Life of Mathematical Genius and Nobel Laureate John Nash* (New York: Touchstone, 1998).

15. Nasar's appearance at a pharma booth stoked controversy, since the film seems to have misrepresented the fact that Nash's "recovery" occurred without the aid of antipsychotic drugs. http://www.namiscc.org/newsletters/February02/JohnNashDrugFreeRecovery.htm, accessed March 10, 2009.

16. Victor LaValle, *The Ecstatic (or, Homunculus)* (New York: Crown, 2002); Natalie Danford, "Review of *The Ecstatic*," *Publishers Weekly*, August 12, 2002, 154–55; Thomas Metzinger, *The Neuronal Correlates of Consciousness* (Cambridge, MA: MIT Press, 2000), 103–10.

17. See, for example, Rev. Don Beaudreault, "We Do Not Stand and Wait, We Move (Sometimes)," Church of Sarasota, April 27, 2003, http://uusara.lunarpages.com/minister/don120.htm, accessed March 10, 2007: "I believe that Dr. King is telling us that the fullness of our humanity lies in the blending of thought and feeling and intention with action. He is calling us to a state of 'congruence' where we no longer live disjointed lives"; Charlie Reilly, ed., *Conversations with Amiri Baraka* (Jackson: University Press of Mississippi, 1994), 127; "Progressive lit.": Amiri Baraka, Bruce Andrews, and the politics of the lyric "I," http://www.thefreelibrary.com/%22Progressive+lit.%22:+Amiri+Baraka,+Bruce+Andrews,+and+the+politics+of . . . -a0110531679, accessed March 10, 2009.

18. The infamous Tuskegee study is often held up as the most obvious example of this fatal duality. Of note, stigma scholars have become increasingly aware of the importance of recognizing disparate cultural meanings of psychiatric terms. In an important 2006 study, Anglin, Link, and Phelan found that "even though African Americans were more likely to endorse stereotypes about individuals with mental illness, they appeared to be more sympathetic and understanding in their views about how these people should be treated . . . It is possible that this increased leniency among African Americans toward people with mental illness reflects a cultural variation that should be considered a strength that can be expanded upon in stigma-reducing interventions targeted to the African-American community." Indeed, one wonders, perhaps the lessons of the African American community might help shape anti-stigma interventions more broadly. Deidre M. Anglin, Bruce G. Link, and Jo C. Phelan, "Racial Differences in Stigmatizing Attitudes Toward People with Mental Illness," *Psychiatric Services* 57 (2006): 857–62.

19. Interview transcription excerpts, former employees of Ionia State Hospital, October 24, 2005; interviewer: Jonathan Metzl; location: Ionia Historical Society, Ionia, Michigan.